Law, Language, and Empire in the Roman Tradition

EMPIRE AND AFTER

Clifford Ando, *Series Editor*

A complete list of books in the series is available from the publisher.

LAW, LANGUAGE, AND EMPIRE IN THE ROMAN TRADITION

CLIFFORD ANDO

PENN

UNIVERSITY OF PENNSYLVANIA PRESS

PHILADELPHIA

Published by
University of Pennsylvania Press
Philadelphia, Pennsylvania 19104-4112
www.upenn.edu/pennpress

Printed in the United States of America on acid-free paper

10 9 8 7 6 5 4 3 2 1

Library of Congress Cataloging-in-Publication Data
Ando, Clifford, 1969–
Law, language, and empire in the Roman tradition / Clifford Ando. — 1st ed.
p. cm. — (Empire and after)
Includes bibliographical references and index.
ISBN 978-0-8122-4354-3 (hardcover : alk. paper)
1. Law—Rome—Provinces. 2. International law (Roman law) 3. Legal polycentricity—Rome. 4. Roman law—Language. I. Title. II. Series: Empire and after.
KJA2918.A86 2011
340.5'4—dc23

2011025556

For John Scheid

Contents

Preface

The civil law was an instrument of empire. It was not, or was not simply, as Roman legal philosophers claimed, a body of rules crafted through communal deliberation and approved by the citizen body for use strictly over itself. On the contrary, many of its most characteristic features—the substructure of formal mechanisms whereby innovation was accomplished in practice and justified in theory; its concern with philosophy of language and the apparatus by which that concern was given expression; its very historical self-consciousness—developed in response to the challenges posed when the Latinate legal system of the single and singular polity of Rome was deployed so as to embrace, incorporate, and govern discrepant people and cultures far afield. This volume attempts to vindicate that position; it illustrates what seem to me significant contours of some, at least, of the problems it raises; and it invites conversation on its themes.

The argument falls into two parts. Chapters 1 and 2 sketch a history of the processes whereby lawyers at Rome, in statute and jurisprudence, grappled with the legal pluralism of the world imperial action had created. They are *not* narrowly an effort to describe practice. (I—and others—are taking up that challenge elsewhere.) Nor do I offer a history of positive law, of legal doctrine, on marriage or dowry or contract or some similar issue, from some antecedent moment when Roman law really was Roman to some late ancient date when it was not. I eschew that problem in part because histories of doctrine abound, and in part because what interests me are rather the means by which Roman lawyers naturalized such changes as did occur, such that civil-law doctrine of late antiquity on marriage, dowry, and contract could easily and legitimately be described as Roman, regardless of the source and nature of the changes it had undergone.

Chapters 3, 4, and 5 examine the relationship between civil, public, and international law in the Roman tradition. Though the latter two categories occupy positions of prestige in ancient and modern legal theory, neither was codified in antiquity. Partly in consequence, neither became the object of jurisprudential scrutiny; nor did either develop an autonomous tradition of argument or interpretation. On the contrary, in the ancient, medieval, and early modern Roman traditions, it was the civil law that provided conceptual resources to those others and whose actions proved paradeigmatic in the articulation of public and international law. At the same time, the manifold implications of the civil law in those systems of domination—its use as archetype in political and legal argument outside its own narrow sphere—opened the door to its own subversion. For when political turmoil at Rome upended its institutions of political and legislative authority and effectively ended its democracy, the concepts and language that the civil law supplied to the project of Republican empire saw their meanings transformed; and by metaphorical recursion, forms of imperial domination once exercised by Romans over others were inscribed in the workings of law at Rome, henceforth to be exercised by the Romans over themselves.

• • •

The focus of the volume overall is therefore not *what* the Romans thought but rather *how* they thought. It is at that level an archaeology of foundational concepts, conceptual archetypes, and modes of argument. Outside the work of Yan Thomas, this is not a topic that has received much attention from Roman legal historians. The reasons for this deserve some scrutiny. On the basis of currently available evidence, the Romans did not write treatises on legal argument or, for that matter, rules of evidence or precedence or procedure *stricto sensu*. Not even allusions to such survive. In consequence, the tendency of historians of law to accept and to function within the imaginative and discursive boundaries of the systems they study has issued, in the case of Roman law, in a remarkably narrow conception of intellectual history.

The second major ambition of the book, the one foregrounded above, is the investigation of the effects on the civil law of its implication in projects of empire. Again, my own concern is *not* with the vastly important questions, in what venues and in what forms the civil law was applied around the empire, or even how its content was known to subjects of Rome. My goal is rather to isolate and study the effects on legal philosophy and legal reasoning that arose from the civil law's implication in those contexts. This again falls outside traditional forms of intellectual-historical inquiry practiced in the field.

To sketch in brief compass two proposals central to what follows, to understand the civil law as an instrument of empire and the product of an imperial state means first situating Roman civil law in all its jurisdictions alongside other codes of law; it requires us to view the Roman Empire, even Rome itself, as legally pluralist; it compels us to understand the operations of law in light of the discrepant legal statuses of the persons whose lives it regulated; and it demands that we recall the populations of the empire to have been linguistically, culturally, and in every other respect heterogenous.

Second, we need to remember that the civil law was at different times and in different ways called upon to codify and sustain systems of differential legal privilege: civil-law arguments were adduced to justify the acquisition of empire, even as civil-law actions were devised and deployed to consolidate its fruits.

This volume is also intended as a celebration of the astonishing creativity of the lawyers and jurists who wrote and reasoned the law at Rome. To read and think in their company is to encounter those ancients who grappled most sincerely and most extensively with the complexity and diversity of the world ancient political action had brought into being. What follows is often a critical reading, but throughout an appreciative one.

Chapter 1

Citizen and Alien before the Law

The object of this chapter is to excavate a body of law that does not exist, namely, the one that governed aliens, particularly aliens in dispute with citizens or with aliens of discrepant citizenship, before Roman courts. In doing so, I hope to advance four interrelated claims beyond the particular work of recuperation I shall perform in respect to legal practice.

First, I urge that a number of the most distinctive formal mechanisms in Roman law and legal language—most notably the fiction and its kin—were developed precisely in order to accommodate before the law persons and things notionally excluded by jurisdictional rules. Second, these mechanisms are visible in statutory language long before they are taken up in jurisprudence and, not surprisingly, they do their most interesting work in the early period of Roman law exactly at those moments and in those places where the Romans sought to incorporate juridically non-Roman populations within their state, namely, in the experimental colonial and provincial landscapes of Greece and Africa in the late second century B.C.E., in the municipalities of Italy created *de novo* as Roman communities in the aftermath of the Social War, and the reorganization of Cisalpine Gaul after the extension of citizenship to its residents and its statutory redescription as part of Italy.

Third, in the hands of the jurists of the classical period, these mechanisms are redeployed to resolve an historically new but structurally similar problem, namely, the resolution of apparent conflicts of law. These arose for the jurists of the classical period prior to the Antonine Constitution principally through the operation at Rome of multiple sources of law: statute, as issued by an assembly of the citizen body; praetorian edict; and imperial utterance. Although these rose to prominence in the order in which they are here listed, none was understood to have superseded the others or, more precisely, none was understood in the classical period to have gone into abeyance or to have ceased functioning altogether. In consequence, despite the existence within Roman legal philosophy of doctrines of desuetude, jurists were reluctant to describe laws from these varied sources as having radically superseded each other. Rather, later laws are described as honoring the principles articulated in earlier legislation, even as they worked in precise but significant ways to subvert those same principles. For that delicate task, the fiction was an ideal tool.

Fourth and last, confrontation with the complicated legal landscapes created by the work of empire and Rome's own complex past spurred the development by Roman jurists and legislators alike of two distinctive traditions that have since proved fundamental to the history of the civil law, in its work both in Europe and abroad, namely, a remarkable historical self-consciousness on the one hand, and a foundational concern for the capacity of legal language to give normative description to the worlds it was called upon to regulate on the other.

Citizenship and Jurisdiction: *Ius Civile* Defined

When I say that the substantive law governing relations between citizen and alien does not exist, I intend the claim in both an historical and a normative sense. At the level of history, the vast bulk of the legal texts that survive from the Roman world were selected and edited for their contemporary utility by scholars working in the sixth century C.E., some three hundred years after the universalization of citizenship. Apart from the trace evidence of a few titles of works quoted exclusively for their civil-law content, such substantive law as once existed to govern citizen-alien relations had long since lost any relevance and was rigorously excluded from the late ancient codifications.

In ideological terms, Roman lawyers understood, and Roman legislators betimes required, civil-law actions to be available exclusively to Roman citizens. Significant moments in this history include laws of 95 B.C.E., the so-called *lex Licinia Mucia*, and another passed by Augustus, called by ancient and modern scholars the *lex Iulia iudiciaria* (these are cited by sources in the Appendix, in passages 6D and 9, respectively).[1] The principle at stake was given decisive formulation in the second century C.E. in Gaius's *Institutes*, in concise wording that bespeaks a common understanding:

> All peoples who are governed by statutes and customs observe partly their own peculiar law and partly the common law of all human beings.

> The law that each people establishes for itself is peculiar to it, and is called *ius civile* (*nam quod quisque populus ipse sibi ius constituit, id ipsius proprium est vocaturque ius civile*), being, as it were, the special law of that *civitas*, that community of citizens, while the law that natural reason establishes among all human beings is followed by all peoples alike, and is called *ius gentium*, being, as it were, the law observed by all peoples. Thus the Roman people observes partly its own peculiar law and partly the common law of humankind. (Gaius *Inst.* 1.1; the Latin text of the whole may be found in Appendix passage 1.)

A civil law is thus the body of law that a community of citizens establishes for and over itself; and access to its actions is largely expected to be restricted to the members of that community, namely, its citizens. The heart of Gaius's claim might thus be said to rest in the distributive *quisque* and reflexive *sibi*: *every civitas* makes a *ius civile for itself*.[2] (As a corollary, it would seem that any political community worthy of the name would have such a body of law.)

This principle of law and legal theory has an important correlate in the fundamental place granted to contractarianism in Roman political thought. In this tradition, a political collectivity, a *populus*, is formed through the consensual commitment of its members to a particular normative order. According to Cicero, for example, "a people is not any coming-together of human beings, herded together for any reason whatsoever, but a coming-together of many *iuris consensu*, united by consensual commitment to a particular normative order and common utility" (*De re publica* 1.39; see Appendix passage 2). Alternatively, in a formulation widely cited by late medieval lawyers, a *populus* is a *collectio multorum ad iure vivendum; quae nisi iure vivat, non est populus*, "a gathering of many in order to live according to law, which, if it does not live according to law, is not a *populus*."[3] Chapter 5 in this volume essays to describe the worlds in which this formulation circulated and whose political cultures it functioned to describe.

The distinctiveness and pervasiveness of this Roman commitment to contractarianism is visible above all in the common use of *civitas*, citizenship, as a metonym for both city and political community. The corresponding term in Greek, *politeia*, which can mean citizenship or governing order, interanimates no such cluster of concepts. The ability of *civitas* to serve as a metonym for political community rests upon the assumption that it is individual possession of membership, and individual commitment to the entailments of membership, that bind one to the community. The failure of *politeia* to serve in the same way suggests that statutory definitions of membership and their entailments were regarded by Greeks as epiphenomenal to whatever essential qualities were understood to unite the community—normally those of kinship, which is to say, of race.[4]

What is more, the unwillingness of scholars to inquire into the civil law's imperial past is at least in part a legacy of this tradition, in which the subjects of the civil law are imagined to be created as such by their own consent. That imperial past is likewise occluded by the tendency of modern historians to echo ancient rhetoricians, for whom the spread of Roman citizenship was an important index of Roman benevolence. The history of its distribution might therefore be told—indeed, its history under the Principate can in fact be told—as an emancipatory narrative.[5] Its Republican past is another story: then, defective or deficient forms of citizenship, entailing obligations without corresponding privileges, were distributed to conquered populations in order to embrace them within the structures of the Roman state. They were thereby made knowable and governable; and in that world, the civil law was, among many things, an instrument of domination.[6]

Legal Pluralism and the Landscape of Empire

Where Roman history is concerned, the importance of the problem on which I focus has been obscured by the existence of rules of jurisdiction based on political geography. Simply put, these generally urge that the legal framework governing social and economic relations was determined by the geographic location wherein any given transaction was conducted.[7] The granting by Rome of authority to such legal systems must have taken place during the formal organization of a province: the commissions that oversaw that process no doubt established jurisdictional boundaries at the same time as they drew boundaries for assize districts, revenue collection, and myriad other purposes.[8] Of that process—or, rather, regarding the legal systems established as a result of it—we have but one extensive description, written by Cicero in 70 B.C.E. when prosecuting Gaius Verres, the immediate past (corrupt) governor of Sicily:

> The Sicilians are subjects of law as follows: actions of a citizen with a fellow citizen are tried at home, according to their own laws. To adjudicate actions of a Sicilian with a Sicilian not of the same citizen

> body (*quod Siculus cum Siculo non eiusdem civitatis*), the praetor (that is, the Roman governor) should appoint a judge by lot, in accordance with the decree of Publius Rupilius, which he fixed on the recommendation of the (commission of) ten legates (sent to advise him at the formal organization of the province), which decree the Sicilians call the Rupilian Law. To adjudicate suits brought by an individual against a community, or by a community against an individual, the Senate of another *civitas* should be assigned, granting the possibility that a *civitas* might be rejected by each side. When a Roman citizen sues a Sicilian, a Sicilian is assigned to adjudicate; when a Sicilian sues a Roman citizen, a Roman citizen is assigned. In all other matters judges are accustomed to be selected from among the Roman citizens resident in the assize district. Between farmers and collectors of the grain tithe, judgments are rendered according to the grain law which they call the Hieronican. (Cicero *Verr.* 2.2.32; see Appendix passage 3)

Regarding Cicero's schema I make but three closely related observations. First, the legal landscape of Roman Sicily is tessellated into jurisdictions, in each of which a different system of civil law is understood to obtain—that is, on a Roman understanding, a body of law generated by, and governing relations among, a political community whose membership is regulated and tracked by the polity itself.

Second, individual subjects of empire hold specific citizenship in polities, but exist also as legal actors holding residency in a specific Roman province—that is to say, they are also Sicilians. The arbitrariness of this new axis of identity is masked for moderns in the case of Sicily by virtue of its being an island, but Sicily was in antiquity politically, linguistically, ethnically, and religiously variegated. Roman success in forging new institutions by which to channel political energies and patriotic aspirations to provinces must count as one of the more remarkable achievements of ancient social and demographic engineering; it was a process impelled in part by the need to establish procedural and doctrinal frameworks for social and economic action in the aftermath of annexation.[9]

The third observation follows upon the second, and that is simply that the *lex Rupilia*, the Rupilian Law, was specific to Sicily. It was necessarily so, insofar as it incorporated and sustained earlier bodies of law and governmental regulation, including the system of taxation on grain established within his kingdom by Hiero, the king of Syracuse in the third century B.C.E. It may have been so in other ways, too, that we can no longer detect, including in matters of jurisdiction. But that very continuity and regional particularity, which was undoubtedly useful in sustaining social order during and after annexation, will have posed substantial hurdles before the progress of legal and administrative homogenization across the empire—a very different but no less desirable form of efficiency.

At the same time as the Romans fixed the boundaries of villages, cities, and districts, they also classified population groups in relation to each other and to the metropole, and modern ancient historians have devoted much energy to the recovery of such systems of classification. But as with rules of jurisdiction, so in respect to the public-law status of cities, the normative framework is a chimaera. For the fact of the matter is that the Romans also gave normative recognition to the necessity that Roman officials resolve disputes among their subjects, even outside the regular framework of the judicial circuit.[10] In so focusing on the status of cities, and further taking the status of cities as an index of the legal condition of their residents, historians systematically misrecognize the principal challenge of Roman government: maintaining order among population groups that were, always and everywhere, internally juridically, ethnically, and linguistically heterogenous. Governing such populations was the principal challenge of Roman government, and discovering the means whereby that challenge was met is a great unsolved problem of Roman history.

The Fiction and Its Kin

The disappearance of substantive law notwithstanding, we are not wholly ignorant regarding the mechanisms available within Roman legal practice whereby aliens might be embraced within the scope of civil and formulary procedure. On the contrary, I argue that the mechanisms used in respect to alien persons, things, and actions were exactly those deployed elsewhere in Roman law both explicitly, to expand the scope of the law, and retroactively, in jurisprudential literature, to resolve conflicts of law. These operations include analogy, contrafactual imperative, fiction, and substitution. These we might analyze separately, by genera formally distinguished, and I have gathered in the Appendix a number of prominent examples from extant Roman legislation (sections 4, 5, 6). I do not discuss these items in detail. I provide them rather to illustrate the early prominence of such operations in actual legislation, both as evidence in itself and by way of background to the widespread invocation of such operations in legal argument in later jurisprudential literature. That is to say, in my view, jurists of the high empire themselves employed fictions and substitutions, and regularly identified the operation of fiction and substitution behind other maneuvers, because these were in actual fact widely deployed in the language and operation of statute law. To the work of fiction in jurisprudential literature I shall turn in a moment. For now, allow me to point out three things.

First, although in any given case, in the immediate context of its composition, it may have been widely known who or what was embraced by any given substitution, the language of statute rarely makes that clear. We do not know, we cannot know—Romans a century after the law did not know—what persons or communities who were neither colonists nor colonies had been treated as if they were through the operations of the *lex agraria* of 111 B.C.E. (Appendix passages 6B, 6C).[11]

Second, formal differences aside, these operations have effects of two kinds, which should be understood as kindred: some transpose individuals above all, but also things and actions from one domain, that of some foreign body of law, to another, to that of Rome; others create legal facts from social ones. The substitutions effected by the *lex agraria* to which I have just referred are examples of the first kind. The clauses quoted in the Appendix from the law on the powers of Vespasian are examples of the second type (Appendix passages 5H, 5I). These prospectively establish that actions taken by the emperor will retroactively be understood as having occurred other than as they did: as having occurred through procedures by which sovereign power had once been legitimately exercised.[12] As with other fictions, the priority of a principle is respected and given formal articulation, even as it is effectively subverted. In a banal but non-trivial sense, one might say that the rule aids to bring into being that which it forbids.

Third, jurists tend to subsume all these operations beneath the conceptual taxon of the fiction. In attempting to clarify for his audience the dangers of the so-called Rubrian law, for example (Appendix passage 4A), Cicero confronts statutory language that ordered the voting of a second law immediately upon the passage of the first. What is more, the first law declared through an exhortatory subjunctive that officials created under its clauses shall possess the legitimacy conferred by the second law, regardless whether it passed or not. Cicero explains this legal chicanery by redescribing it as operating through the use of fiction: "they shall have the same legal status without a curiate law *as they would have had if* they had been created by the people according to strict procedure."

Although modern law—in particular modern common law—shies from the use of fiction as being somehow radical, fiction and its kindred operations were employed so widely at Rome because they were understood as conservative in scope.[13] Allow me to explain in what sense this was true, and then to illustrate.

In the view of the jurists, the two most prominent uses of fiction and substitution in Roman law were first, contingently to extend the scope of a statute, and second, to alter the scope of some outmoded legal framework. In both cases, what the operation in question permitted was the continued existence of, indeed, continued respect for, that earlier statute or framework. The fiction that an alien was in fact a citizen, which Gaius calls the *fictio civitatis* and which was adopted in order to move a given case into a civil-law framework, was thus understood to respect, rather than to subvert, the principle that the civil law should be available only to citizens (Appendix passage 7). Of greater interest to the jurists, because they recognized their revolutionary potential, were the fictions that in their view lay behind praetorian formulae that revised or replaced earlier statute law. Those cases possess a structural resemblance to what modern lawyers call conflicts of laws, such as arise when two sources of law notionally operate within the same jurisdiction or (more commonly in the modern world) a dispute between private parties could conceivably be resolved within a number of legal frameworks, each arising from a different national authority.[14] By masking revision or replacement, the fiction in such cases worked to preserve the legitimacy of the varied sources of law operational at Rome in the classical period. And naturally these are not mutually exclusive explanations for the ideological work performed by any given operation.

The Roman jurists had their own language for describing the powers of, as well as constraints upon, these formal moves in argument and interpretation. In the words of Julian, a jurist of the first half of the second century C.E., for example, such changes to the framework or taxonomic structures of prior legislation occurred *aut interpretatione aut constitutione*, "either through interpretation or by legislative act."[15] And where statute has once gone, thence might a jurist proceed *ad similia*, "to similar problems."[16] In all cases, to adopt the wording of Ulpian, it was the jurist's duty "to frame an interpretation that fits the individual words" of earlier law.[17] To the gap that would seem to yawn unacknowledged between the wording of legislation and the situations it was called upon to address, I return in closing.

Let me now provide two illustrations of the conservatism of Roman legal fictions, both thematically connected with the issues at the heart of this inquiry.

One example involving issues of personal status internal to the citizen community arose in civil law regarding the devolution of property.[18] A Roman male's heirs in civil law, strictly speaking, were those of his descendants who became full legal actors upon his death—in Roman terms, they passed out from under his power and became *sui iuris*. These individuals were related to the testator by *agnatio*; and strictly speaking, relations of *agnatio* (what we might call the agnatic line) pass through male descendants from a common ancestor. *Postumi*, descendants born after the testator's death, had *de facto* never been in his power and could not in civil law succeed to their father's or grandfather's property as *sui heredes*, as his heirs. One can imagine a variety of remedies to this situation. The solution devised at Rome is typical not only of its conservatism, but of the respect accorded by its different agents to problems of legitimacy among the sources of law. Hence, this "injustice in the civil law"—that *postumi* cannot be heirs—was "corrected by the praetor's edict," as Gaius records in his *Institutes*: "But these injustices in the civil law were corrected by the praetor's edict. For he summons to inheritance all children deficient in statutory title, *proinde ac si*, *exactly as if* they had been in their father's power at the time of his death, whether they stand alone or whether *sui heredes*, that is, persons who actually were in his power, come in with them" (Gaius *Inst.* 3.25–26; Appendix passage 8). Gaius elsewhere describes the work of this fiction with language that acknowledges at once the work of analogy in its operation, but also the inability of existing terminology and taxonomic structures to accommodate the world created by it. *Postumi* were admitted to inheritance, according to Gaius, by *quasi agnatione*, and *eo modo iura suorum . . . nanciscuntur*, "by sort-of agnation, and in that way their rights (as quasi-heirs?) were born."[19]

My second illustration is likewise of direct thematic relevance: it concerns jurisdiction. In the late first century of this era, as a result of a decision at Rome, the cities of Spain were incorporated as Roman towns, and a standard charter was written to guide their self-governance. In a late chapter of that document, rules are given to shape the administration of justice:

> if judgment has not taken place within the time laid down in Chapter XII of the *lex Iulia* that was recently passed concerning *iudicia privata* and in the decrees of the Senate that relate to that chapter of the statute, so that the matter be no longer under trial; the statute and law and

> pleading is to be as it would be if a praetor of the Roman people had ordered the matter to be judged in the city of Rome between Roman citizens. (*lex Flavia municipalis* chapter 91; Appendix passage 9)

I discuss this text further in Chapter 2, in studying metropolitan conceptions of the legal landscape of the empire, in particular in seeking to address the question concerning what resources were available at Rome for conceiving the institutions of law and government as permeating uniformly throughout its territory. In the present context, I draw attention to this fact only, that the text explicitly cites the *lex Iulia iudiciaria*. Indeed, it genuflects before its principles: Roman justice is best administered by a Roman praetor, judging a case between Roman citizens in the city of Rome. Nor does the Flavian law subvert or revise that earlier text. It merely urges that the law be administered in Spain *exactly as if* the litigants were Roman citizens arguing their case before the Roman Praetor in the city of Rome.

In a legal climate so ordered, in which the principle that civil law forms should be available only to citizens was so oft invoked, the *systematic* extension of civil-law rights and actions to aliens might well have been felt too radical. Indeed, it is a program for which no explicit advocacy survives. Even the extension of the franchise remained a controversial topic well into the first century C.E. But civil-law rights and actions were, in fact, extended, on a massive scale; and that history, I suggest, contributed to make the universal extension of the citizenship conceivable and ultimately possible.

This came about from two causes. First, for multiple reasons, Roman practice in adjudicating disputes in the provinces had long since come to follow the principle outlined by Julian in the eighty-fourth book of his *Digest*, where he probably dealt with attempts by citizens of municipalities to use Roman courts to escape local liturgies: "Regarding cases where we do not follow written law, the practice established by customs and usage should be preserved. And if this is in some way insufficient, then one must adhere to whatever is most analogous to it and follows from it. If even this is obscure, then the law observed by the city of Rome should be applied."[20] Alas, the extract as it is preserved for us provides no explanation why the Roman magistrate might *not* "follow <local> written law." Regardless, local law failing, Julian provides a sequence of alternate sources of norms that a magistrate might consult in reaching a decision. The ultimate recourse is the law of the city of Rome. My own suspicion is that Roman magistrates, schooled in

Roman law and culture and alien, as it were, to the local cultures that they governed, would have turned quickly to the familiar over against the foreign. As a formal matter, I shall urge, this application of Roman law occurred through the massive deployment of transpositions, whether reified in any given case through analogy, fiction, substitution or some other operation.

The iteration of these operations contributed in turn to a second revolution. For while the fictional nature of legal fictions was well understood in antiquity—please pardon the tautology—the habitual construal of the world other than as it was ultimately brought a new social reality into being. This occurred first in the perceptual framework of the Romans themselves, who gradually made what cognitive linguists would call an ontological commitment to the fictional world crafted by the language of the law, and so created new truths from fictional ones.[21]

Personal Status and Past Lives in Roman Law

I wish now to discuss in some detail two examples of the operation of fiction in Roman law to illustrate the sophisticated ways in which seemingly rigid distinctions in the juridical status of persons were regularly and systematically reimagined before the law.

Bracketing the granting of citizenship to freeborn aliens, there were two common circumstances in which individuals passed in and out of the Roman citizen body: slaves appropriately freed by Roman citizen owners themselves became citizens, and Roman citizens lost their citizenship when captured in war. The complications that arose from those transformations demanded complex legal solutions, and these illustrate, I suggest, the range of mechanisms available in Roman law for negotiating across status distinctions.

Rome was a slave society, but in many respects a peculiar one. Among other things, manumission was extremely common, and *liberti*, freedmen, who were manumitted by one of several formal processes received Roman citizenship. Their citizen rights were, however, prejudiced in several respects. Most importantly for my purpose here, they continued to owe various duties to their former owners, now styled their "patrons." Among those were *obsequium*, respect; *operae*, "works," meaning regular or periodic labor; and their savings. For freedmen could not have heirs; they had to leave their estates to their patrons *manumissionis iure*, by law of manumission.[22] (Patronal rights were passed along the patron's agnatic line, but the duties on the part of the freedman were not so passed to his descendants.)

Slaves freed informally did not receive citizenship, or any civil-law rights. Indeed, at civil law such freedmen remained slaves. But in a gesture typical of praetorian law's role "to aid, supplement or correct *ius civile*,"[23] and typical also of the respect accorded each other by the different sources of law, it became regular in the late Republic for informally manumitted freedmen "to be protected in a framework of freedom by the aid of the praetor."[24]

The emperor Augustus seems to have thought the rate of manumission at Rome too high—or, rather, he seems to have thought too great a percentage of the free population to be of servile extraction—and his reign saw the passage of two statutes regulating manumission, the more important of which, the *lex Aelia Sentia* of 4 C.E., imposed very substantial restrictions on manumission, of many kinds.[25] But his reign (or that of his adopted son, Tiberius) also saw the formalization of the protection that the praetor had previously extended on an informal basis to improperly freed slaves. For by a *lex Iunia* it was provided that henceforth informally manumitted slaves (except those known to have committed violent crimes) should become "Latin." What in the world does that mean, and what consequences did it have?

In this context, "Latin" was a legal status named for a confederation of cities located near Rome and united by ethnicity and language (the region was Latium; their language was Latin), with which Rome maintained an alliance and which Rome ultimately brought to heel in the late fourth century B.C.E. After that date, according to the treaties that settled the war, the citizens of any one of those cities were forbidden to forge certain types of social and commercial bonds with citizens of any other, but they were permitted to forge such ties with Romans. They therefore existed in a special relationship with the Roman state, and their status came to be regarded in complex ways as intermediate between citizen and alien. In point of fact, it only becomes clear that the composite of rights and obligations created in that settlement *was* a status, as opposed to a purely contingent agglomeration, when the Romans began to assign the so-called *ius Latinum* to people who were neither ethnically nor juridically Latin. That is to say, the term Latin once had a referent whose ontological status was prior to any grant of *ius Latinum*, but the operation of law wrenched that term from a realist usage to a nominalist one, even as it created people as Latin through the actions of government.[26]

Though the text of the *lex Iunia* does not survive, the analysis of it provided by Gaius reveals it to have operated by a double fiction. The first operated to effect the change in status:

> We proceed to consider the estates of (Junian) Latin freedmen. In order to make this branch of law clearer, we must call to mind that, as we have said elsewhere, those who are now termed Junian Latins were in earlier times slaves by Quiritary law (that is, civil law in the strict sense), but that they were maintained in a framework of freedom by the aid of the praetor; and therefore their property used to go to their patrons by law of *peculium*; later, owing to the *lex Iunia*, all who used to be protected in a state of freedom by the praetor came to be free and to be styled Junian Latins: Latins because the law made them free *exactly as if* they were free-born Roman citizens who, by migrating from the city of Rome to Latin colonies, had become colonial Latins; Junian because it was by the *lex Iunia* that they were made free, though not Roman citizens. (Gaius *Inst.* 3.55–56; Appendix passage 10)

The author of the *lex Iunia* seems thus to have declined to emend civil-law doctrine on manumission. (He may also be declining to correct the *lex Aelia Sentia*, if, in fact, the *lex Iunia* postdates that law.) That is to say, the *lex Iunia* did not imagine an alternate outcome to manumission to citizen status. Rather, the law posited a new life history to informally manumitted slaves: they were *ingenui*, freeborn, and had voluntarily surrendered their citizenship in order to enroll in a Latin colony. The legitimacy of the legal system seems to have trumped any concern over the ideological consequences of thus redescribing the prior life of slaves.

Beyond the operation of this fiction lay a further problem. Previously, the property of informally manumitted freedmen "used to go to their patrons *peculii iure*, by law of *peculium*." A *peculium* was the personal property of a slave, who possessed but did not own it. (The same term embraced the property of children while they remained "in the power" of their father.) The "framework of freedom" by which the praetor protected such freedmen evidently permitted the description and control of their property according to the rules of civil law, by which those freedmen were, in fact, still slaves; and thus owners who manumitted informally did not have to forego the material rewards available to those who manumitted properly.

But Junian Latins were not understood to be ex-slaves, or to have *ever* been slaves, and so did not have *peculium*. As Gaius observes, the author of the law foresaw this difficulty.

> Realizing that as a result of this fiction the estates of deceased Latins would no longer go to their patrons, because of course they would die neither as slaves, whose property would go to their patrons *iure peculii*, nor as freedmen, whose estates would go to their patrons (*manumissionis iure*), the author of the *lex Iunia* therefore deemed it necessary, in order to prevent the benefit given to them from being turned to the injury of their patrons, to provide that their estates should go to their manumitters *exactly as if* the *lex* had not been passed. Hence under the *lex* the estates of Latins go to their manumitters in some fashion by the law of *peculium*. (Gaius *Inst.* 3.56; Appendix passage 11)

Here, then, is the second fiction. In order to create an obligation exactly parallel to the law of *peculium*, the *lex Iunia* requires conduct in its aftermath to be carried out in one crucial respect as if it had not passed. The fiction of the law is of its own nonexistence.[27] Gaius shies from calling the resulting obligation an operation of *ius peculii*: it occurs, rather, *iure quodammodo peculii*, "in some fashion by the law of *peculium*."[28]

About prisoners of war I can be more brief. By long-standing tradition, Roman citizens captured in war lost their citizenship status. (If they returned to Roman territory, they could recover their citizenship by right of *postliminium*, a word whose etymology suggests a meaning like "beyond the threshold"). But the loss of citizenship left the civil-law status of their wills, their property, and their heirs in question—for non-citizens could not write valid wills. This situation was remedied by a *lex Cornelia* of the late Republic, perhaps c. 80 B.C.E. That statute provided that the testamentary dispositions of prisoners of war should be treated *perinde . . . atque si in civitate decessissent*, "exactly as if they had died in citizenship." *Propter quam fictionem*, "because of that fiction," all civil-law enactments regarding testation were held to apply to the wills of those captured in war.[29] In the case of the *lex Cornelia*, then, live non-citizens are imagined as citizens, albeit dead ones.

Of course, not everyone who died on campaign was *sui iuris*, an independent legal actor. Some were "sons in power," males who remained under the control of their fathers, who therefore had no right of ownership of property but, like slaves, had a *peculium*, property they controlled only. The jurist Paul, writing in the first decades of the third century C.E., imagined a complex situation regarding just such a son-in-power, who left behind a codicil containing a *fideicommissum*, a trust, asking his father to give the savings of his military pay (his *peculium castrense*) to one Titius:

> A son in power who died while serving in the military charged his father by means of a codicil with a trust, to deliver to Titius his *peculium castrense* after death. It is asked whether the heir (namely, the father) could deduct a quarter. I said that the *lex Falcidia* had been extended by the Divine Pius in respect to trusts even to cases of intestate succession. That said, in the case before us, there was no inheritance, although I would have agreed that, had someone outside the family been named heir, his acceptance would have created an inheritance. As the son in our case remained in the power of his father, the erstwhile legal framework obtained and the property was *peculium*. Nor is this contrary to the fact that the *lex Falcidia* governs the wills of those who die as prisoners of war, for the fiction of the *lex Cornelia* creates both an inheritance and an heir. (Paul *Quaestiones* bk. 11 fr. 1373 Lenel = *Dig.* 35.2.18.*pr.*; Appendix passage 12)

Paul asks the question whether the father can deduct from his son's military savings, left in trust to Titius, "the Falcidian quarter." (A *lex Falcidia* of 40 B.C.E. required that testators leave at least one quarter of their estate to their heirs, and this rule was extended to trusts in the second century C.E.) The answer is simple, according to Paul: in the hypothetical situation, there is no inheritance. The property is *peculium*. That is to say, the son, being a son-in-power, did not as a matter of law own the property, and could therefore not dispose of it.

But Paul is not content with that answer. As he sees it, had the son-in-power instituted an heir outside his family, acceptance by that nominal heir would have created an inheritance. Then, indeed, his father could have withheld the Falcidian quarter, but likewise the son's wish that his property should pass to Titius would have been respected. No matter, says Paul, that the *lex Falcidia* here regulates the will of someone who died as a prisoner of war: "for the *fictio legis Corneliae*, the fiction of the *lex Cornelia* creates both an inheritance and an heir."

Given that, by what justification can we understand the situation to create an obligation upon the father? That is to say, how might we understand the situation—how might it be redescribed using the operations of law and legal language—to permit the son to bequeath, and to require the father to respect the bequest? Paul continues: "But I also said that I did not doubt but that the charity of the law should also be satisfied, if the father were required to transfer the assets *as if* those of a *paterfamilias* and, being instituted as heir but declining acceptance under the will, he were then sued in respect of legacies on the pattern of the edict" (Paul *Quaestiones* bk. 11 fr. 1373 Lenel; Appendix passage 12). Paul's answer is to carry the fiction of the son's emancipation to its natural conclusion: if the son is imagined to be *sui iuris* and the father is recipient of his *fideicommissum*, then the father must needs be imagined as his heir—indeed, most simply as his son. The obligation upon the father to honor his son's *fideicommissum* is thus understood by Paul to be entailed by the fiction of the Cornelian law, and not as a consequence of this peculiar family's peculiar legalitarianism.

The power Paul grants the fiction is remarkable. The desire to respect what he terms *legis beneficium*, the spirit or charity of the law, permits the fiction to trump civil law twice: for the son-in-power died an alien, and absent the fiction could not write a will; and had he died *in civitate*, in citizenship, he had no civil-law status to write a will in the first place.

The Junian and Cornelian laws thus transferred individuals across status boundaries of many kinds, and imagined them embedded in networks of legal relations across prior and future life histories whose operations were made to depend on the susceptibility of citizenship, the civil law, and the Roman state itself, to the transgressive work of fiction.

Fiction and Empire

A proper history of citizenship in the Roman Empire remains to be written. Even today, the simple fact of its universal extension defies explanation. To be sure, the privileges of citizenship were gradually evacuated over the first two centuries of this era, the most significant index of that change being the exposure of lower-class citizens to progressively more savage and violent remedies at law.[30] But the scale of that act—the simultaneous incorporation of so vast a congeries of nations—surprises nonetheless, whether we regard it solely in light of the ethnic, cultural, and linguistic heterogeneity of the empire's residents, or also in comparison with policies on citizenship in other empires, ancient and modern.

My argument is that Roman law played a paradoxical role in that history.

Conceived internally as a set of norms regulating the affairs of citizens, the civil law would seem a tool that could only disjoin, and never unite, citizens and aliens. But in point of fact, despite never shedding that commitment to citizen privilege, Roman law in practice came to embrace an ever widening portion of the population. This happened at different moments for different reasons—among communities of citizens far from the praetor, among aliens seeking the prestige and power of Roman courts, or among the Romanizing municipalities of Spain. Ultimately, I suggest, the endless construal of aliens as citizens naturalized the truth of that fiction, and a new political and cultural landscape was born from that revolution.

This came about quite in spite of an awareness on the part of Roman lawyers that the operation of legal fictions required precisely that the false be taken as true.[31] Nor did Roman lawyers maintain any illusions about the power of legal language to change the world beyond itself, as it were, whether that were some higher, ontologically more stable realm of ideas, or the realm of nature itself. As Gaius was provoked to write about the invention of a usufruct of money and a subsequent *senatusconsultum* establishing regulations for such: "The *senatusconsultum* did not bring it about that there might strictly speaking be usufruct of money—for *naturalis ratio*, natural reason cannot be altered on the authority of the Senate—but, this remedy being introduced, quasi-usufruct was established."[32]

The power of the law over social reality was a different matter. There, in words of Ulpian excerpted twice in the Digest, *res iudicata pro veritate accipitur*, "legal decisions are accepted in the place of truth." By that he did not intend that legal decisions are necessarily false, or themselves rest on falsehood. But it is noteworthy that his obiter dictum in fact emerged to explain the commitment of legal institutions in respect to changes in the legal status of persons, as is made clear from its other use, which provides a context for its utterance: "We must accept as freeborn someone concerning whom there is a judgment to that effect, even if he was born a freedman: for legal decisions are accepted in the place of truth."[33]

The gap Ulpian here observes, between social facts and legal facts, has an important correlate in the gap between the language of the law and the social realities it was called upon to regulate, a problem made visible to the jurists in one prominent form in the aftermath of the Antonine Constitution, when the Latinate law of Rome was called upon to give normative description to social and economic relations in the Greek-speaking east (their reflections on this topic are taken up in Chapter 2). It is this latter gap between law and social realities that fiction and substitution elided, and to which words like *quasi* and *quoddammodo* draw insistent attention. How to theorize that gap, as a matter of legal philosophy, was disputed: for every lawyer like Ulpian, who insisted that new situations could—always? only?—be embraced by adhering to "the individual words" of legislation, there were others, like Celsus, who insisted that "knowing the law" consisted in adhering *not* to their words but to their force and import.[34] *Potestas legis*, the import or tendency of a law, is likewise the term used by Paul to explain what part of statute law was preserved or respected by the praetor when he extended its usage to situations theretofore or inadvertently unimagined.[35]

That said, the extraction of a legal principle from statutory language and its application to new situations had perforce to be reified in language, and that act created legal facts—Latinate legal facts—where none had been before. The question what is the power of law as a system of language to make social facts out of legal ones is taken up most explicitly by Gaius in a passage not on fiction but theft (Appendix passage 13). A statute established that refusing to allow one's property to be searched for stolen goods rendered one liable for the action against manifest theft. (Merely being caught with stolen goods made one liable for a lesser degree of theft.) This caused some writers to ask whether theft was manifest *aut lege aut natura*, "by statute or in reality." That is to say, was manifest theft a particular form of theft, or could any act of theft be not merely classified as but in fact transformed into manifest theft through statutory language? Gaius denounced the question:

> The truer answer is that manifest theft is understood as such in reality. For statute can no more bring it about that a non-manifest thief is manifest, than it can make someone who is altogether not a thief into a thief, or someone who is not an adulterer or a homicide into an adulterer or a homicide. Rather, what law can do is simply this: it can make someone liable to punishment exactly as if he had committed theft or adultery or homicide, even if he had committed none of those things. (Gaius *Inst.* 3.194; Appendix passage 13)

It could also bring it about that aliens existed in law, and in the world the law ruled, exactly as if they were citizens, even if they were in reality no such thing.

Chapter 2

Law's Empire

This chapter pursues several interrelated problems at the intersection of law and the articulation of the late ancient state. They may be framed as an inquiry into the consequences, intended and otherwise, of Caracalla's decision to grant citizenship to all—or nearly all—freeborn residents of the empire. For the Antonine Constitution would seem to mark, or should have marked, a turning point in the history of the empire: put concisely, one might ask whether the empire still was an empire when it no longer ruled over anyone. Put more elaborately, was there a corresponding shift in the perception, ambitions, and actions of the state in keeping with the universalization of citizenship? Did acts or agents of government, or depersonalized institutions of the state, penetrate more deeply or spread more uniformly to match the universalization and homogenization of political culture that the spread of citizenship would seem to entail? What resources did the Romans have even to conceive, let alone to pursue, such an aim, if they had it, in whatever form they did?

In pursuing these questions, we face a number of obstacles, both ideological and evidentiary, that I mention simply to set the stage. These are, first, that Roman law was throughout this period a moving target, its doctrines and procedures undergoing constant revision and change. Second, Roman law—like so many fields of our discipline—has its own classical ideal, which urges us to esteem virtually all periods of Roman law about which we can actually know something as instantiating debased and degenerate forms of some earlier, pure and pristine law.[1]

Third, even if we stand apart from the modes of valuation that gave us so-called vulgar law, bureaucratic law, and the like, we encounter an even more serious obstacle at the level of evidence: the very great bulk of legal texts at our disposal were edited at one or another of two periods in late antiquity so as to speak to formal issues of substantive law as it was then in force. That is to say, the texts we have—the huge bulk of which come in the form of something like a Routledge sourcebook—were systematically edited so as to provide or conduce the formulation of decision rules. Such material as jurists and lawyers once wrote that spoke directly to problems of justification, legitimation, or implementation has been rigorously excised.

This is, of course, a well-known problem. But it is perhaps not often enough remarked that in consequence the texts we possess seem scarcely to speak to two great historical problems of Roman law, namely, the adjudication of disputes between individuals of divergent legal status, whether citizens and aliens or aliens of divergent citizenship; or the administration of social and legal relations among formerly peregrine populations in the aftermath of the Antonine Constitution. For if one thing was emphatically true of the legal landscape of the early sixth century as it was imagined by the Justinianic compilers, it is that the individuals who would come before the law would all be citizens. It is hard to believe that many texts on legal relations between citizens and aliens survived to the sixth century—a scant handful of titles can be recovered—and when those few are quoted, it is for their reflections on the civil law alone.[2] In the rest of their content—in the very issues that motivated their composition—there was simply and understandably no interest.

Quite in spite of this, my ambition in this chapter is to address to the late antique compilations the questions I framed at the outset; to suggest a way to read them, by which they might be made to answer those questions; and to gesture, at least to what their answers might be.

My approach in brief is this: I propose to sidestep the question of what changes were made in substantive law or its interpretation and investigate instead how those changes were made: what pressures impelled them; how they came about; and how those changes were understood, described, and justified in later legal and jurisprudential literature. My second question—how they came about—would have to be taken in at least two directions: what was the source of law that enacted the change—statute? rescript? edict? interpretation?—and what was the conceptual mechanism by which that change was effected? Was some new species of person, thing, or action integrated within an existing taxonomy? Was a wholly new legal action created? Did some jurist create a work-around, through analogy or fiction? And so forth.

My argument will be that in post-Antonine legal literature, in the form we have it, the mechanisms developed in the late Republic and early Principate to constrain and channel pressures for change into particular formal outcomes were redeployed in the third century and beyond, continuing robustly into the age of Justinian. Or so it appears: for here we encounter some very substantial problems of evidence, arising most obviously from the editing and selection performed by the Justinianic compilers. One possibility is that the apparent continuity in forms of practical and theoretical elaboration across the corpus is a product of their work, by virtue of their conscious recognition in these texts of conceptual and linguistic forms that they viewed as legitimate and current. To credit this last claim would amount to arguing that the Justinianic editors privileged in their editorial work a vision of the law and in particular of what counted as legitimate reasons for change and mechanisms for realizing such. To this problem I shall return in closing.

This remarkable continuity in theoretical position and interpretive practice was achieved, I argue, despite the very considerable historical differences between the situations Roman lawyers confronted in the late Republic and early Principate on the one hand, and the post-Antonine world on the other. In the former, as we have seen in Chapter 1, the principal challenge to the system lay in the arrival on the scene of new sources of law, first the praetor and later the emperor. This is in fact an altogether common problem in almost all legal systems: it produces what might catachrestically be called conflicts of law, and in general the concern within any given tradition is their resolution in a fashion that respects the legitimacy of the separate sources of law and thus conduces the legitimacy of the system as a whole. In the classical period, the praetor is thus often described as acting in pursuit of greater adherence to principle that is either assumed or explicitly described as animating statute law, but in practical terms what praetorian action or the occasional statute or jurisprudential interpretation did was to ignore that same principle. In Roman law, I have argued, this work was usually performed by means of fiction, analogy, or mere substitution: the principle at stake is thus nominally sustained by virtue of an avowedly ad hoc and limited translation of objects, things, or persons across whatever taxonomic divide the principle was intended to articulate.

The twin pressures on post-Antonine law were the need to sustain social order in the formerly discrepant legal landscapes of the empire, while insisting wherever possible on the superordinate normative status of Roman law. Jurists, legislators, and judges needed, in other words, to acknowledge the fact of contingent divergence from Roman practice by nominal Roman citizens at some primary level of analysis in such a way that permitted the redescription and reorientation of that practice over time into alignment with Roman norms. Homogeneity had to be produced out of heterogeneity, unity out of plurality, without disruption to preexisting social and economic relations.[3]

The product of the effort so described was the development of legal actions that occasionally explicitly—and in aggregate implicitly—accorded legitimacy to the normative codes that had structured local life in the pre-Antonine age. At the same time, Antonine and immediately post-Antonine jurists recuperated for this project a set of legal-theoretical categories with which to describe this new landscape: custom, natural law, and *ius gentium*, the law of nations. None of these was new, of course; but none had been made to do such heavy lifting before, nor had any been so robustly characterized at any point in the Roman past. The turn to these categories was necessitated above all by the prominence formerly given in political and legal philosophy to *ius civile*. For in the system adumbrated by Cicero and given full-fledged articulation by Gaius, every community of citizens, every *civitas*, had its own *ius civile*: in an age of multiple citizenships, this explained the tesselation of the legal landscape of the empire into several *civitates*—indeed, it offered the whole ontological security of a most interesting kind—but the construct had to be radically rethought, even rebuilt from the ground up, to remain useful in a world in which there were no separate citizenships.[4]

Beyond these more abstract conclusions, one thing I hope to highlight is the remarkable historical self-consciousness of Roman lawyers, a feature of their intellectual make-up little remarked and generally obscured by their fondness for writing lemmatic commentaries rather than monographs. But the jurists early and late thought long and systematically about the need for law to evolve in response to new social and political realities. This sensibility was combined with a quite fascinating sense of the limitations of discursive language. In the words of Julian, Ulpian, and Celsus, "Neither statutes nor decrees of the Senate can be written so as to embrace every eventuality that might at some time occur." "For it inheres in *natura rerum*, in the nature of things, *ut plura sint negotia quam vocabula*, that the forms of conduct are more numerous than the terms for them." In consequence, the law must provide recourse, even when the *actionum nomina* or *appellationes* provided in civil law fail.[5]

Jurisdictional Rules and Legal Pluralism before the Antonine Constitution

Law as such is a neutral tool, perforce inherently conservative in the most banal sense. In imperial contexts, however, the law of the metropole is generally assumed to be a tool of oppression, designed to disjoin rather than unite populations and to sustain distributions of wealth and power that favor its own interests. That said, interest in this context is hard to assess: spread of civil-law forms across the empire would likely have reduced transaction costs to macro-regional trade still further, and this would almost undoubtedly have produced greater revenues for Rome, and there is evidence for such thinking in antiquity in terms not so blatantly economic.

At the same time, there is very considerable testimony to a reluctance on the part of Romans to allow aliens access to civil law for partisan reasons; to a kindred reluctance on the part of aliens to take up the law; and likewise evidence that Romans believed that sustaining local traditions, including legal relations, conduced social order in some fundamental and probably profitable sense.[6] Against vague rhetorical claims in Roman sources both early and late (in Livy, say, and Servius) that laws and language are the victor's to impose, one might therefore set widespread invocation of the principle—and insistence in practice—that basic structures of civil- and even public-law relations were expected to map citizen status of individuals and communities.[7] Hence Trajan offered to Pliny the general principle that *id ergo, quod semper tutissimum est, sequendam cuiusque civitatis legem puto*, "it is always safest, I think, for the law of any given citizen community to be observed" within its jurisdiction (Pliny *Ep.* 10.113). In short, non-citizens were to use their own laws. The principle is concretized in historical narrative in Livy's language in book 9, when he describes the aftermath of Rome's war with the Hernici: preferring their own laws, Rome's allies declined the offer of Roman citizenship.[8] Similar in equating change of citizenship with entry into a new legal regime, and of direct relevance to the period at hand, is the assertion by the Tetrarchs in a text on marriage preserved in the *Collatio*, to the effect that *cunctos sub imperio nostro agentes*, everyone living under their rule "should be mindful of the need to conform themselves to the lifestyle and laws of Rome and should know that only those marriages are licit that are permitted *iure Romano.*"[9]

In point of fact, law in the classical period over and over again exhibits a similar schizophrenia, working at once to universalize norms but also along multiple axes to fragment the empire. In consequence, the Romans eventually crafted impressive theoretical resources for conceptualizing the empire as permeated by a uniform legal culture, even as multiple firewalls disjoining Rome and Italy from the provinces in the availability of civil-law actions were erected and enforced. As I hope to show in closing, these very rules and resources remained alive in the reign of Justinian, when just those resources were reactivated and employed to dismantle those same firewalls.

Perhaps the best index of the conceptual work performed in this arena in the late Republic and early empire is the distance traveled, as it were, between the laws on jurisdiction of the late Republic on the one hand and the Flavian municipal law on the other.[10] A schematic view of the former might outline their content as having the following form: (1) In communities of types A, B, and C, in area D, (2) in which jurisdiction rests with magistrates of types G or H, (3) legal actions of type K shall be handled locally, using procedure M, if conditions P and Q are met, or (4a), if conditions P and Q are not met, procedure R should be used locally, or (4b) the case shall be sent to Rome. The Veleia fragment, a text of the mid-first century B.C.E., gets to the heart of what these texts contribute to my story, for in that text it is very nearly the words *quei ibei* alone that confirm its identification as a late Republican law on jurisdiction: the end of the clause may confidently be restored *ius deicet*: "he who holds jurisdiction *there*" (*Roman Statutes* no. 29).

In the ninety-first chapter of the Flavian municipal law, by contrast, the following rule is laid down regarding various points of procedure: "if judgment has not taken place within the time laid down in Chapter XII of the *lex Iulia* that was recently passed concerning *iudicia privata* and in the decrees of the Senate that relate to that chapter of the statute, so that the matter be no longer under trial; the statute and law and position is to be as it would be if a praetor of the Roman people had ordered the matter to be judged in the city of Rome between Roman citizens" (see also Chapter 1 and Appendix passage 9). Written perhaps a hundred years apart, these texts offer startlingly different visions of the legal landscape of the empire. The Veleia tablet distinguishes explicitly between Rome and everywhere else; in line with other legislation of its era, it reserves the power and capacity of judgment in matters of import to the metropole. Only its judges, sitting in its forum, animated by its soil, could decide. Late Republican jurisdictional clauses also cleave the empire socially, for it is not all disputes, nor even all disputes between citizens, that are removed to Rome for adjudication, but only those in which the matter in dispute, converted to monetary terms, was worthy of Roman attention.

In contrast, the Flavian municipal law preserves the distinction between Rome and elsewhere only to upend it, by means of a fiction that operates on two levels, geographic and social: it dissolves both distance in time and distinctions in the legal status of persons: disputes between potentially alien *municipes* are to be resolved "as if a praetor of the Roman people had ordered the matter to be judged in the city of Rome between Roman citizens." Provinces and provincials are thereby assimilated to Rome and Romans. What is more, there is considerable evidence for the ongoing use of just this fiction—what Gaius calls the *fictio civitatis*—part of whose attraction must have been that it permitted the principle of restricting civil law to citizens to stand, while freeing Romans with jurisdiction in the provinces to judge in light of the law they knew.

That said, evidence in textual sources for the role of law in disjoining the empire is far more substantial. Perhaps the most important distinction lay between Italy and the provinces: any number of civil-law rights and actions could be performed or actualized only on Roman or Italian soil. Consider, for example, the famous correspondence between Pliny and Trajan regarding the scruple involved in moving the temple of the Mother of the Gods in Nicomedia. Pliny hesitated to approve the act, he wrote, because the temple had no *lex*, as the *morem dedicationis*, "the method of consecration," practiced in Nicomedia was *alium apud nos*, "different from that practiced among us." Trajan responded that Pliny could be "without fear of violating religious scruple," as the *solum peregrinae civitatis capax non sit dedicationis, quae fit nostro iure*, "as the soil of a peregrine city cannot receive consecration as it is performed according to our law."[11]

The "soil" in question in Trajan's response was that of Italy, in which inhered some quality of Romanness that more perfectly animated both Roman law and affection for Rome than soil elsewhere ever could. In consequence, persons exiled in the provinces were excluded not simply from the particular province whence they were banished, but from Rome and Italy as well—a rule articulated by Hadrian in a rescript, which was quoted and commented on by Ulpian, whose text was cited in full by the *Collatio* but edited to produce an erroneous attribution in the *Digest*.[12] The special place of Rome and Italy in both affective and legal terms is repeatedly rehearsed in the Code of Justinian: in 225 for example, Alexander endorsed the continuation of an exclusion from Italy of slaves whose masters had freed them for the purpose of sending them away.[13]

With this framework disjoining Italy and empire still in place, the scope for action by the Antonine Constitution in producing legal homogeneity was limited, regardless of its intent. That said, the homogenization of legal structures in the provinces, in relation at least to each other if not to Italy, that followed in its wake does appear to have enabled a new jural-political geographic consciousness: for it is, I think, first in jurisprudence after 212 that we find the term *in provincia* to refer to the collectivity of provinces, which usage in turn enabled the binarism common in the post-Antonine jurists, *in Italia::in provincia.*[14] A number of other conceptual obstacles must have fallen along the way to make that possible, but it seems meaningful nonetheless.

Naturally, insofar as the provincial::Roman distinction was a matter of law, it was also surmountable at law. And that is precisely what we find in Gaius. At the start of his second book, a brief comment on the distinction between what is *sacer* and what *religiosus*, what is sacred and what is religious, leads to a digression on the meaning of those terms on precisely provincial soil:

> That alone is thought to be sacred which is consecrated on the authority of the Roman people, either by law or by decree of the Senate. We make things *religiosum* in private actions by bearing our dead to particular sites. . . . But *in provinciali solo*, on provincial soil it is generally agreed that the soil cannot be *religiosum*, since there ownership rests with the Roman people or with Caesar, while we seem to have only possession or use. *Utique tamen, etiamsi non sit religiosum, pro religioso habetur.* Nevertheless, even if it is not *religiosum*, it is treated as though it were. Similarly, whatever in the provinces is not consecrated on authority of the Roman people is properly not sacred, but it is nevertheless treated *pro sacro*, as if it were. (Gaius *Inst.* 2.5–7)

Here it is the simple use of substitutive *pro* that does the work, a nearly ubiquitous usage in Roman law. But the effect was not innocent, for what Gaius enabled by its usage—as with the fiction in the Flavian municipal law—was the regular and consistent overcoming of precisely the principle he nominally upheld.

One might have thought that the distinction between Italian and provincial soil would gradually lose its power to articulate truths about the affective and legal landscape of the empire over the course of the fifth century, if not before—for all, perhaps, but antiquarian pedants like Justinian. But that is not what happened. Rather, the language in which that distinction was expressed was taken up from below, as it were, to give expression to the realities of the late ancient state under siege. This had effects both within and without the empire. That is to say, the metaphorical association of soil, system of law, and affective bond as mutually implicated ways of articulating membership in a Roman political community remained strong, and its ongoing usage by provincials to voice their attachment to the empire ultimately demanded revision of the system that had theretofore employed this same language to keep them at a distance. The power of this network of associations is laid bare, for example, by its repeated use in the middle of the fifth century by Salvian, who construed the condition of being conquered by barbarians as subjection to *ius hostium*, to the enemy's laws, and thus as creating him and his fellows as non-Romans: his condition was therefore that of an alien, living *in alieno solo*, on foreign soil. A few decades earlier Eugippius described Saint Severinus admonishing civilians in the face of barbarian onslaught to migrate *in Romani soli provinciam*, "to a province of Roman soil."[15]

Theorizing Plurality after Universal Citizenship

Considered in these terms, the challenge confronting Justinian in providing a vision of the empire as integrated by law was articulable in classical language of immediate contemporary relevance. The solutions available to him were multiple, and some were simple: he might, for example, have redescribed all soil as Roman, and thereby assimilated procedure and principle within Italy to that without. But even had he undertaken some such revision by sleight of hand, its narration would naturally not tell the whole story of late ancient law, even at the level of legal philosophy. On the one hand, massive historical changes had taken place in the realm of law between the Antonine Constitution and the sixth century, and no reckoning with Justinianic language alone can map those changes; and on the other, the problems of the legal system even in the sixth century were not to be resolved solely through figurative language.

Turning first to the landscape of law and historical change in the earlier period—and reacting against a body of literature that diminishes the importance of the Antonine Constitution—it is worth stressing that the world of the law after 212 was in fact different, utterly different, than the world before: the landscape of actual legal relations remained fully as heterogenous as before, but the participants to those relations now had full and undeniable standing before the law in Roman courts. What resources did classical law provide to conceptualize and administer this system, what new ones were crafted, and how did they fare in the third and fourth centuries?

It is important first of all to recall that the most prominent mechanism for acknowledging and controlling legal heterogeneity in the world before 212 now failed. I refer to the simple recognition of the existence and legitimacy of separate bodies of law and the assigning to them of non-overlapping jurisdictions. The clearest shorthand gesturing at this apparatus is surely that of the

Tabula Banasitana, an inscription of 177 C.E. recording a grant of Roman citizenship to one Aurelius Iulianus, which grant is said to occur *salvo iure gentis*, "without prejudice to local law" (*IAM* 94). Quite apart from our ignorance what the ramifications of this clause in fact were, one thing is clear: after 212, there *were* no separate *iura* in the empire, neither of *gentes* nor of *civitates*. This new present naturally had recursive effects on how one viewed the past, and I will turn in a moment to consider that problem.

But the mere death of systems of local law is not the end of the story. For one thing, existing relations of a very great portion of the empire had until a moment ago been structured by non-Roman normative codes of some description, and these had to be respected before the law: one problem was therefore how to name them—indeed, how to know what they were—if their (separate) existence *as law* was no longer possible.

It is of course well known—or might be expected—that jurists and lawyers should turn to the categories of *mos*, *consuetudo*, and *ius naturale*, of custom and of natural law. That said, even those moves had outcomes little studied and perhaps not to be expected, and in what follows that story will run in counterpoint to the others I seek to tell.

Allow me first simply to point out how extensive were the shock waves of Caracalla's act in legal philosophy. For what the Antonine Constitution required was nothing less than the wholesale imposition of a code of law upon highly developed cultural and political systems whose existing social-material relations it did not accurately describe. Viewed in these terms, this moment had a loose structural analog in the aftermath of the Social War, in the process captured for well or ill in the phrase "the municipalization of Italy." But the problem in 212, measured along any one of a number of axes, was wholly different in scale.

Grappling with this task provoked thought of two kinds relevant to this chapter, at whose bare outlines I can only gesture. The first concerns language and consists in reflections of the sort I cited earlier, to the effect that the language of the law, and the taxonomic efforts to which it gives voice, must needs fail to capture the complexity of even present social-material relations, let alone future ones. It is here that a gap was created, wherein late antique legislators inserted their interest in principles of one kind or another—equity, humanity, what have you—over against the *subtilitas*, the punctiliousness, of the law.[16]

The second form of legal-philosophical reflection provoked among jurists confronting the world that Caracalla created was more abstract in orientation. It was occasioned, it seems to me, precisely by the lack of fit between the ambitions, shape, and social-theoretical consciousness of Roman law and the varied local legal systems it had now to map and replace. If those systems were neither homologous in their principles nor homeomorphic in their structures, how should one then account for such fit between law and society as does arise? More fundamentally, what was the ontological status of law or for that matter of culture? Not surprisingly, the most extensive meditations on these themes are to be found in the eastern jurists, whose rise in just this period was described some years ago by Fergus Millar.[17] Consider, for example, Marcian's description of the legal capacity of exiles, of ex-citizens, in a work likely of the 220s C.E.:

> *deportatus civitatem amittit, libertatem retinet et iure civili caret, gentium vero utitur. itaque emit vendit, locat conducit, permutat, fenus exercet aliaque similia. unde etiam recte obligat, quae post condemnationem quaesivit: quibus in rebus creditores quoque, qui bona fide contraxerunt cum eo, praeferuntur fisco deportatis defunctis succedenti. nam bona, quae condemnationis tempore inveniuntur, deportatus alienare non potest.*

> A deported person loses his citizenship but retains his freedom, and while he loses the *ius civile* he employs the *ius gentium*. He accordingly buys, sells, leases, hires, barters, lends money and does other things of this same kind. Hence, he may also lawfully pledge those things that he acquired *after* his condemnation; and in these dealings, his creditors who have contracted with him in good faith are preferred to the imperial treasury as successors when a deported person has died. For a deported person cannot alienate the goods that are found in his possession at the time of his condemnation. (Marcian *De iudiciis publicis* bk. 2 fr. 214 Lenel [the book attribution is that of Lenel; the citation is missing from the *Digest*] = *Dig.* 48.22.15)

What Marcian provides is an enumerative definition of *homo economicus* as he existed between legal systems in the mind of a man who knew more than one, who had been brought by circumstance to reflect on the range of legal actions commonly available, which is to say shared, between bodies of law in the Roman east. Reflections on the content of *ius gentium* before the Antonine Constitution are empty shells by comparison.

By way of parenthesis, let me add that there exist a wide range of texts in the *Codex Theodosianus* on just this problem, with the opposite intent: that is to say, the law in question imposes a sentence of *infamia*, and goes on to specify what civil-law rights one should imagine guilty parties losing: they lose *omnem facultatem testandi ac vivendi iure Romano*, "all capacity to write a will or live in accord with Roman law"; or guilty parties are henceforth *intestabiles*, "forbidden to write a will or enter into an inheritance," and possess *nullam potestatem alicuius ineundi habere contractus*, "no power to enter into a contract"; and so forth.[18] Although marked by a different ambition, namely, that of cutting off their victim from human society, these laws exhibit a clear continuity with Marcian in their conception of the forms of human sociability of interest to the law.

The Future History of Prior Law

I turn now to custom, with an example in a moment on contract, to continue the theme. Custom, *consuetudo*, had not been a preoccupation of pre-Antonine jurists. On the contrary, with the possible exception of some very limited reflections on *desuetude*, Roman jurists had almost no interest in custom: as evidence of its alienness within Roman legal thought, one might point to its conjoining in extracts in the *Digest* with "unwritten law," a category self-consciously flagged by Roman jurists as borrowed from the Greeks.[19] This was true even when the jurists turned their attention to the provinces: after all, if even the Zagrenses could be credited with possessing *ius*, a body of law, what need had one of their customs?

In the aftermath of the Antonine Constitution, I have argued, the separate and continued existence of other bodies of law could not be permitted, at least at the level of theory. At the same time, social and property relations—social order—demanded that now notionally Roman courts throughout the provinces uphold within some attenuated civil-law framework legal agreements formed under those earlier bodies of law. I want here to discuss briefly two features of the rulings and writings that emerged from that process: first, of necessity earlier provincial law, whatever its origin, is characterized in post-Antonine legal writings *as* custom, and this is likely to have affected the work of courts in crafting decision rules in specific cases; second, more remarkably, this had effects on what came to count as *civil* law.

The transformation of prior law into custom in doctrinal texts is at some level not surprising: it has precedent in the language of late Republican Roman law, where non-Roman marriages are described as taking place according to *mos*, at times explicitly in light of the grant of *civitas* to the communities where the marriage took place.[20]

Where provincial law is concerned, I cited earlier the rule handed down by Trajan to Pliny, that local law should prevail. Similar in vocabulary—because, I suspect, of an oversight on the part of the compilers—is Paul's suggestion that in the interpretation of a statute, one should especially consider *quo iure civitas retro in eiusmodi casibus usa fuisset*, "the law that the *civitas* had previously applied in cases of the same kind." The sentence that follows, the last of the extract, seems in contrast clearly post-Antonine in its vocabulary: *optima enim est legum interpres consuetudo*, "for custom is the best interpreter of laws."[21] The equivalence here struck between *consuetudo* and the law that had once been applied gets to the heart of the historical process I seek to analyze.

The consequence of the Antonine Constitution in the practice of law is well known: an enormous case law sprang up, seeking to determine which prior practices and principles could survive, at least for the lifetime of individuals and contracts grandparented in. As has often been observed, the result in Justinian's Code is an enormous body of rescripts merely restating standard doctrine, even when the judgment in the case at hand was that the illicit practice of the individuals in question would be permitted to stand. What I would stress today is the complete replacement in those texts of the vocabulary of law with that of custom, from the reign of Alexander clear through to the reign of Diocletian: pre-Roman norms are described as *mos regionis, mos locorum, praeterita consuetudo, Graeco more*, and so forth.[22] One example from the reign of Alexander is particularly apt, as it rehearses in new language, as it were, the principle of Paul:

> *Praeses provinciae probatis his, quae in oppido frequenter in eodem genere controversiarum servata sunt, causa cognita statuet. nam et consuetudo praecedens et ratio quae consuetudinem suasit custodienda est, et ne quid contra longam consuetudinem fiat, ad sollicitudinem suam revocabit praeses provinciae.*
>
> After a case has been heard, the governor of a province shall decide in accordance with established practices, such as have been frequently confirmed in the same type of dispute in the town. For both *consuetudo praecedens*, preexisting custom, and the *ratio* that established the custom should be taken into consideration, and the governor of the province shall recall to his own attention the need not to allow things to occur in contravention of *longa consuetudo*, long-established custom. (*Cod. Iust.* 8.52.1 [Honoré Palingenesia 665/8/47], from 224 C.E.)

Particularly charming in this body of material are the trial balloons, when someone attempted and failed to associate an anomalous act with a fictitious local custom and got shot down: *Nec apud peregrinos*, not even among aliens, insisted Diocletian and Maximian, could someone make another brother to himself by adoption.[23]

This recuperation in actual legal practice of what had been at best occasional musings regarding the relationship between the *consuetudo civium* and the statutes those *cives* make for themselves was a time bomb waiting to explode on the civil law. For the customs now being upheld *as customs* were perforce the customs of citizens, albeit recently enfranchised ones. Who was to say their customs were not law?

And this, remarkably, is just what happens. In an extract from book 4 of Ulpian's commentary on the edict, contained in the chapter of the *Digest* called *De pactis*, he takes up the problem of honoring non-civil-law forms of contract before the law:

> (pr) By *ius gentium*, *conventiones quaedam* some agreements give rise to actions, some to defenses.
>
> (2) But even if the matter does not fall under the head of another contract and yet a ground exists, Aristo in an apt reply to Celsus states that there is an obligation (*obligatio*). Where, for example, I gave a thing to you so that you may give another thing to me, or I gave so that you may do something, this is, Aristo says, a συνάλλαγμα, a *synallagma* and hence a civil obligation arises (*civilis obligatio*). And therefore I think that Julian was rightly reproved by Mauricianus in the following case. I gave Stichus to you so that you would manumit Pamphilus; you have manumitted; Stichus is then acquired by a third party with a better title. Julian writes that an *actio in factum* is to be given by the praetor. But Mauricianus says that a civil action for an uncertain amount, that is, *praescriptis verbis*, is available. For the contract described by Aristo with the word συνάλλαγμα has been made and hence this action arises. (Ulpian *Ad edictum* bk. 4 fr. 242 Lenel = *Dig.* 2.14.7)

The problem before Ulpian is the need to provide a generic action for disputes arising from non-Roman forms of bilateral agreement: hence his invocation of *ius gentium*, and the preservation within the jurisprudential (and textual) tradition of the Greek term *synallagma*. What must have been a largely theoretical problem for Aristo was a very real one for Ulpian.

What is remarkable here is the two-fold embrasure—perhaps not all of Ulpian's agency—of this new action within *ius civile*. For the non-Roman contracts in question are said to give rise to a *civilis obligatio*, a civil-law obligation; and the generic action on agreements—the so-called *actio praescriptis verbis*—is itself granted status as *civilis*, too. Equally stunning was the intuition by Julian to subsume the problem of non-Roman contracts under the umbrella of the *actio in factum*: for that action was itself an omnibus category, designed in the classical period and understood precisely as allowing adjudication before the law of cases that could not, by hook or by crook, be described in the language of contemporary formulae. Despite its (intentional) vagueness of definition, it was emphatically recognized as a legitimate civil-law action; and in both origin and application it provided exactly a precedent for the situation confronted by Ulpian and others across the third century.

The Work of Integration in the Age of Justinian

The issues raised in these texts of the third century, and the methods employed by jurists and lawyers to negotiate them, had a long life in late antiquity. Let me give two quick examples, which hearken to terms and themes I have already raised, and by that means return to the conclusions I sketched at the start.

First, in 529 Justinian attempted a correction to the law of dowry. The difficulty he sought to address was partially one of fairness: he wished to grant to women getting divorces the right to recover their dowries before any other claims were made upon their ex-husbands' property. And the problem existed or, rather, was apparent in part because in this area as in so many others, Roman and Greek practice diverged, and attempts to assimilate the two provoked reflection and revision in the law.

The law opens with a statement of the substantive revision it enacts—that wives should have a prior claim, in order to recover their dowries—followed by a blatant assertion of fact in denial of law: wives are so entitled

> *cum eaedem res et ab initio uxoris fuerant et naturaliter in eius permanserunt dominio. Non enim quod legum subtilitate transitus earum in mariti patrimonium videtur fieri, ideo rei veritas deleta vel confusa est.*

> because the property belonged to the wife in the first place and it naturally, *naturaliter*, remains in her *dominium*. For the truth of the matter, *veritas rei*, is not destroyed or confused by the subtlety of the law, in which a transfer of the wife's property into the estate of her husband appears to have occurred. (*Cod. Iust.* 5.12.30.*pr.*)

This is a deeply sloppy piece of legislation: in effect, Justinian wholly overturns all prior law on dowry by denying that ownership of it passes to the husband in the first place. On the understanding he adumbrates, the husband possesses only usufruct of it, and it is important to observe that the long history of law on dowry had been heading in this direction. But Justinian shied from revision on that scale. He resorted, rather, to the standard toolbox of the Roman lawyer: like a classical lawyer, he left prior law standing, only to upend it by fiction; and like a third-century jurist, he justified that action by asserting a gap between some social reality and the world the law would or could describe:

> *Volumus itaque eam in rem actionem quasi in huiusmodi rebus propriis habere et hypothecariam omnibus anteriorem possidere, ut, sive ex naturali iure eiusdem mulieris res esse intellegantur vel secundum legum subtilitatem ad mariti substantiam pervenisse, per utramque viam sive in rem sive hypothecariam ei plenissime consulatur.*
>
> Therefore we desire that she have an action *in rem* relating to property of this kind, as if it were her own, and possess, too, an hypothecary action prior to all others, so that regardless whether the property of the wife is considered to be hers in accordance with natural law, or is held to have become part of the estate of the husband through the subtlety of the laws, her interest shall be fully protected by one or the other of these two actions, that is to say, the one *in rem* or the hypothecary action. (*Cod. Iust.* 5.12.30.1)

It's a fascinating text, but a sorry piece of legal reasoning. In light of my suggestion regarding Ulpian's domestication of Greek forms of contract, it is worth noting that when Justinian boasted of his revisions to marriage law in the *Institutes*, nowhere does he suggest his revisions betray foreign influence: unknown to the ancients, he writes, the practices he codified were simply the enactments *a iunioribus divis principibus*, by more recent emperors (Justinian *Inst.* 2.7.3).

As with dowry, so with Italy. In a series of laws in 530 and 531, whose success he vaunted in the *Institutes*, Justinian attempted to dismantle the legal schemes that distinguished ownership on and of Italian and provincial land and hence, too, the actions and rules that governed transfer of said ownership.[24] One important difference *between* the two schemata had lain in the systems whereby possessors of certain goods could claim ownership of them; another distinction had been drawn *within* each schema between moveable and non-moveable goods.

Expressing repeated frustration with the *inutiles ambiguitates et differentiae*, useless ambiguities and distinctions that the ancients had imposed upon the law in contravention of *ius naturale*, Justinian declared it pointless to permit usucapion *in Italicis solis* but to exclude it *in provincialibus*, to permit it on Italian soil but exclude it from provincial soil. He also removed as merely "antiquated" the distinction between forms of ownership previously restricted to Italian soil, which had distinguished there between moveable and non-moveable goods.

But here he involved himself in a difficulty: for though he desired to homogenize the full range of existing practices around the simplest rule possible—*sit et rebus et locis omnibus similis ordo*, "let there be the same scheme for all things in all places"—and chose for that reason to universalize usucapion—the Italian action, as it were—for various reasons he actually compromised the simplicity of this scheme in two related ways. First, he redefined usucapion so as to include the timetables, plural, that had governed the provincial rule of *longi temporis praescriptio*; and second, he did this in part because he ultimately decided to (re)impose a distinction between moveable and non-moveable goods. One reason to take these actions, beyond mere common sense, was that individuals were even then shaping actions that extended into the past and future in light of prior law—the same problem, one might say, that jurists and lawyers had confronted across the third century.

Justinian and his lawyers were less flexible thinkers, though they deployed the same tools in resolving this impasse: rather than admit that a *similis ordo* did not, in fact, pertain *rebus omnibus*, he allowed that ownership of moveable goods passed to long-term possessors ***quasi*** *per usucapionem ei adquisitam*, "*as if* they had been acquired by him through usucapion."

Conclusion

I conclude with two brief thoughts, one about the Justinianic corpus and one about the late ancient state.

On my reading, Justinianic law emerges as surprisingly classical: in particular, the formal moves employed in it to enact change or mere revision echo those adopted in earlier periods of upheaval—the municipalization of Italy and the aftermath of the Antonine Constitution—as well as those brought forward by legal philosophers in calmer moments, when they sought in earnest reflection to resolve conflicts of law provoked by the praetor or for that matter the emperor. But the corpus also appears to me, at any rate, suspiciously homogenous: for one thing, there are too few aliens and too little law about them. More seriously, I worry that the Justinianic compilers excerpted and retained those passages in which the *arguments* (in distinction to mere rules) appeared to them legitimate.

Described as in some respects grappling with problems similar to those that confronted lawyers in the early empire, and furthermore as employing tools that are themselves logical developments upon classical ones, the law of the later Roman Empire may thus be understood as more Roman—less vulgar, less Byzantine. At the same time, the texts that preserve classical law emerge from this inquiry somewhat less trustworthy: not so much as saying things that are not true, but as *not* saying things no longer applicable or, rather, no longer intelligible, to sixth-century lawyers.

Where the late ancient state is concerned, the world the law sought to create was more unified in its legal structures, of course, but also in fundamental respects more inclusive: for within the normative superstructure that Justinian sought to universalize were embedded non-Roman concepts and non-Roman rules that were often enough self-consciously redescribed as Roman at the moment of their taking up. In this way, legal-philosophical tools devised to justify decision-rules in the present worked continually to rewrite the past.

If the state so created appears nevertheless less flexible, more univocal, than its classical ancestor, that is because emperors from Constantine onward, but particularly those commencing with Theodosius, explicitly co-opted nongovernmental institutions and personalized networks of power in the project of state-building, and so robbed public life of its constitutive outside, and themselves of the notionally disinterested chorus that had earlier hymned their legitimacy.[25] But this was not the lawyers' fault.

Chapter 3

Empire and the Laws of War

Alberico Gentili's extraordinary work *De armis Romanis* takes the form of a pair of speeches, the first an indictment of the injustices committed by the Romans in war, the second a speech of defense, on the justice of those same actions. The work lacks an introduction or conclusion in propria persona; the reader is thus left without guidance as to how to award the palm of victory. That said, Gentili did not write in a spirit of postmodern indeterminacy. His concerns were rather source-critical: "it is necessary," his first speaker insists, "that I consider their own histories suspect. For they openly admit that they were hostile to all those who stood forth as enemies of the Romans" (*De armis* bk. 1, chap. 1, in David Lupher's fine translation).[1] How can one trust Roman claims to have adhered to the laws of war—to have fought, in their terms, only wars that were just—when they can be shown to have lied about fundamental issues in their past? And what might one conclude about war and imperialism in general, when that most paradeigmatic of empires felt such shame, even before itself?

Gentili was far too sophisticated merely to accuse the Romans of mendacity. On the contrary, he brings to bear upon the ancient sources a number of critical tools, some with distinct and important modern analogs. Here I single out three, which will in altered form guide my own reconstruction and critique of the institutions invented at Rome to actualize principles of justice in war.[2]

First, in reading ancient texts Gentili distinguishes between "bare narrations of deeds and opinions that are added on," and proposes mechanisms for adjudging the reliability and cogency of each. Importantly, he does not allow one to claim that the Romans lied only in their judgments but may be trusted in their facts. On the contrary, comparison even of Roman texts reveals widespread disagreement about basic information; and some portion of that confusion must surely stem from invention (see especially bk. 1, chap.

5). What more might one learn from Carthaginian sources, or any by "those other peoples with whom the Romans had their disputes and wars?" "But I have access to nothing" from them, is the reply (bk. 1, chap. 1).

Second, although Gentili more or less accepted the historicity of the conceptual and institutional frameworks described in Roman sources for adjudicating questions of justice in war, and in particular those concerned with declaring wars that were just and striking treaties that were fair, he recognized the scope such frameworks gave to interested manipulation: invented by the Romans, their language and rules were regularly deployed in patently self-serving fashion. The aftermath of the battle of the Caudine Forks, when the Romans surrendered a Roman general to their enemies, only to have him kick the Roman ambassador and by that violation of *ius gentium* permit the Romans to wage war "the more justly," was only the most famous such case (bk. 1, chaps. 6–7).

Third, Gentili insisted again and again that the less robustly attested institutions of international law at Rome might be understood in light of the categories and concepts of the civil law. The concept of restitution is a case in point (bk. 1, chap. 6). As I shall show momentarily, a demand for reparations lay at the heart of Roman declarations of war, and the failure of Rome's opponents to give satisfaction made those wars just. But while Roman sources expend much effort showing that such demands were made, received and rejected, they never entertain the question whether the demands were *themselves* just. Gentili urges recourse in just that matter to the concept of restitution in private law; and on that understanding, his first speaker insists, Roman wars were anything but just.

Gentili's instincts on these issues were superb. And yet, modern formulations of his concerns, as well as the methods one might devise to address them, would naturally take a different form. As regards Roman knowledge of the early Roman past, for example, contemporary scholarship exhibits a deep and justified skepticism. To illustrate the magnitude of the problem, contemporary ancient historians generally rehearse the attested length of histories of Rome written between the late third century B.C.E., when Roman historical writing seems to have begun, and that of Livy, written between 30 B.C.E. and 14 C.E. and the first extant in any reasonable degree. As late as the 120s B.C.E., Lucius Calpurnius Piso Frugi could tell the history of Rome in 7 books; his contemporary Cn. Gellius took 30 books to reach the Second Punic War (218–201 B.C.E.). But a generation later, Valerius Antias covered the same span in 75 books, while Livy's history famously consumed 142. It is of course possible that through diligent research Valerius Antias and Livy uncovered substantial sources of information their predecessors had overlooked, but it is by no means clear what those sources would be. Among other things, Livy himself allows in the preface to his sixth book, some four hundred modern pages into the History, that virtually all written sources for Roman life before 390 B.C.E. were lost when the city was sacked by the Gauls.[3]

We thus rely primarily upon sources written in the final decades of the first century B.C.E. for knowledge of the age of conquest—from roughly 400 to 50 B.C.E.—despite knowing at some level that their authors cannot have known a considerable number of the facts they purport to relate. What is more, within this schema, the earlier the event, the less reliable the evidence for it is likely to be.

As regards bias, it is now fairly widely recognized that Roman conceptions of the empire—as both political form and political and cultural project—underwent profound change across the last century B.C.E. John Richardson has rehearsed with commendable care the evidence for one aspect of this transformation, that regarding conceptions of empire as state. Hand in hand with that development went another, in which the Romans came to regard themselves as responsible not only for themselves, but for their empire, that is, for the ongoing life of conquered places and societies. That is to say, it was in the ages of Cicero and Augustus—the age of Livy—that the Romans began to speak of an imperial project, and so came to write histories in which the acquisition of empire took place according to rules that made the fact of empire morally supportable.[4]

Finally, as regards the history of law in particular, two modern claims related to Gentili's purely heuristic strategy of interpreting Roman international law in light of civil law deserve special attention; one is source-critical, the other historical. The source-critical claim may be simply put: for multiple reasons, not least the lack of any vigorous capacity to imagine their own society in archaic, bronze- or iron-age form, the Romans tended to retroject into the remote past the institutions of the classical city, and thus to narrate intervening events as though conducted through those same institutions. The historical claim is more complex in its defense and likewise its ramifications, but may also be simply stated. Where scholars once assumed that many institutions and practices of religion at Rome were genuinely archaic or at least had roots in some prepoliadic past, some now argue—and I heartily concur—that, on the contrary, it is the institutions of the classical city-state that have the best claim to ancientness, while the customs and institutions attributed by the Romans to remote antiquity are often enough inventions, their supposed aetiologies merely interested attempts to legitimate innovation in the present by assigning it roots of hoary antiquity.[5]

As it happens, the ritual the Romans claim to have used throughout their history to ensure their wars were just is precisely an institution of this kind: one barely if at all attested throughout the centuries when it supposedly governed declarations of war but robustly described by historians at the very end of the age of conquest. What is more, the Romans themselves—and scholars in the aftermath—have compared it superficially to a genuinely archaic civil-law action, the so-called *legis actio sacramento in rem*, the "legal action for title to a thing conducted by oath." Assuming the religious ritual to be ancient and yet eschewing its explication precisely on grounds of its enigmatic ancientness, scholars make the comparison merely to illustrate that which they should have worked to prove, namely, that archaic civil-law actions derived from statal religious ones.[6]

In this chapter, I follow Gentili's lead in asking what we might learn—indeed, what questions we might be provoked to ask—if we refuse to accept at face value Roman histories of that ritual—the ritual of the fetial priests, the object of so-called fetial law—and instead subject those histories to scrutiny. What is more, I follow Gentili's lead again in assigning hermeneutic if not historical priority to the civil law. If, as seems highly probable, the Romans invented for themselves and retrojected into the past a legal-religious ritual for declaring just wars on analogy with a well-attested civil-law action, it behooves us to ask what light that action might shed upon the justice of Roman wars and relations of law and empire in the Roman world.

Fact and Fiction in Histories of the Fetial Priests

If we turn now to both the data for, as well as Roman histories of, the laws of war, the evidence is perhaps best described twice, first as they understood it and second in relation to the source-critical concerns I laid out above.[7] For even if we come to regard those Roman histories as largely the product of middle and late Republican invention, the form of those inventions is nevertheless an object of very great historical importance, not least for the history of laws of war in Europe in the aftermath.

The story the Romans told has more or less two parts; the story that we would reconstruct, two more. That is to say, the Romans themselves described their laws of war as having a single moment of origin and as having undergone a single significant revision. Speaking strictly about the data organized in relation to the periods they describe and without concern for their reliability, we can describe two further, seemingly significant patterns in appeals to those laws down to the age of Augustus at the end of the first century B.C.E.

First, the Romans claimed that at some point in the eighth century B.C.E.—a good half millennium, in other words, before on their own estimation historical writing was first practiced at Rome—the Romans adopted wholesale from a neighboring people, the Aequicoli, a priesthood charged with supervision of piety in international affairs. In a story of quite typical form, a Roman king decided that his people lacked something—in this case, some constraint on their aggressive instincts—and so he imported a practice or, rather, a priesthood, from elsewhere. There is no evidence for this tale before the first century B.C.E., but it was much celebrated then. Indeed, the emperor Augustus honored the Aequicolan inventor of fetial law with a statue in his forum.[8] As we shall see, he had reason to do so.

The bailiwick of the fetial priests, and hence of the *ius fetiale*, of fetial law, comprised three arenas, only two of which—declarations of war and the striking of treaties—are assigned by our (late) evidence to this very early period. The third arena, safeguarding the sacrosanctity of ambassadors, emerges to real prominence first in late accounts of the Samnite wars; I cited above Gentili's discussion of those events (p. 38).[9] Turning first to their role in the striking of treaties, Livy described the practice of the early fetials thus:

> **a.** *fetialis regem Tullum ita rogavit: "iubesne me, rex, cum patre patrato populi Albani foedus ferire?" iubente rege, "sagmina" inquit "te, rex, posco." rex ait: "pura tollito." fetialis ex arce graminis herbam puram attulit.* (1.24.4)
>
> The fetial addressed a question to King Tullus as follows: "Do you command me, king, to strike a treaty with the *pater patratus* of the Alban people?" The king so commanding, the fetial said, "King, I demand of you *sagmina* (a clump of grass torn from the earth with its roots and soil)." The king said, "Take it pure." The fetial took from the citadel pure grass.
>
> **b.** *fetialis erat M. Valerius; is patrem patratum Sp. Fusium fecit, verbena caput capillosque tangens. pater patratus ad ius iurandum patrandum, id est, sanciendum fit foedus; multisque id verbis, quae longo effata carmine*

> *non operae est referre, peragit. legibus deinde recitatis, "audi," inquit, "Iuppiter; audi, pater patrate populi Albani; audi tu, populus Albanus. ut illa palam prima postrema ex illis tabulis ceraue recitata sunt sine dolo malo, utique ea hic hodie rectissime intellecta sunt, illis legibus populus Romanus prior non deficiet. si prior defexit publico consilio dolo malo, tum illo die Diespiter populum Romanum sic ferito ut ego hunc porcum hic hodie feriam, tantoque magis ferito quanto magis potes pollesque." Id ubi dixit porcum saxo silice percussit. Sua item carmina Albani suumque ius iurandum per suum dictatorem suosque sacerdotes peregerunt.* (1.24.6–8)
>
> The fetial was Marcus Valerius. He made Spurius Fusius *pater patratus*, touching his head and hair with the *verbena*. The *pater patratus* is appointed to swear the oath, that is, to sanction the treaty. He does this with many words that it is not necessary to relate, the *carmen* being long to recite. The terms of the treaty having been recited, he said, "Listen, Jupiter; listen, *pater patratus* of the Alban people; listen, too, Alban people. As these things have been recited from first to last from these wooden or wax tablets without malice aforethought (*sine dolo malo*), and as they are most properly understood in this place on this day, the Roman people will not be the first to depart from their stipulations. If the Roman people does depart by public decision with malice aforethought, then on that day let Diespiter strike the Roman people even as I strike this pig in this place on this day; and may you strike harder by as much as you are stronger and more powerful." When he had said this, he struck the pig with the flint. The Albans completed their own *carmen* and swore their own oath through their own *dictator* and their own priests.

Livy turned later to their role in declaring war:

> **c.** *legatus ubi ad fines eorum venit unde res repetuntur, capite uelato filo—lanae uelamen est—"audi, Iuppiter," inquit. "audite, fines"—cuiuscumque gentis sunt, nominat—"audiat fas. ego sum publicus nuntius populi Romani; iuste pieque legatus venio, verbisque meis fides sit." peragit deinde postulata. inde Iovem testem facit.* (1.32.6)
>
> When the envoy comes to the boundaries of those from whom reparations are sought, he covers his head with a fillet—the veil is made

of wool—and says, "Listen, Jupiter; listen, borders"—he names the people whose borders they are—"listen, Righteousness: I am the official envoy of the Roman people; I come as ambassador justly and piously; let trust attend my words." He then goes through the demands. Then he makes Jupiter witness.

d. *tum is nuntius Romam ad consulendum redit. confestim rex his ferme verbis patres consulebat: "quarum rerum litium causarum condixit pater patratus populi Romani Quiritium patri patrato priscorum Latinorum hominibusque priscis Latinis, quas res nec dederunt nec fecerunt nec soluerunt, quas res dari fieri solui oportuit, dic," inquit ei quem primum sententiam rogabat, "quid censes?" tum ille: "puro pioque duello quaerendas censeo, itaque consentio consciscoque."* (1.32.10–12)

Then the envoy returned to Rome for consultation. Straightaway the king consulted the Fathers with words such as these: "Concerning the goods, suits and disputes about which the *pater patratus* of the Roman people, the Quirites, has spoken with the *pater patratus* of the ancient Latins and the ancient Latin peoples, they have neither given nor performed nor paid the things that ought to be given, performed or paid." Addressing him whose opinion he asked first, the king said, "Speak! How do you vote?" Then that person said, "I vote that those things should be sought in a pure and pious war, and I so move and so propose."

e. *fieri solitum ut fetialis hastam ferratam aut praeustam sanguineam ad fines eorum ferret et non minus tribus puberibus praesentibus diceret . . . id ubi dixisset, hastam in fines eorum emittebat. hoc tum modo ab Latinis repetitae res ac bellum indictum, moremque eum posteri acceperunt.* (1.32.12, 14)

It was customary for the fetial to carry an iron-shod spear or fire-hardened shaft of cornel-wood to the borders of the people in question and to say in the presence of not less than three men of military age . . . When he had said this, he hurled the spear into their territory. In this way reparations were sought from the Latins and war was declared, a custom later generations have received.

About these texts, please observe the following: in passage **a**, note the synecdochic relationship between the *sagmina* from the Capitol and the soil, the stuff, of Rome itself. In passage **b**, note the stipulation that violations of the treaty are to be considered meaningful in relation to the agent's state of mind, whether, that is, the Roman people act with or without malice aforethought. (This was an issue of great interest to Gentili: see *De armis* bk. 1, chap. 1.) In passage **c**, observe first the curious metonymic address of the boundaries rather than people, and second the collocation of terms of legal, religious and moral valuation: *fas, iuste, pie, fides*.

In passage **d**, notice again two things: first, the assumption (visible also in passage **a**) of a strict homology between the institutions of the contending parties—both sides have a *dictator*, a *pater patratus*, and so on; and second, that the purity and piety of the war seems to follow directly upon the refusal of the other party to accede to the Romans' construal of the situation. That is to say, whether a war is "just" depends crucially not on any assessment of the legitimacy of Rome's demands, but solely on the enemy's response to those demands. Finally, in passage **e**, note first the ritualization of violence in the form of the throwing of the spear, not in substitution for real violence but to establish a bookend by which the war itself is ritualized: closure will come when the same college of priests is ordered by the relevant magistrate *foedus ferire*, to strike a treaty. Second, observe how the declaration of war is conceived as an end to a process of *rerum repetitio*, a seeking of return of goods or reparations for grievance. (I will consider Isidore of Seville's musings on just these themes in conclusion.)

According to Roman sources, fetial ritual underwent one substantive change in the long history of war at Rome. This took place in the early third century B.C.E. when Rome began to fight *bella transmarina*, wars across the sea.[10] At that point, it became inefficient to send so many delegations to the enemy, not least the last, to throw the spear. I will consider below the one detailed description of the change undertaken in response to this problem, but in summary what the Romans are supposed to have done is this, to have required a prisoner of war to purchase land at Rome, so as to create a plot there of notionally hostile territory; and henceforth they threw the spear into it.

About the history of the fetials in particular, but also the laws of war and international law more generally in the aftermath of this change, extant sources are nearly silent. This is not to say that Rome did not go to war, or strike treaties, or for that matter participate in legal disputes in the international arena in this period. But neither the fetials nor any superpoliadic or superstatal understanding of norms of justice in international affairs is ever mentioned, nor more importantly are any specific contents of a codified body of such law ever cited.

Then, rather startlingly, after an absence from even Roman sources of some two centuries, the fetials reemerge in the mid-first century B.C.E., first in asides in literary texts of the mid-50s B.C.E., and then quite possibly in their role striking a treaty in 38 B.C.E.—the evidence for this event, a Greek translation of an official Roman document, cannot offer definitive proof as there were no fixed correspondences in Greek terminology for Roman institutions even at this late date. Finally, the fetials appear in all their glory—declaring war!—in the lead-up to the battle of Actium of 31 B.C.E., when the forces of the future emperor Augustus, joining Rome, Italy and the West, went to war against Antony, Cleopatra and the theriomorphic gods of Egypt.[11]

That one can describe the moment in such clear-cut terms, however, belies the fraught realities of the age. It was, rather, the last—or better, the latest—in a sequence of civil wars. The deliberate assimilation of Antony's forces to those of his Egyptian ally was only the most obvious of the mechanisms deployed by the future Augustus to win support among Romans for the renewed slaughter of other Romans. On some readings, the revival—or even the invention—of a ritual for declaring war, and its handing off to priests, was another such mechanism. For as it happens, if one orders the testimonia for the fetials' role in declaring war by the dates of their authors, then it is revealed that the earliest testimonium derives from Lucius Cincius Alimentus, a Roman senator who wrote a history of Rome in Greek at the start of the second century B.C.E. The passage from Cincius refers to an event of the eighth century B.C.E. Not only can we not establish any means by which knowledge of that event would have passed to Cincius; in no case other than under Augustus can we establish that the ritual was even performed, let alone that knowledge of it did not come from Cincius. Such is the tenuous thread on which hangs the history of the laws of war at Rome.[12]

That said, Augustus was not the only person who sought to endow morally and legally dubious action with legitimacy by invoking religious law. Livy, Augustus's exact contemporary, clearly rewrote the history of Roman warfare in light of this concern, and the retrojection of the fetials into situations where we have no evidence—and very likely he had no evidence—of their involvement was the principal means by which he did this. That said, even if the Romans do not appear to have had any mechanism to actualize principles of justice and piety in war, it is not unimportant that they came eventually to feel they should have had some. Nor is it by any means obvious how fetial ritual might achieve this end: whose justice was served by the formal delivery of demands for reparations? Is the reading above correct, that the vote on war rested solely on the question whether the enemy had satisfied that demand, rather than on the justice of the demand itself? Whose law was satisfied by the legalitarian trick of selling Roman land to a foreign soldier?

These questions are equally meaningful—and their answers equally elusive—if we accept the facticity of Roman claims regarding the origin and actions of the fetial priests in the archaic period. To answer them, I follow Gentili's lead, as it were: turning to a comparatively well-attested civil-law action, I seek to extract from the logic of its performance a key by which to understand the place of fetial law specifically and international law more generally at Rome.

The *Legis Actio Sacramento in Rem*

As I have already observed, fetial procedure for declaring war has an important comparandum in an ancient legal action known as the *legis actio sacramento*, namely, the action conducted via *sacramentum*, by oath. (Two asides: I describe the action as "ancient" because it formed part of the system of civil-law actions in use, as it seems, already in the fifth century B.C.E., a system in many ways replaced, but in some narrow respects merely supplemented, by the so-called formulary system introduced by the *lex Aebutia* sometime in the second century B.C.E.; and the shifting meanings of the term *sacramentum* are precisely one of the curiosities of this history.) Indeed, the resemblances between the two are so striking, at the level of both form and function, that scholars have sought generally to establish the two in genealogical relation and not by means of comparison to shed light, each upon the other. Rather, the bulk of opinion has more or less unreflectively assumed, in this case as in others, that the civil-law action must derive from the statal or religious one, despite what seems to me fairly overwhelming evidence to the contrary. In what follows, I want to establish the comparison in two respects: between the rites in their ancient form or, rather, in what is represented to us as their ancient form; and later, to compare changes to the rites and the construals placed on those changes already in antiquity.[13]

According to Gaius, the author of an idiosyncratic textbook of Roman law of the mid-second century C.E., the *legis actio sacramento* was a general action available when no other action was suited. It had two basic applications: *in rem* and *in personam*, in regard to things and to persons. Where things were concerned, the plaintiff claimed ownership of an item in the possession of the defendant. In cases involving persons, the plaintiff claimed that the defendant *dare facere praestare oportere*, "ought to convey, do, or answer" for something. Alas, only one substantial description of the *legis actio sacramento* survives, that in Gaius's *Institutes*, and the section on actions *in personam* is lost. More crucially, from what we do know the action appears to have been designed precisely to provide an opportunity for redress at the law to those who had no evidence to support their claim. This affects not only the procedure followed but the consequences of settlement. Consider the description provided by Gaius:

> *Si in rem agebatur, mobilia quidem et mouentia, quae modo in ius adferri adduciue possent, in iure uindicabantur ad hunc modum. qui uindicabat festucam tenebat; deinde ipsam rem adprehendebat, uelut hominem, et ita dicebat:* HUNC EGO HOMINEM EX IURE QUIRITIUM MEUM ESSE AIO SECUNDUM SUAM CAUSAM. SICUT DIXI, ECCE TIBI, UINDICTAM IMPOSUI. *et simul homini festucam imponebat. aduersarius eadem similiter dicebat et faciebat. cum uterque uindicasset, praetor dicebat:* MITTITE AMBO HOMINEM. *illi mittebant. qui prior uindicauerat, ita alterum interrogabat:* POSTULO ANNE DICAS QUA EX CAUSA UINDICAUERIS. *ille respondebat:* IUS FECI SICUT UINDICTAM IMPOSUI. *deinde qui prior uindicauerat dicebat:* QUANDO TU INIURIA UINDICAUISTI, QUINGENTIS ASSIBUS SACRAMENTO TE PROUOCO; *aduersarius quoque dicebat similiter:* ET EGO TE.

> If the action was *in rem*, movables and self-moving things, provided they could be carried or led into court, were claimed in court in the following manner. The claimant picked up a *festuca*, a rod, grasped the *rem* itself—a slave, for example—and spoke thus: "I affirm that this human being is mine by Quiritary right, according to his proper title. As I declare, look you, I have laid my claim." At the same time he laid his rod on the slave. His opponent declared and did the same things in the same way. When each had laid his claim, the praetor said, "Unhand the human being, both of you." They let him go. The first claimant then addressed the other claimant as follows: "I demand that you say on what basis you have laid claim." The other responded, "I have exercised my right as I laid my claim." Then the first claimant said, "Since you

> have laid a claim unjustly, I challenge you by a *sacramentum* of five hundred *asses*." His opponent for his part spoke similarly: "And I you." (Gaius *Inst.* 4.16; translation after F. de Zulueta)

About the action thus far depicted, observe three things. First, it is the stuff, itself, that seems to matter. The laying of claim—the speaking of force, in an ancient etymology—took the form of an address to one's opponent accompanied by physical contact with the property in dispute. No substituent representation was permitted. In this respect, the commitment to materiality at work in the archaic form of the *legis actio sacramento* mirrors that operative in the fetial ritual for the striking of treaties, in which the priest took a clump of Roman soil, with shoots of grass, roots and all, to the location where the treaty would be struck (passage **a**, p. 41).

Second, the absence of evidence creates a dynamic in which plaintiff and defendant observe a meticulous procedural equivalence: the defendant says and does *eadem similiter*, the same things in the same way; or responds, *et ego te*, "And I you." (Compare the parallelism asserted by Livy, again in his account of the striking of treaties [passage **b**, pp. 41–42 above]: "The Albans completed their own *carmen* and swore their own oath through their own *dictator* and their own priests.") A further consequence is that the loser suffered more than a loss of the property in dispute. He was also adjudged guilty of perjury. Such might seem in many legal proceedings a logical entailment of the verdict—namely, that witnesses for the losing side said things that in the reality created by the verdict turn out to be untrue, whatever they were before—but rarely was this entailment pursued. But the evidentiary regime of the *legis actio sacramento* virtually required this. For the claim of each party was ultimately grounded solely in the *sacramentum*, the oath given concrete form in the monies sacrally deposited, and because loss revealed the loser's oath to be falsely sworn, he was held guilty of *falsum* and his deposit, by the classical period also designated by the term *sacramentum* by commonplace metonymy, reverted to the state treasury.[14] Loss in the *legis actio sacramento* thus came in the Roman legal imagination to symbolize loss of the most total kind, of case, property, and face.[15]

Third, an understanding of the stakes in the civil-law action clarifies the nature of fetial ritual, with its elaborate embassies to and fro, its demand for reparations and prescribed periods of inaction, during which Rome's opponent might consider its options. Those options were two: total surrender, which is to say, the performance of reparations under whatever conditions

Rome stipulated—in the *legis actio*, the equivalent would be surrender of the *rem*, not commencing the ritual and certainly not offering the *sacramentum*—or war, the staking of everything on a contest. In other words, we are led once again to see that priestly action, in the form of an embassy by the fetial priests, was understood to come into play only when fatal violence had become overwhelmingly likely and required legitimation.

Within the unitary legal community of the city, however, recourse to oath and deposit, to *sacramentum*, effected a displacement by which a third party, the gods, were momentarily drawn into the dispute. As a consequence, the potential for violence, which might always threaten the stability of a merely juridical decision, was legally and symbolically contained: the violence of the decision, by which one party was dispossessed of face and possibly goods, bracketed victor from loser precisely by animating a new entanglement between loser, gods, and community, which was, however, settled in virtually the same motion as it was opened. The originary act that gave rise to the dispute, whatever it might have been, whether crime or no, yields at the announcement of the verdict to oath-breaking, and the retaining of the *sacramentum* by the state effects atonement in the same act of closure that seals the restitution.

In this perspective, we can see that the *festuca* in the *legis actio*—the rod, an unshod and unsharpened piece of wood—carries two meanings. It did stand, as Gaius says, *quasi hastae loco*, "as it were in the place of a spear,"

> *signo quodam iusti dominii, quando iusto dominio ea maxime sua esse credebant, quae ex hostibus cepissent; unde in centumuiralibus iudiciis hasta proponitur.*
>
> the spear being one symbol of lawful ownership, as they believed those things especially to be theirs by lawful ownership which they had seized from an enemy. It is for this reason that a spear is displayed in centumviral court. (Gaius *Inst.* 4.16)

Gaius hedges because, as his remarks make clear, the best symbol of a spear is a spear, nor were Roman courts shy to display spears to symbolize their authority and their bailiwick. But the use of the *sacramentum* in the *legis actio* required that the vindication be understood *not* as an act of violence. The acting out by plaintiff and defendant of the speaking of force was not even directed at each other; it was, rather, a gesture not least before the gods. Indeed, such an understanding of the rite seems to lie behind the language of the essayist Aulus Gellius, of the second century C.E., in a remarkable commentary he wrote nearly contemporaneously with Gaius's *Institutes* on the phrase *ex iure manum consertum*, "to lay on hands in accordance with the law." Gellius needed to understand the phrase because it occurred in the *Annales* of Ennius, a poet of the early second century B.C.E.:

> *pellitur e medio sapientia, vi geritur res;*
> *spernitur orator bonus, horridus miles amatur.*
> *haud doctis dictis certantes, nec maledictis*
> *miscent inter sese inimicitiam agitantes.*
> *non ex iure manum consertum, sed magis ferro—*
> *rem repetunt regnumque petunt—vadunt solida vi.*
>
> Wisdom is driven forth; the matter is debated through violence;
> the good speaker is spurned; the rough soldier is loved.
> Contending not with learned words or curses,
> the sides commingle and stir up enmity.
> Not by laying on of hands in accordance with the law,
> but with iron rather they seek rule and reparations
> and on they rush with heavy force. (Ennius *Ann.* ll. 248–53 = bk. 8 fr. i Skutsch)

Gellius understands the phrase "laying on of hands in accordance with the law" to refer to an action *in rem* of the Twelve Tables in which, as in the *legis actio sacramento*, the property itself was brought to court and ritually seized. He therefore interprets Ennius as constructing a polarity in which legal and martial action are taxonomically related as two kinds of *vis*, two kinds of force, though Ennius mentions only one. What is more, Gellius articulates this reading with vocabulary that draws on the symbolism precisely of the *legis actio sacramento.*

> *idcirco Ennius significare volens gestum, non, ut ad praetorem solitum est, legitimis actionibus neque ex iure manum consertum, sed bello ferroque et vera vi atque solida rem repeti dixit; quod videtur dixisse, conferens vim illam civilem et festucariam, quae verbo diceretur, non quae manu fieret, cum vi bellica et cruenta.*

> Hence Ennius, wanting to describe action of this kind [namely, legal], says that reparations were sought not after the fashion customary before the praetor, through legal action or by a laying on of hands in accordance with the law, but through war and iron and actual and heavy force. He seems to have spoken thus in order to compare civil and *festucaria*, rod-ly force, which is spoken with words and not conducted by hand, with the force of bloody warfare. (Gellius 20.10.10)

Fetial ritual was thus not designed to forestall violence. Far from it. Its function was rather to inaugurate wars that were, in Roman terms, *purum piumque*. It remains to investigate the connection drawn by its ancient commentators between the fetials' role in producing wars that were pious and pure and wars that were just. Whose justice? Which gods? The question is not pure pedantry. For example, in Livy's description of the *devotio* of Decius, a rite whereby a general vowed self-destruction and called upon the gods similarly to destroy his enemies, Decius concludes the invocation that opens his prayer by describing the gods he has named as "gods whose power embraces both us and our enemies"; and, as we have seen, Livy's description of early fetial ritual suggests not surprisingly that it was organized on the assumption that Rome's enemies, too, had fetials, that their language and gestures would be immediately intelligible. But neither assumption of parallelism can have obtained for long. It is in modifications to the ritual as these assumptions broke down, and the interpretation of those modifications, that we might seek an answer; and it is by triangulation with other rituals and their exegesis that we should find our way.

As noted earlier, the most famous *emendatio* to fetial ritual is that ascribed to the early years of the third century B.C.E. when the Romans first undertook a *transmarinum bellum*, a war across the sea. The fullest description is that provided by Servius, a commentator on Vergil of the fourth century C.E.:

> *PRINCIPIUM PUGNAE hoc de Romana sollemnitate tractum est. cum enim volebant bellum indicere, pater patratus, hoc est princeps fetialium, proficiscebatur ad hostium fines, et praefatus quaedam sollemnia, clara voce dicebat se bellum indicere propter certas causas, aut quia socios laeserant aut quia nec abrepta animalia nec obnoxios redderent. et haec clarigatio dicebatur a claritate vocis. post quam clarigationem hasta in eorum fines missa indicabatur iam pugnae principium. [post tertium*

> *autem et tricesimum diem quam res repetissent ab hostibus, fetiales hastam mittebant. denique cum Pyrrhi temporibus adversum transmarinum hostem bellum Romani gesturi essent nec invenirent locum, ubi hanc sollemnitatem per fetiales indicendi belli celebrarent, dederunt operam, ut unus de Pyrrhi militibus caperetur, quem fecerunt in circo Flaminio locum emere, ut quasi in hostili loco ius belli indicendi implerent.]* (*Ad Aen.* 9.52)
>
> BEGINNING OF BATTLE: this is what one needs to know concerning the Roman rite. When they wanted to declare war, the *pater patratus*, that is, the chief of the fetials, would set out for the enemy's border. There he would speak certain solemn pronouncements, saying in a clear voice that the Romans were declaring war for specific reasons, either because they had harmed allies of Rome, or because they had not returned animals they had stolen or captives they had seized. This is called the *clarigatio*, from the *claritas* of his voice. After the *clarigatio*, a spear is hurled into the enemy's territory, to indicate the commencement of hostilities. [The fetials throw the spear at any time after the thirty-third day from the one on which they demanded restitution. Finally, when in the time of Pyrrhus the Romans were about to wage war against a *transmarinum hostem*, an enemy across the sea, and could not find a place where they might perform through the fetials this ritual for declaring war, they compelled one of Pyrrhus's soldiers, a captive, to buy a plot of land near the *circus Flaminius*, so that they might fulfill the law of declaring war *quasi in hostili loco*, as if in foreign territory.]

Servius finds a logical correlative to this ritual in the seizure of enemy land in order to conduct on it Roman rites. This information he attributes to Varro's *Calenus*, and it is from Varro, a contemporary of Cicero, that much of Servius's information on fetial ritual is likely to have come.

> *Varro in Caleno ita ait duces cum primum hostilem agrum introituri erant, ominis causa prius hastam in eum agrum mittebant, ut castris locum caperent.*
>
> Varro in his *Calenus* says that when generals were about to enter hostile territory, they first threw a spear into it, to seize land for a camp, for the taking of auspices. (Varro *Calenus* = *Logistorici* fr. 2 Semi)

In counterpoint to this history one should eventually set the other significant evolution in literature on the fetials, that they were increasingly described as supervising Roman adherence to *ius gentium*, charged in particular with oversight of the sacrosanctity of embassies.[16] For the moment, however, two features in these accounts stand forth. First, as regards the ritual itself, observe what we might call the strong nominalism of Roman ritual and legal language: the formal purchase of land by a prisoner of war suffices to create enemy territory. The effectiveness of language in the rite of sale thus creates a new reality—regardless of the mental state of the enemy participant, who cannot have been willing even if he were not acting with malice aforethought. Second, the category "enemy territory" is in the language of Servius violently abstracted from the particular. In Livy's description of the original rite, it was the enemy of the moment who had to be warned, and the requirement of warning was satisfied only when three males of military age among its populace heard the declaration.

In point of fact, this change in fetial practice has a parallel in the *legis actio sacramento*. For as we have seen, litigants had recourse to the *actio* also to claim things inconvenient or impossible to move, and practice in regard to them repays comparison to fetial law in several respects. There is first the logic of the ritual itself, for as Gaius makes clear, it rested upon the synecdochic use of parts of the disputed objects as stand-ins for the whole, whether clods for fields or wool for flocks.

> *Si qua res talis erat, ut sine incommodo non posset in ius adferri uel adduci, uerbi gratia si columna aut nauis aut grex alicuius pecoris esset, pars aliqua inde sumebatur eaque in ius adferebatur, deinde in eam partem quasi in totam rem praesentem fiebat uindicatio; itaque ex grege uel una ouis siue capra in ius adducebatur, uel etiam pilus inde sumebatur et in ius adferebatur; ex naue uero et columna aliqua pars defringebatur; similiter si de fundo uel de aedibus siue de hereditate controuersia erat, pars aliqua inde sumebatur et in ius adferebatur, et in eam partem proinde atque in totam rem praesentem fiebat uindicatio, uelut ex fundo gleba sumebatur et ex aedibus tegula, et si de hereditate controuersia erat, aeque res uel rei pars aliqua inde sumebatur.*
>
> If the disputed object were such that it would not without inconvenience be brought or led into court—for example, if it were a column or ship or

> herd of animals—some part could be taken and that could be brought into court, and the claim could be laid on that part as if on the whole thing. So from a herd either one sheep or goat was led into court, or even a hair might be plucked and brought into court; from a ship or column, some part was broken off. Likewise, if the dispute was over a field or building or legacy, some part was taken and brought into court, and the claim was laid on that part as if on the whole, present thing. For example, a clod was taken from a field and a tile from a house, or if the dispute concerned a legacy, some article was taken from it. (Gaius *Inst.* 4.17)

The second fulcrum of comparison lies not so much in the logic or components of the ritual, but in the historical understanding of the ritual devised by its exegetes in the classical period. The most notable of these is located not in jurisprudential literature but in Gellius, who found himself unable to comprehend the logic that tied the speaking of a claim, the laying on of hands, and the presence of a nearly absent object.

> *Correptio manus in re atque in loco praesenti apud praetorem ex duodecim tabulis fiebat, in quibus ita scriptum est: si qui in iure manum conserunt. Sed postquam praetores, propagatis Italiae finibus, satis iurisdictionis negotiis occupati, proficisci vindiciarum dicendarum causa ad longinquas res gravabantur, institutum est contra duodecim tabulas tacito consensu, ut litigantes non in iure apud praetorem manum consererent, sed "ex iure manum consertum" vocarent, id est alter alterum ex iure ad conserendam manum in rem de qua ageretur vocaret atque profecti simul in agrum de quo litigabatur, terrae aliquid ex eo, uti unam glebam, in ius in urbem ad praetorem deferrent et in ea gleba tamquam in toto agro vindicarent.*

> According to the Twelve Tables, a seizure by hand of thing or place took place in the presence of the praetor. For there it is written, "If any lay on hands in court." But later, after the boundaries of Italy were extended, the praetors became preoccupied by legal matters and were reluctant to travel for the sake of hearing claims to far-off objects. As a result, it was decided by tacit agreement, contrary to the Twelve Tables, that litigants would not lay on hands in court before the praetor, but they would call for "a laying on of hands according to the law." That is, one litigant would summon the other to the disputed object for a laying on of hands in accordance with the law. Having set out at the same

> time to the field in question, they would bear back from it some bit of earth—a clod, for example—to the city, into court before the praetor and on that clod, as if on the whole field, they would speak their claim. (Gellius 20.10.9)

What Gellius cannot understand is not the need for the disputed object itself to be claimed—that is to say, he comprehends natively the need that a claim to an object should be made through physical contact with the object itself. It is rather the realism, as it were, underlying the synecdoche of clod for earth that he finds incomprehensible. There is of course no evidence that this synecdoche is an accretion to an earlier phase of ritual practice in which the materiality of object and vindication were actually respected. But Gellius feels that such must have been the case, so much so that he labels the work-around of part-for-whole *contra duodecim tabulas*, "contrary to the Twelve Tables."

In fact, the explanation he advances for this change also recalls the history of fetial ritual, if not its reality then certainly its historiography. For like those writers who posited a change in response to the practicalities of transmarine warfare, so Gellius understands ritual in law to have been modified in response to the new geographic and practical realities of the growing Roman state. In this the arguments of Gaius and Gellius harmonize with standard ancient visions of legal history: in Pomponius's shorthand, *augescente civitate*, as the civic community grew, *deerant quaedam genera agendi*, some types of legal action were found to be lacking.[17] What is more, as Gellius himself maintained in another essay, *longa aetas verba atque mores veteres oblitteravit, quibus verbis moribusque sententia legum conprehensa est*, "the great expanse of time (since the writing of the Twelve Tables) has brought to oblivion the language and customs of antiquity, and it is in light of language and customs that the sense of the laws is understood" (Gellius 20.1.6).

So it is, by the middle of the second century C.E., that the logic of archaic ritual, in its forms and language—its efficacy in bringing into being an internally consistent reality and then acting upon it—was slipping from intelligibility. The distance Gaius and Gellius felt between themselves and some other state in which that logic was clear was posited by them as principally chronological, nor were they unreasonable in so thinking. The most compressed expression of their incomprehension before the identism on display in these rituals is not even their insistence that what is taking place are substitutions: that the *festuca* is used *hastae loco*, in place of a spear. It is rather their sense that this is not, in fact, correct: hence, what Gaius actually asserts is that the rod is used *quasi*, *as if* in place of a spear; the plot of land near the circus Flaminius functions *quasi in hostili loco*, *as if* on enemy territory; claims are made *in eam partem proinde atque in totam rem praesentem*, on the part *as if* on the whole, present thing; or *in ea gleba tamquam in toto agro*, on that clod *as if* on the whole field.

In speaking of identism, I seek to open debate regarding a practice in which I myself have participated, even in this volume. Heretofore I have identified the two practices misconstrued by Gaius and Gellius as synecdochic or realist on the one hand, and nominalist on the other. But the metaphorical borrowing of concepts developed in rhetoric and linguistics to discuss problems of materiality and representation in ritual seems to me here and elsewhere unhelpful. For the terms virtually require that we see between these two practices some radical difference, where in fact, I have argued, they should be understood as deeply and multiply aligned. The problem, I urge, is that the metaphysics of ritual at Rome presumes a very different ontology than does the metaphysics of modern linguistics, where what is generally at stake is precisely the gap between the ontologically distinct entities of word and thing.

The Justice of the Civil Law

When the *pater patratus* created by the fetial announced in the course of his oath sealing a treaty that only actions committed with malice aforethought should or would count as violations proper, and only they should provoke retaliation by Diespiter, how did he imagine that determination would be made? Was this a recognized standard in international law? Was there somebody to judge the matter? Would the other party to the treaty or transaction have a say?

As a reminder of what was at stake in these transactions, I cite the report by Tacitus of the Romans' deliberations near the end of a successful siege in 49 C.E. of Uspe, a small town in the kingdom of Bosporus:

> *Postero misere legatos, veniam liberis corporibus orantes: servitii decem milia offerebant. quod aspernati sunt victores, quia trucidare deditos saevum, tantam multitudinem custodia cingere arduum: [ut] belli potius iure caderent. datumque militibus, qui scalis evaserant, signum caedis.*

> On the next day envoys [from Uspe] were sent, begging pardon for the free and offering, too, ten thousand slaves. This the victors rejected, because it would be savage to slaughter the surrendered, and likewise difficult to surround so great a number with a guard: better they should fall by the law of war. And so the soldiers who had scaled the ladders were given the signal for slaughter. (Tacitus *Ann.* 12.17.1–2)

On Tacitus's view, the Roman commanders weighed a number of factors—moral, legal, and practical—and satisfied themselves that indiscriminate slaughter of the defeated was unobjectionable on all scales, so long as they rejected the offer of surrender. The principle involved was presumably that "surrender and gift have no meaning without acceptance"—but neither the citizens nor the gods of Uspe can have found much consolation in such legalitarianism.

On these issues, namely, the place of intention and determinations of it in fetial law, we must once again fall back on the evidence of legal instruments and interpretation outside international law. Two issues at least deserve attention: who was thought to establish the conceptual and definitional framework within which to adjudge individual cases, and what agents—what sort of agents—did the judging?

The fate of the loser's *sacramentum* in the *legis actio sacramento* provides one clue. Notably, the money was not handed over to the successful litigant. It was not in that sense an additional penalty, nor an emollient for the successful litigant's expenditure of time and effort. Rather, because its donor was deemed to have sworn falsely, the deposit was accepted by the state in expiation for the injury done the gods. Similar frameworks were employed to provide for individual fault in public and private contexts. The most famous articulation of any such rule was provided early in the first century B.C.E. by Quintus Scaevola the pontifex (fr. 10 Huschke-Seckel-Kuebler). Varro for one cited it in elaborating on the consequences of performing legal acts on days when such actions were forbidden:

> *quod si tum imprudens id verbum emisit ac quem manumisit, ille nihilo minus est liber, sed vitio, ut magistratus vitio creatus nihilo setius magistratus. praetor qui tum fatus est, si imprudens fecit, piaculari hostia facta piatur. si prudens dixit, Quintus Mucius aiebat eum expiari ut impium non posse.*

> But if he unwittingly speaks that word and manumits someone, that person is nonetheless free, but with a bad omen, just as a magistrate elected with a bad omen is nonetheless a magistrate. A praetor who so speaks, if he does so unwittingly, may be expiated through the sacrifice of an expiatory victim. If he speaks wittingly, Quintus Mucius says that he is *impius* and so cannot be expiated. (Varro *Ling.* 6.30)

Varro's account leaves open the possibility that a deliberate violation of scruple receives no expiation whatsoever. But this was not in fact true: Scaevola's rule merely provided that the agent of such a crime could not himself perform the relevant sacrifice. On the contrary, the rule articulated here that only inadvertent crimes may be expiated by their agent has an important correlate in other bodies of law, to the effect that it was the community as a whole or, rather, its designate who then had to act.[18] One such example comes from the *lex*, the regulations of the sacred grove at Spoleto:

> *honce loucom nequ<i>s uiolatod neque exuehito, neque exferto quod louci siet, neque cedito nesei quo die es deina anua fiet; eod die quod rei dinai cau[s]a [f]iat, sine dolo cedre [l]icetod. seiquis uiolasit Ioue bouid piaclum datod, si quis scies uiolasit dolo malo, Iouei bouid piaclum datod et a(sses) CCC moltae suntod; eius piacli moltaique dicato/[ei] exactio est[od].*

> Let no one violate this grove, or export or take away what belongs to the grove. Let no one cut (wood) except for the requirements of the annual divine service; on that day it shall be allowed to cut without malice for the requirements of divine service. If someone violates (this rule), let him offer a *piaculum* of an ox to Jupiter; if someone violates (it) with malice aforethought, an expiatory sacrifice of an ox shall be offered to Jupiter, and three hundred asses shall be as a fine. The offering of the *piaculum* and the collection of the fine shall be the responsibility of the *dicator*. (*CIL* I^2 366 = *ILS* 4911, revised in Panciera 1994)

Bracketing for a moment the problem of who makes the determination with regard to the mental state of the perpetrator, it is clear that within this system sacrilegious acts always require expiation. The mental state of the perpetrator enters into consideration only insofar as the knowing criminal renders himself *impius*: he can no longer act in public cult on his own behalf, and the community must take responsibility for making atonement.

As for the determination of mental state, that task presumably fell to the community, while the gods in question, who would in any event receive an expiatory victim, were expected to be satisfied with the community's judgment. This was, importantly, not an implicit expectation in Roman religion but a central tenet of its practice. It is reified in the regulations of cult as preserved in documentary and literary texts above all in the form of third-person imperatives: whatever errors might take place in performance, *(tamen) probe factum esto*, "(nevertheless) let it be held to have been performed properly."[19] The legal declaration brings a particular reality into being, at least for those within the community that holds that language efficacious. The willingness of the gods of Rome to be bound by such language was held a principal sign of their citizenship and goodwill. On this understanding, the standards by which the Romans expected to be judged in their decision at Uspe, and likewise the Romans who struck the treaty with the Alban people (pp. 41–42), were Roman standards, and the gods, Roman gods. It thus bears mention that no Alban god is called to witness the Roman oath.[20]

Understood in relation to its ongoing life in the classical period—and not, that is, purely for what it can or cannot reveal about the distant past—the *legis actio sacramento* suggests a different way to understand fetial law. Here it merits recalling how little we actually know about the conduct of the action in practice. The features that attracted the attention of antiquarians and jurists alike concerned neither the manner, frequency, purpose, nor practicalities of its use, but simply aspects of its form. We do not know what sort of proofs or pleadings the parties presented, or how judges reached their decisions. The insistence that the loser forfeited his *sacramentum* rests on two assumptions, that parties offered no proof other than their oath (whatever that would mean), and that each party wished to win.

What if neither assumption held? In seeking to understand the place of the rod in the context of the action, Gaius invoked the symbolism of the spear: it signified ownership, he wrote, "as they believed those things especially to be theirs by lawful ownership which they had seized from an enemy." Set aside the problem that Gaius has no authority whatsoever for this claim: like all fictions of an original position or state of nature, the world in which such beliefs obtained was a logical postulate alone. (Like many such, it has probably more often than not been invoked by the strong against the weak.) In this case, the ownership of things seized in war can only be the purest form of property in relation to legal title. In that sense, seizure of property in war mirrors the surrender, indeed, the creation of title on judgment in a case at law. This, I suggest, is in fact the explanation for the survival into the classical period of the *legis actio sacramento*, a legal action of an otherwise outmoded form of procedure. For what Gaius implies is that parties had recourse to it when neither could prove ownership, which deficiency was precisely rectified in the outcome of the case. What neither he nor Gellius takes seriously is that deficiency in title was a liability at sale, one that could be redressed at the law. The utility of the *legis actio sacramento* as a mechanism for the creation and transfer of title lay in its ability to resolve just this difficulty.

That said, such an understanding of the *legis actio sacramento* points very precisely to the utility, as also to the limitations, of fetial law. For it served—indeed, I would maintain that it was invented, directly in imitation of the civil-law action—to satisfy ethical and moral demands that the Romans placed on themselves, but we should never forget that the demands were framed, and the degree of their satisfaction adjudicated, by the Romans themselves.[21]

In closing, I quote the fascinating final paragraph of the remarkable chapter *De bellis*, "On war," in Isidore of Seville's *Etymologies* (18.1.11):

> *Quattuor [autem] in bello aguntur: pugna, fuga, victoria, pax. pacis vocabulum videtur a pacto sumptum. posterius autem pax accipitur, foedus primum initur. foedus est pax quae fit inter dimicantes, vel a fide, vel a fetialibus, id est sacerdotibus, dictum. per ipsos enim fiebant foedera, sicut per saeculares bella.*
>
> Four things are done in war: fighting, flight, victory, and peace. The term "peace" seems to be taken from *pactum*, pact. Moreover, a peace is agreed upon later; first, a *foedus*, a treaty is entered into. A treaty is a peace made between warring parties; it derives from *fides*, trust, or from *fetiales*, that is, the priests of that name. For through them treaties are made, just as wars are made by *saeculares,* by lay people.

As it happens, for all his learning, Isidore is useful to me above all because of his errors, which are of two kinds. Some are factual, the most important of which in this passage is one of omission, namely, that the fetial priests were instrumental not only in ending wars but also in starting them. Other errors lie in the realm of background presumption. The most important statement of this latter kind is the assertion that (at Rome) treaties were made by priests but wars by *saeculares.*

Read this way, Isidore offers us one perspective among many on a gap, visible in different ways at different times in European history, between an expectation that among human institutions religion and law, too, should play a role in constraining violence, and historical reality, in which that expectation is variously cheated. In Rome of the middle and late Republic, this expectation was generally articulated through discussion of one of two related topics: debate over the legality or prudence of specific actions in foreign affairs on the one hand, and investigations into the practice and doctrines—or "laws," as the Romans would have it—of the fetial priests on the other. For example, in a fragment of book 3 of Cicero's *De re publica* preserved, as it happens, by Isidore, the principle is announced that

> *illa iniusta bella sunt quae sunt sine causa suscepta, nam extra <quam> ulciscendi aut propulsandorum hostium causa bellum geri iustum nullum potest. . . . Nullum bellum iustum habetur nisi denuntiatum, nisi indictum, nisi de repetitis rebus.*
>
> those wars are unjust that are undertaken without cause, for no just war can be waged except for the sake of revenge or driving off an enemy. No war is held just unless it is announced, declared and concerns the recovery of goods. (Cicero *De re publica* 3.25 Powell = 3.35 Ziegler)

And yet, as Cicero made clear a decade later, when in *De legibus* he listed the statutes of his ideal state, the messengers and the judges are one and the same, and they are Roman:

> *Foederum indutiarum †ratorum† fetiales iudices nuntii sunto, bella disceptanto.*
>
> Of treaties, truces and †legal affairs† let the *fetiales* be judges and messengers; let them judge concerning war. (*De legibus* 2.21)
>
> *Sequitur enim de iure belli, in quo et suscipiendo et gerendo et deponendo ius ut plurimum valeret et fides, eorumque ut publici interpretes essent lege sanximus.*
>
> What follows concerns the law of war. In that field, regarding the taking up, waging and ending of war, we have laid down that *ius . . . et*

> *fides*, law and good faith should prevail as much as possible, and that there should be public interpreters of these. (*De legibus* 2.34)

That fetial law existed in the age of conquest, if it existed at all, solely as part of discourse on warfare internal to Rome is displayed most clearly by the story of its amendment in the age of transmarine warfare. That tale displays not simply the subjection of religious law to processes of abstraction and manipulation in vogue in secular law, but the consequences of its description *as* law.[22] For the change described by Servius in fact involved two conceptual revolutions. In one, a soldier captured from a current enemy purchased land, and so a strict, formal demand was met, that the "hostile territory" into which the fetial would throw his spear did as a matter of law belong to the particular enemy on whom the Romans were declaring war. But unless we believe that a different soldier purchased that land in each conflict, the fetials must soon have resolved upon a work-around—one that appears in hindsight, at least, as prototypically Roman—namely, the abstraction of a category "enemy territory" from multiple particulars.

On this reading, even bracketing the interpretation of the *rerum repetitio* offered above (pp. 48–49; see also 44), it is hard to avoid the conclusion that the ethical standards which the so-called laws of war were designed to meet were Roman ones alone; and far from any early modern aspiration that laws of war might in themselves constrain or forestall violence, in the Roman case, the application of law issued not in an avoidance of violence but in an evasion of responsibility.

Not surprisingly, fetial law features at key moments in both books of Gentili's *De armis Romanis*. In book 1, although the speaker praises the importation of fetial law as motivated by a desire to constrain Romans' appetite for profit through conquest, he also endorses the criticism of the fourth-century Christian apologist Lactantius, to the effect that fetial law, in its status as law and its condition as a Roman institution, was regularly and easily manipulated to provide cover for unjust wars, launched by a people who, "always craving other peoples' things," "acquired for themselves possession of the entire world" (bk. 1 chap. 3). The charge is not quite met by the speaker in the second book (bk. 2 chap. 3). The second speaker instead indicts the first for a factual error, having assigned Lactantius a birthplace in Italy rather than Africa. In having left the first speaker vulnerable on these grounds, but likewise having allowed the second speaker such a limited response, Gentili permits the bulk of the critique to stand, in somewhat discredited form.

As it happens—indeed, as Gentili knew well (bk. 1, chap. 6)—the passage in Lactantius cited by the speaker in book 1 was itself inspired by a passage in Livy, an indictment precisely of Roman manipulation of law in self-serving ways: "You always cloak your deceits with some semblance of legality."[23] That passage is in fact one of a very large number in Roman literature in which savage indictments are leveled against Roman imperialism in its every aspect, largely but not exclusively vocalized in those texts by opponents of Rome, marked at once by nobility and inefficacy. If, as I have argued, one legacy of Gentili's work in modern scholarship should be renewed attention to the influence of the civil law upon the multiple and problematic births of international law, another might be the recuperation of those voices—the lawyers of Salamanca come to mind—who sought in the law some humility for their own people before the world.

Chapter 4

Sovereignty and Solipsism in Democratic Empires

In late medieval and early modern Europe, Rome existed as exemplar among empires in two guises: one tacitly pagan, polite and powerful, urbanized and urbane; the other Christian, at war against heretic and infidel within and without, the proud and sinful instrument of Providence. In elisions typical of historical memory, the major revolutions that produced the Christian empire from the pagan were largely forgotten, while the wars of conquest and the domestic turmoil that issued from them were sidelined completely. This interested portrait has its roots in Christian recollections of Roman antiquity, in which the seizure and mastery of empire by Augustus, enacted above all in the Lukan census, were portrayed by many as preparing the world for Christ. In the world created anew by his arrival, the Roman Empire emerges into history fully realized, without pangs of war, domestic or foreign.

Kindred elisions have long operated in scholarship on the Roman Republic and not coincidentally the Athenian empire. In the case of Rome, part of the problem was evidentiary: the story of the Republic was the one the Romans told, of citizens and nobles pursuing domestic honors, motivated by ambition and tempered by virtue. In the case of Athens, problems of evidence have been compounded by a willful blindness. Admirers of Athenian democracy do not wish to see in Athens what the Romans simply ignored about themselves: both states were at their most aggressively imperialistic when their respective democracies were most radical.

Reflection on that fact raises questions of several kinds regarding the self-understanding each polity possessed of its status in the world; what doctrines of sovereignty defined for each legitimate action at home and abroad; and how claims to empire were legitimated, in relation to one's own and the wider past and to the varied audiences of the present. Taking the Athenian empire as a foil, my principal object in this chapter is to reflect on two of these questions in respect to Rome. First, wherein did Romans—and Athenians, for that matter—imagine the legitimacy of their expansionist impulses to lie? In particular, do legal and diplomatic instruments attest doctrines of sovereignty in respect to those states, their interlocutors and their opponents that might shed light on that question? And second, did Rome's increasing awareness of itself as an empire, kindred in form to past empires, shape the articulation at Rome of an imperial project?

My argument in brief is as follows. The Romans developed and deployed arguments for the legitimacy of their actions and empire in at least two distinct arenas, namely, diplomatic conduct and historical debate. In diplomacy, what was at stake was Rome's self-understanding vis-à-vis its neighbors; in historical and philosophical literature, the question was rather contemporary Rome's position in relation to the past, both its own and that of its subjects. In both cases, a survey of Roman evidence reveals complex and interrelated changes across time. A comparison of public-law instruments from Athens and Rome suggests that both states in their most democratic and imperialist phases justified their actions by appeal to an essentially solipsistic conception of sovereignty. In each case, what legitimated action in foreign relations was nominally the same factor that did so at the domestic level, namely, the will of the people. The Athenians, moreover, signally failed to develop an understanding of statehood and kingship that recognized in many of their peers foci of sovereignty that persisted through time. At Rome, by contrast, diplomatic practice evolved in the late Republic in ways that recognized, in form, at least, the like sovereignty of neighboring states, as well as a homology of institutional forms between those states. This appears to have resulted from pressure internal to legal argument, which required a rationale for the ongoing validity at law of treaties and other arrangements with foreign powers. In that context, doctrines that accorded sovereignty exclusively to Rome were simply unhelpful. In roughly the same period, Romans' self-consciousness regarding themselves as holders of an empire encouraged the development of a historical self-awareness of their position in relation to earlier empires.

Translatio Imperii

Within ancient historiography, the conceptual juxtaposition of empires in comparative or analogical relation occurred most often through simple claims to succession. In literature written in the period of Roman hegemony, such theories may be classified under roughly three rubrics. The most prominent is also the oldest, namely, that of the four empires, which received its most influential articulation in the book of Daniel. It was there eschatological in orientation, and so featured then and thereafter among the themes of oppositional literature, first to Antiochus IV and later to Rome.[1] But it was not only that: already in the first century B.C.E. Greek writers at Rome deployed the scheme in order to exalt Rome as the fifth and most perfect empire, the one, moreover, destined to last forever. It served in that form as one of two popular justifications for writing universal history under Rome.[2] The other justification, it should be noted, was that Rome was in fact the first empire of note, and in that telling Rome succeeded no one.[3]

The Romans also knew a tradition, originating in Greece, that summarized the story of that nation by identifying the sequence of states that had exercised either hegemony or rule over the whole. Perhaps the most pithy articulation of that theme derives from a handbook to rhetoric of the early first century B.C.E., where it serves to illustrate the figure of *gradatio*, or climax: "The *imperium Graeciae*, the empire of Greece belonged to the Athenians; the Spartans took it from the Athenians; the Thebans defeated the Spartans; the Macedonians conquered the Thebans and, having conquered Asia rapidly in war, added it to the empire of Greece."[4] This tradition is distinguished from the first by a perspective foreshortened both chronologically and geographically: the kingdoms of Greece are by any standard late and small-scale.

Finally, Greeks and Romans alike obsessed about Alexander: would he have beaten the Romans of his day? And how did the Roman Empire compare with his? To the latter question we have in fact the response of the emperor Augustus himself. Upon hearing that Alexander had completed his conquests before the age of thirty-two and found himself at a loss what to do next, Augustus marveled that Alexander had not regarded the administration of empire a greater task than its acquisition.[5] In quite different ways, these latter two means of telling the history of empire in the ancient Mediterranean, the one focusing on the empire of Greece, to which Asia is figured as an appendage, the other concentrating on the evanescence of Alexander's conquests, both construct the succession in such a way as at once to lead to Rome and yet distinguish it utterly from its antecedents.

With a single possible exception, appeals to imperial succession as a legitimating device for Roman rule appear in ancient literature, whether Greek or Latin, starting only in the first century B.C.E., a good half millennium after

Rome's conquest of its neighbors had commenced.[6] (That historians *in* the ancient world—as well as many *of* the ancient world—tend to view Roman expansion as having commenced later, particularly with one or another of its initial wars overseas, is a problem to which I shall return.) This might, of course, result from the scant survival of earlier Roman literature. But more significant is likely to be the rise in just this period of something like an imperial project[7]—the development of a principled awareness and practical program to promote the flourishing of conquered societies and populations.[8] It is, of course, precisely this sense of mission that animates Augustus's reproach of Alexander. This ideological construal of empire as stewardship is then instrumental, I would argue, in the rise in just this period of an aspirational literature by Romans ascribing to their polity an infinite extension in time. Far more prominent earlier—and prominent, indeed, in Roman literature of all periods—are diagnoses of decay and testimonials to decline and fall.[9]

The most famous Roman to predict the fall of his own state was Scipio Aemilianus, who when witnessing the death throes of Carthage in 146 B.C.E. famously took the hand of his friend Polybius, the historian and statesman, and lamented the likelihood that his own city, too, would fall. Either he or Polybius—the text is uncertain—also quoted at that moment Hector addressing Andromache in the *Iliad*, "A day will come when sacred Ilion shall perish, and Priam and the people of Priam of the strong ash spear."[10] In the text of Appian, writing in the second century C.E., Scipio is said first to have wept and reflected on the necessity that cities, nations and empires all should fall, including those of the Assyrians, the Medes, and the Persians, as well as the most recent and brilliant, that of the Macedonians. Appian's account is generally not credited, despite his explicit citation of Polybius, who was present with Scipio throughout the siege (as Appian knew). But it is in any event a notable deployment of the four empires theme, and is perhaps its only articulation in which the fall of the fifth empire, too, is imagined as historical necessity. Scipio is likewise responsible for perhaps the most famous example of *gradatio* in Latin literature, provided in voicing a theory of politics equally famous among students of empire: *ex innocentia nascitur dignitas, ex dignitate honor, ex honore imperium, ex imperio libertas*, "From virtue is born esteem; from esteem, public honor; from public honor, power of command; and from power of command, freedom."[11]

About that problematic passage I say here very little. I draw attention to two difficulties only in its interpretation. First, it effects an elision of the boundary between individual and collective.[12] (That elision occurs also in

Greek political thought, but for different reasons and, I suspect, less self-consciously, a point to which I shall shortly return.) Even within a purely Latin tradition, that elision proves several times slippery: for *dignitas*, *imperium*, and *libertas* are all properties of both individuals and communities, while public honor and power of command tend to be held by individuals but are legitimate only when granted by the collective. The second problem raised by the passage is the predication of *libertas* upon *imperium*, of freedom upon power of command—in the strictest sense, the power to command Roman citizens. Setting aside for the moment the logical or practical relationship between the two concepts and their exercise, I suggest that they may each separately be translated by "sovereignty," and yet conjoined express that concept not through hendiadys but through aggregation.[13]

I thus return to the program that I outlined at the start of this chapter, which I can hopefully now refine. Imperial succession as a legitimating device acquired traction at Rome some centuries after Rome had embarked on the conquest of the world. It did so in a period of profound change. The first century B.C.E. witnessed inter alia the final conquest and annexation of Spain, Gaul, the northern coast of Asia Minor, Syria, and Egypt, as well as the collapse of republican government at Rome and its replacement by a constitutional monarchy. In this period, too, Romans of the governing class came to see their state *as* an empire, in crucial respects homologous with other empires, and so capable of comparison with them. These processes were complexly related.[14] The violence and social and economic upheaval unleashed by the wars of conquest contributed to the distortion of norms and practices that had theretofore sustained republican government; and up to a point, the arrival of monarchy may have contributed to the capacity of Romans to see analogies between their own state and the empires of Asia and Hellenistic Greece. That said, Romans' understandings of the jural-political structure of their empire could not be divorced from its history, even if that history was in important respects periodically rewritten to accommodate contemporary ideological pressures. Despite such rewritings, Romans nevertheless retained specific ideas about when their empire began—the plurality of those ideas is not crucial but noteworthy nonetheless. In addition, the concept of *imperium*, of empire, abstracted as the legitimate exercise of state power, existed in Roman thought as a fundamental component of sovereignty. It remains to be seen whether sovereignty so conceived might be conceded to others.

The capacity to recognize historical empires as political formations both structurally and juridically parallel to oneself thus has as a theoretical correlate the capacity to see oneself within a network of likewise sovereign states. It is the object of this chapter to examine this matrix of sovereignty, memory and imperialism at Rome in the period of the empire's acquisition, namely, in those years when Roman politics was at its most radically democratic. I frame my concern in this way to gesture toward two further aspects of my project. First, I want to break (ancient) historians of their habitual privileging of constitutional change at Rome in denominating historical periods. In the parlance of contemporary ancient historians, "Roman empire" refers not simply to a state, but to that state in its monarchic phase. On this reasoning, Rome was an empire when it had an emperor, despite the fact that it acquired the vast bulk of its conquests while still a republic.[15] Proper acknowledgment of both the democratic and the imperialist aspects of Roman republican government would trigger the posing of questions kindred to those we might ask of Athens, the other most famous, but not nearly only other, democratic empire of antiquity. In particular, we might ask how they justified to themselves their exercise of dominion over others, whether those people were Greek, Roman, or barbarian, and their polities governed by democracy, monarchy or oligarchy. We might likewise wonder why voters in each community regularly sent themselves, their families, and their friends to war, despite the horrific cost in human life they paid with apparently abundant enthusiasm.[16]

The second aspect of this project I wish here to highlight is the measuring of ancient experience against an apparent anachronism, namely, the concept of sovereignty.[17] In so proceeding what I do not want to produce is some purely negative conclusion, that neither Greek nor Roman conceptions of international law contained more than an embryonic conception of sovereignty (or, just as undesirable, the self-deceptive conclusion that either or both did possess something like our own), or even some register of sameness and difference between Greeks, Romans, and moderns. Rather, I seek to ask on the one hand whether sovereignty provides a useful hermeneutic in the study of ancient empire, and on the other whether the conceptions of sovereignty sustained by ancient democracies were not inherently solipsistic, and the range of actions they might legitimate did not always include the unilateral and imperialistic. Where theories of sovereignty are concerned, the question I might seem to beg—though I raise it here so as not to do so—is whether Athens or Rome or any ancient polity qualifies as a state. That is a question I have attempted to answer elsewhere in respect to Rome, especially with respect to the concept of territoriality and the practice of the census.[18] I should like my argument here to stand as a further contribution to the project of thinking about ancient polities in light of modern theories of the state.

That said, sovereignty as now understood *is* a modern concept, and as so often in such projects, a large part of our work must consist in taking the measure of the gap separating our notions of sovereignty from their ancient correlates. To that end, I turn first to the constituents of sovereignty in Greek thought, namely, *eleutheria* and *autonomia*, freedom and autonomy; and second, to the dissonance between Greek and Roman thought and practice in international law.

As in Latin, so in Greek sovereignty was not a unitary concept, nor was it mapped by any single term. Again, as in Latin, so in Greek the most robust form of state sovereignty was described by a pair of terms, autonomy and freedom. Autonomy referred exclusively to the right of communities to use their own laws and try their citizens in native courts,[19] and a sophisticated and widely recognized language and practice developed already in the fifth century B.C.E. to regulate the exercise of such autonomy within networks of states, whether those networks were voluntary or compelled, provisional or long-term.[20] The conceptualization of Greek freedom, *eleutheria*, however, remained embryonic even to the twilight of the classical world.[21] Among other things, idealizations of the freedom of communities within Greek political thought remained derivative to the end of the simple binarism free and slave in respect of individuals.[22] At its most basic, and very nearly at its most complex, it consisted in the freedom to make war and hence, as we shall see, the power to subjugate others. We get some sense of this at an early phase in the classical period from the description provided by Herodotus of the constraints placed on the Greek cities of Ionia by the Persian Empire—this *after* they had revolted with Athenian aid and later been brought to heel when that aid evaporated: the satraps Artaphernes and Mardonius forced the cities of Ionia to make treaties with one another, to the effect that they would be subject to jurisdiction in disputes with each other and would not attack each other over them; and they put an end to all tyrannies and established democracies throughout the *poleis*.[23] What was apparently not compromised under Persian rule early in the fifth century, but regularly was under Athens half a century later, was the crucial juridical component of their *autonomia*: their right to regulate internal aspects of social and economic life under domestically generated norms, and to enforce those norms through local institutions.

That in making war and pursuing empire the freedom of other communities was necessarily compromised is a theoretical problem that the weak often voiced against the strong, particularly in the long and sordid struggle for supremacy that preoccupied and ultimately weakened peninsular Greece between the defeat of Athens and rise of Macedon.[24] But the ideal of strong sovereignty, of autonomy conjoined with freedom, remained alive in the fourth century nonetheless. It was the experience of diaspora in the aftermath of Alexander's conquests that strained and ultimately robbed that ideal of its universalism. For the Greek cities established and aided by Alexander and his successors outside peninsular Greece were more than sites of Hellenic culture; they were also nodal points in a political economy that worked to subjugate non-Greek peoples, upon whose labor, brutally exploited, the efflorescence of Hellenism directly depended. In that perspective, one of the historical roles of the Hellenistic kingdoms was to collaborate with the elites of subject cities in preserving an ethnic hegemony of Greeks over multiple non-Greek populations, and one of the prices paid for that concentration of spectacular power in the hands of kings was the loss of freedom of action in foreign affairs on the part of individual cities. It was a small price to pay.[25]

The pressure on the archetypal structures of Greek political thought created by post-Alexandrian geographic dispersal—and the attendant sundering of historical connections between individuals, their ancestors and the land—impelled developments in Greek politics in three areas relevant here. First, in peninsular Greece in particular, there was renewed experimentation with forms of collective action among city-states, most notably the so-called league: some of these respected a more or less robust sovereignty on the part of their members, while others required the surrender of sovereignty in one or more respects to a collective council. In the final analysis, these must be adjudged a failure, and not simply because Greece collapsed so swiftly and completely in the face of Roman aggression. Rather, outside Achaea and Aetolia the Greeks signally failed to discover the means to legitimate supra-poliadic structures of interstate cooperation, military or otherwise. What we find instead are repeated invocations of a liberationist ideology—but in both historical and theoretical terms, these proved time and again self-subverting.[26]

In the second development consequent upon diaspora, the strict genealogical logic of kinship, so prominent in classical theories of citizenship and cultural identity, foundered in the face of the new geographic realities of post-Alexandrian Hellenism, and opportunities were thereby created for new conceptions of cultural identity and new models and practices of citizenship to come to the fore.[27]

The third development in Greek politics and political thought impelled by the geographic dispersal of persons in the aftermath of Alexander's conquests is as follows. Seemingly motivated by the experience of removal from the affective and mythical loci of Greek identity, there arose in the Hellenistic diaspora a generation of individuals who rejected membership in a *polis* as the foundation of political identity but whose thought found expression in two distinct and irreconcilable traditions. One valorized the status of ξένος, legal alien, or of being *apolis*, literally an uncitizen; the other located the irreducible core of political identity in humanity itself.[28] But neither of these traditions produced in the Hellenistic period a political or juridical program. For that, Greece awaited Rome. If in that light cosmopolitanism has had a longer life than existential atomism, that is because having been conceived in the context of diaspora, it became under Rome a feature of empire.[29]

As it happens, what changes took place in Greek conceptions of freedom came about not through the work of political theorists, but in public and international law under pressure from Rome.[30] Here two different issues were at stake. First, Greeks confronted the problem that Roman sovereignty and its constituents did not map well onto their Greek counterparts, despite the apparent ease with which word-to-word correspondences for particular terms of law were found.[31] Regarding sovereignty, for example, Greeks may well have grappled more carefully and more accurately with the concept of *imperium*, differing as it did quite starkly from its counterpart *autonomia*; but the seeming overlap between *libertas* and *eleutheria* left them befuddled. (In point of fact, I suspect there is more to be said regarding the affinities between modern autonomy and Latin *imperium* than might at first glance appear.) The second problem lies in the cultural specificity of their respective legal traditions. For reasons that I shall attempt momentarily to isolate, no Greek legal tradition accessible to us today developed systems of construal or a doctrine of autonomous law or one regarding precedence or even systems of definition before the Roman period. These gaps left Greek politicians ill-equipped to negotiate the constituents of freedom for their communities before Roman magistrates who sought to give it to them.

Greek Freedom, Roman Majesty

In what consisted Roman freedom? And how was its widespread bestowal compatible with the exercise of *imperium* and the holding of empire?

Regarding the freedom of cities, we have a schematic definition from Sempronius Proculus, a jurist of the first century C.E.:

> A free people is one that is not subject to the power of another people (*liber autem populus est is, qui nullius alterius populi potestati est subiectus*). An allied people is either one that has entered into friendship under an equal treaty or one embraced by a treaty such that one people should with good will respect the *maiestas* of the other. Note moreover that the one people is understood to be superior; the other is not to be understood as not free. So, just as we understand our clients to be free, even if they do not excel us in authority or dignity, so those who are bound to respect our *maiestas* with good will should be understood to be free. (Proculus *Letters* bk. 8 fr. 30 Lenel = *Dig.* 49.15.7.1; trans. after O. Robinson)

Proculus supplied this definition as part of an attempt to diagnose with what states Rome had relations of *postliminium*, rules governing the loss and recovery of citizen status when citizen soldiers were captured on foreign soil. The passage was, moreover, written at a time when, we are told, the geographic use of the term *imperium* to mean something like our "empire" had long since consolidated.[32] A modern reader, and even many ancient ones, might therefore be surprised to discover that the free and allied peoples here described exist within, not without, the borders of the empire—this despite the fact that Proculus himself earlier acknowledged that they were without doubt "foreign to us." Part of the difficulty arises from the dissonance between rhetoric and reality, between Roman claims to possess an "*imperium* of the entire world, to which *imperium* all nations, kings and races have assented," and the patent reality of autonomous nations, kings and races existing beyond the boundaries of the empire (*Rhet. ad Herennium* 4.13). Part, too, springs from the existence at Rome of many registers by which the foreignness of land and people might be assessed.[33] But a further important contribution is made also by the extra-juridical nature of assent encapsulated in Proculus's invocation of *maiestas*, the ancestor of our "majesty," famously defined in a rhetorical treatise of the early first century B.C.E. as "that which comprises the dignity and grandeur of the state" (*Rhet. ad Herennium* 4.35: *maiestas rei publicae est in qua continetur dignitas et amplitudo civitatis* [trans. Caplan]).

Maiestas emerges from this reading of Proculus as a crucial component in Roman foreign relations. If it was indeed incumbent on foreign powers to respect the (greater) dignity and grandeur of the Roman people, and if the litmus test for such respect was in fact obedience to Roman *imperium*, that power of command held uniquely by the people and surrendered by them to and into their elected magistrates, then in *maiestas* we should have located a crucial tertium quid distinguishing Roman from Greek conceptions of sovereignty, as well as a mechanism by which Romans might legitimate to a domestic audience, at least, wars of aggression against notionally neutral foreign powers. Nor is there any reason to doubt but that it did occasionally perform that role. Indeed, the temptation to freight it with heuristic value is only sharpened by the discovery that *maiestas* is attributed by Roman writers nearly exclusively to the Roman people.[34] The reason for this is revealing: *maiestas* emphatically does *not* mean mere "dignity and grandeur." It is, rather, a rare, perhaps even unique abstraction formed from a comparative: it means literally "greaterness." It was for this reason that only one party to any bilateral negotiation—and only one party within a network of potential interlocutors—could have it. For the same reason, a comparative presents an obstacle to dialogue more insurmountable than any superlative: all manner of nations might be great or greatest, just as all manner of sovereigns might be most, best or highest, or for that matter rulers of the world. But only one party could have "greaterness." If *maiestas* was a constituent of Roman conceptions of sovereignty, then we must conclude that in Roman theory, at least, only Rome was a sovereign state.[35]

That said, *maiestas* as a solution to the puzzle of ancient imperialism must remain a chimaera, for at least two reasons: it signally fails to differentiate Greek from Roman *practice* in wars of aggression, and legitimating imperialism is in general not the work it was called upon to perform. (Proculus, one must recall, wrote well after the age of conquest had come to an end.) We must look elsewhere.

I turn instead to instruments of public and international law, in which, I note, *maiestas* is little in evidence, and I seek there to diagnose two problems: wherein was sovereignty within the Athenian and Roman states understood to lie, and why was it not conceived as existing in reciprocal relation with other states. Athens and Rome must here be studied using fundamentally different bodies of evidence, for though the public use of monumental writing at Rome predates its employment at Athens (so far as we can tell), verbatim transcripts of statutes and treaties survive from Rome starting significantly later than at Athens. And while a significant number of Roman instruments from the sixth, fifth and fourth centuries B.C.E. are quoted or paraphrased in literary texts, many of those appear in Greek, and the translation of those documents from Latin to Greek works to obscure precisely the development of constitutional theory and language that I seek here to chart.

That said, we confront even at Athens a crucial gap in our knowledge. The Athenian empire was born of its unilateral transformation of an alliance for common defense, a ξυμμαχίς, into an ἀρχή, a rulership of one state over others. The instability of the fifth-century Athenian empire no doubt resulted in part from its historical foundation upon an ideology of liberation, and the same problem in different forms plagued attempts at hegemony in mainland Greece throughout the fourth century as well. About the timing of this transformation, the language and self-consciousness with which it was debated, and its reception among the allies-turned-subjects, we are equally in the dark.[36] As late as 453/2 B.C.E. (probably—the date is uncertain), the Athenians referred to their allies and the alliances in just those terms, namely, as free states, joined by treaty relations freely undertaken.[37] But commencing sometime just after 430 B.C.E.—again, the condition of the texts permits only approximate dating—Athenian decrees regulated the internal affairs of a general category of "the city-states over whom the Athenians exercise power," and Athenian magistrates in the subject cities of the empire were being directed to take unilateral action on matters of currency and trade.[38]

But the path leading to that transformation may in fact be charted. For such instruments of public law and international relations as do survive unfailingly locate the source of their legitimacy in their recording of the will of the Athenians, by which is meant the will of the citizen body, properly organized and duly expressed. Crucially, no distinction of genre and no difference in parliamentary or documentary protocol distinguishes instruments of public or private law, international treaties, or purely honorary decrees.[39] Instead, we find an unvarying, justificatory announcement at the start of all such documents, ἔδοχσεν τῶι δέμοι, "it seemed to the people."[40] That is to say, the only legitimate constraint upon Athenian action is Athenian will, and no difference in the legal or moral status of subjects of that will is recognized.

These documents gesture at two further features of Athenian thought relevant here. The first concerns the taxonomic distinctions they make between forms of states, and the second the timelessness of temporality at Athens. As regards the first, the Athenians generally identified kings by name only: Dionysius of Syracuse, called "the ruler of Sicily" in 393 B.C.E., and Hebryzelmis, identified as the king of the Odrysians in 386/5 B.C.E., are exceptions.[41] Otherwise it is nearly impossible to distinguish individual citizens of democratic states from kings. In the treaty struck between the Athenians and various kings of Thrace, Paeonia and Illyria in 356 B.C.E., forming an alliance against Philip of Macedon, for example, nothing about the text apart from sheer improbability suggests that the Athenians are not swearing "to fight against Philip with all their strength, as much as possible" in alliance with three remarkably brave individuals, one of whom has brothers of an unspecified number.[42] Regarding Athenians' conceptions of their own state, the term *archê*, "rulership" or possibly "empire," may be useful as an index in pointing to a conscious evolution away from an alliance and toward authoritarian rule, but it lacks specificity at the level of constitutional or institutional arrangements. That, combined with this apparent unwillingness to conceive kings of states as occupiers of an office existing beyond the life of its occupant, crippled any incipient perception of a homology between the Athenians and the regional dynasts with whom they interacted, such that both groups might be regarded as sovereign powers ruling aggregations of subordinate states that we would call an empire. The one terribly important exception to this rule is the king of Persia, who in legal instruments is always identified as "the king" and never by name.[43]

The personalization of kingly power, and corresponding institutionalization of the *demos*, points to my second concern. For kings and kingdoms exist in these documents as evanescent presences in history: it is the king, himself, and never a state that is party to a treaty, and any relationship formed between such an individual and the Athenian people had to be renewed with the king's successor. The Athenian *demos*, in contrast, is radically dehistoricized. It is only in the late 420s B.C.E., for example, that the Athenians began regularly to date public documents, and so reconstructed (and in large part invented) a list of eponymous magistrates going back to the early years of their community.[44] This, it seems to me, is another expression of the ideology of autochthony that Nicole Loraux has done so much to excavate, and which finds expression in the fourth century in what J. K. Davies has called the Athenian "ideology of static institutions."[45] For it is essential to Athenians' conceptions of themselves and the origin of their culture that they exist outside of time, unchanging. That is why Athenian thought proves so hostile to theories of socialization or, for that matter, to the Socratic elenchus: for nothing imperiled Athenians' self-understanding so much as attempts to identify the contingent in their culture. Herein, too, lies the explanation why the development of both historiography and law at Athens remains so abortive. Here I side with Loraux against other students of temporality at

Athens—Christian Meier, Louis Gernet, Eric Csapo and Meg Miller—who locate in the birth of democracy some new historical self-awareness.[46] But Athens produced no historical writing of any note before Aristotle (the exile Thucydides obviously excepted), nor, *pace* Josiah Ober, does Athenian memory of the fifth and early fourth centuries record the transition to democracy as a revolution. That came later.[47]

From Republican Empire to Imperial Republic

About Rome we must tell a different kind of story. From the early years of the Roman Republic, in the years, namely, of the classical Athenian democracy at its most expansionist, we have two sources of knowledge regarding Roman legal and diplomatic practice in foreign relations, each suspect. First, Polybius provides Greek summaries, including translations of select clauses, of six early treaties between Rome and Carthage, three predating the first Punic War (264–241 B.C.E.), the others coming between that war and the second (218–201 B.C.E.). The first treaty he dates "to the consulate of Lucius Junius Brutus and Marcus Horatius, the first consuls established after the expulsion of the kings, by whom the temple to Jupiter Capitolinus was dedicated," but he cautions that "the difference in language among the Romans between then and now is so great that only the most intelligent can puzzle it out, and even then partially and with difficulty" (Polybius 3.22.1–3). For that reason among others, I set the earlier three treaties aside, though I observe as an aside in support of Polybius that there is some reason to think that the Romans did, in fact, establish a new historical era at the start of their democracy.[48] The problem for historians of early Rome in making use of these documents is that, so far as I can tell, the system of dating in use in the archaic Roman democracy did not rely on eponymous magistrates; the Capitoline temple was not dedicated in the first year of the Republic; and the earliest high magistrates were not called consuls.[49] In other words, though we have reason to believe that important changes did in fact take place in Roman practice in respect to the calendar at the foundation of the Republic, the memories of those changes preserved at Rome are almost undoubtedly false.

Our second source of knowledge consists in narrative histories of early Rome, all dating from the first century B.C.E. and later, though many cite, and some quote, sources written earlier. These are variously reliable, but they fail us in one crucial respect. As with virtually all ancient historiography, the authors of these texts bridge rather than respect the gap between the culture and institutions of their own day and those of the archaic past.[50] They therefore represent Roman relations with other Italian city-states as mediated by homologous institutions and conducted through diplomatic forms that all parties receive as intelligible and legitimate. They do this in spite of a purely antiquarian awareness that Italy had once been diverse, and in many respects remained so. But Latin had long since come to dominate and had in many places simply replaced the many dialects that had once tessellated the Italian peninsula; and in the crucial matter of public law, municipal practice had largely homogenized within the lifetime of many of the writers concerned. This in itself made the real past of Roman-Italian relations much more difficult to imagine, as the institutional diversity of Italy's communities would have to be recovered from records written in languages then in the process of being lost, or from memories themselves almost undoubtedly rehearsed in a Latinate Roman framework. But there was more to this rewriting of the Italian past than some methodological failing in the technologies of memory. It was also motivated, at least in part, by the political and ideological aftermath of the Social War, that bitter struggle between Rome and its Italian allies at the end of the first decade B.C.E., whose paradoxical and tragic outcome was a Roman claim of victory and a Roman concession of all that the vanquished had sought.[51]

This collaborative forgetting of Italy's past then worked in harmony with other trends in historiography to fix a history of Roman imperialism somewhat at odds betimes with the data ancient historians themselves recorded and, indeed, with sheer probability. For instance, writers of the second and first centuries B.C.E. agree that the progression of Roman arms across the water marked a turning point in Roman culture. But a turning point of what sort? And which body of water? For Polybius, echoing Roman moralists, it was the turn eastward, and in particular the influx of wealth from conquered Hellenistic kings commencing in 168 B.C.E., that altered Rome.[52] For Cicero, writing in this case in 70/69 B.C.E., the body of water was the Sicilian strait and the change was, remarkably, the turn to empire itself: "for Sicily was the first of all foreign nations to place itself in the friendship and trust of the Roman people; Sicily was the first province to be so named, an ornament, as it were, of empire [in 241 B.C.E.]; Sicily it was who taught our ancestors how outstanding a thing it is to exercise imperial power over a foreign race" (2 *Verr.* 2.2).[53] And for many others, it was the crossing of the Adriatic, because it was no longer possible endlessly to adapt the religious and diplomatic institutions of a city-state to the logistical realities of transmarine warfare.

The religious institution most often cited in these contexts is the fetial law.[54] As was rehearsed in Chapter 3, its most important use—very nearly its entire bailiwick—was the protection of ambassadors and the regulation of declarations and endings of war. In particular, fetial law required that declarations of war proceed through an elaborate sequence of embassies demanding redress for whatever grievance motivated the exchange; and the sequence ended with the ceremonial hurling of a spear into foreign territory. This ritual had an essential correlative in the need for Roman magistrates to be on Roman soil in order to take the auspices—to inquire, as best as could be done, whether divine favor existed for the action planned for any given day. Had either regulation been sustained, Roman arms might never have advanced beyond a day's march from Rome. But in Roman narrative, a legalitarian solution was found in the selling of a piece of land in Rome to a foreign soldier, and the corresponding appropriation by Roman generals of enemy land, that each ritual might be performed according to the letter, if not the spirit of the law.

Again, according to the data provided by Roman annalists, by the first century B.C.E., fetial law as it governed the embassies seems to have been largely abandoned, even as it was revived or invented to regulate declarations of war. What we find instead in narratives of diplomatic practice commencing at the very end of republican government at Rome in the late 50s B.C.E. and continuing thereafter are highly ritualized performances, in which Roman magistrates meet foreign rulers or their legates on the exact border between their territories—often on bridges or boats in the middle of rivers—and there negotiate the terms of future relations. If these narratives are to be believed, the same form is observed regardless whether the foreign party is a Germanic chieftain, an African nomad, or an Armenian or Parthian king—regardless, that is, whether the foreign leader, his people, or his state had stable borders, censused its population, or possessed institutions in any way homologous to those of Rome.[55]

In historical writing of the first century B.C.E. and later, Roman relations with other peoples in Italy are narrated as though all parties to those events had similar institutions and a shared understanding of something we might call international law. (It is, in fact, a notable achievement within Roman culture that it developed a conception of international law and that legal theorists so heatedly debated the source of its content and its force.) That those narratives are largely supplied by individuals juridically Roman but in all probability of extra-Roman Italian extraction is in itself an important part of the story I wish to tell. And quite possibly, Romans of the sixth and fifth centuries B.C.E. did in fact conduct themselves on the presumption that neighboring city-states were organized along parallel lines to their own, and in all likelihood this presumption turned out *de facto* to be correct. By contrast, by the late first century B.C.E., theory and practice had evolved so that other parties to diplomatic exchange were treated as though they and Rome existed in a network of similarly ordered states, despite clear evidence to the contrary. In other words, the presumption operated *de iure* at a time when it clearly failed *de facto.*

In point of fact, this presumption of similarity must have failed already when Roman war making extended beyond central Italy. But in Roman memory and in many important respects in Roman law, Rome nevertheless remained in this period a city only, in large measure, I suppose, because land conquered in war was either appropriated, and so became Roman, or given away, and so remained foreign. And yet Rome *did* become an empire, and Romans retained an awkward, partial and perhaps dissatisfying sense that this transformation had worked substantial ruin on the character of their culture, even as it impelled the dissolution of their system of governance. In grappling with those changes, however well or poorly diagnosed, Romans came to recognize that theirs was no longer a city-state, even as they encountered farther and farther afield people less and less like themselves. In crafting practices to surmount that difference, and theories to render those practices narratable in Roman language, foreign powers became Roman states, and Rome became a state among states, and an empire intelligible in a sequence of empires.

Allow me to acknowledge in closing that I have answered a somewhat different set of questions about Rome than I did about Athens. I could have attempted to align Rome more closely with Athens—I could have presented Rome as having started, like Athens, with something other than an empire, and as having transformed it by solipsistic fiat into one. I might then have asked how that act was justified. But that would have been false to history, in two significant and related respects. First, Rome did not transform its allies into subjects. This is not to say that Rome's allies did not suffer or were not exploited; but the difference between Roman and Greek policies on the legal status of persons was non-negligible and a source of particular fascination precisely to the Greeks. Second, evidence survives not solely through accidence. What we know of how Rome *became* an empire is in part a product of how it *ceased* to be one—not, as at Athens, in violent conflagration, but through the sudden and still remarkable assimilation of all free-born subjects to citizens.

Chapter 5

Domesticating Domination

Chapter 3 urged that civil-law actions might usefully be situated in hermeneutic relation to international law in Roman antiquity, indeed, that civil-law forms and arguments played a paradeigmatic role in its initial elaboration. This chapter turns that historical argument back on itself: a principal claim of this chapter is that forms of domination that the Romans of the Republic exercised over foreigners came, in the establishment of monarchy, to be exercised by Romans over themselves. But this occurred within a political and legal regime that insisted on the vitality of the Republican forms through which social, political and legal conduct continued to be organized. The result, I urge, was the codification within the civil-law tradition of practices of domination and social differentiation whose nature and source the tradition has worked systematically to elide.

As it happens, this is a project of considerable contemporary relevance. The last quarter century has witnessed a stunning rebirth in the so-called Republican tradition; indeed, it has been so robust that its adherents may now be sorted into multiple camps—the civic Republicans, the neo-Romans, and so forth.[1] But one thing common to nearly all these theorists is their belief in the existence of such a tradition; and, remarkably, a common element of their intellectual practice is the grounding of their varied normative projects in one or another strand of that tradition.[2] Another object of this chapter is thus to subject their historical projects to scrutiny, but not simply to check facts, as it were. Rather, I seek to call into question the historical methods they have used—to indict them not least for failing to attend to the contingent languages of classical, imperial and late medieval republican thought; and in consequence to open up specific lines of scrutiny into the normative framework they have elaborated on the basis of that so-called tradition. These projects proceed along two lines.

First, advocates of Republican liberty and Republican citizenship have on the whole failed—indeed, failed radically—to attend to the contexts within which the texts of their tradition were written and its languages developed. As a result, I shall argue, they have failed to perceive the extent to which the languages and institutions of Republicanism were developed in support of monarchical rule and imperial domination, to say nothing of the almost complete lack of interest on the part of republicanism's ancient exponents in fostering civic engagement among citizens at large. This is perhaps most emphatically true of citizenship. The narratives that we commonly tell regarding Roman citizenship adopt its spread as an index of political change under the empire; they are therefore emancipatory in character. But experimentation in the law of persons under the Republic was perhaps the principal instrument by which subject populations were embraced within the structures of the expanding Roman state.[3]

Second, the dominant conception of the tradition is too narrow, its models of intellectual history too strictly genealogical. Not for nothing have the major developments in the field resulted largely from periodic efforts to expand the range of material embraced by its "tradition": on this reading, the recuperation for Republican scholarship of the Aristotelian tradition by John Pocock or of the glossators and rhetorical handbooks of the twelfth and thirteenth centuries by Quentin Skinner amount to always partial, sometimes interested, acts of recovery. But little or no systematic debate has been conducted regarding the boundaries of the tradition; developments in the field thus appear as purely happenstance events, each incremental move being subjected to wholly contingent modes of evaluation.

To anticipate a point to which I shall momentarily return, one area of late medieval, Humanist, and Renaissance intellectual endeavor almost entirely neglected by these scholars is rather paradoxically inquiry directed toward the Roman Republic in particular, and toward the sources of late medieval knowledge of Rome more generally.[4] In consequence, as I shall attempt to demonstrate more fully in what follows, the vision of Roman politics and political culture held and propounded by contemporary republican theorists derives almost entirely from imperial sources, and what is more, often from normative sources of the imperial period directed at the governance of conquered populations. A similar indictment might be issued against scholars of Roman history: to my mind, the privileged position granted to a particular notion of public law and constitutional thought in the study of the Roman Republic derives at least in part from the role public-law arrangements played in the Augustan settlement, perhaps especially in Cassius Dio's brilliant analysis of it.

As a result, neo-Roman theorists, but civic Republicans, too, systematically misrecognize, or simply fail to recognize, the dangers inherent in their projects of historical recuperation. On my reading, far from providing resources for an emancipatory rejuvenation of some pre-Hobbesian conception of liberty, the Roman and neo-Roman traditions instead offer cautionary lessons, in the ease with which imperial domination may be cloaked in the languages of liberty and of law.[5]

That it should be necessary to make this fundamental point surprises for several reasons. The most important, if also the most obvious, is simply that Rome was a deeply hierarchical, sexist, imperialist, and slave-owning society: the Romans saw no tension in advocating liberty of whatever kind for the very few, knowingly to be purchased at the cost of liberty for the many. Why should we rely upon their articulations to aid in emancipatory projects today, not least when such different jural, socioeconomic and communicative regimes obtain? Why should we think their formulations disarticulable in some unproblematic way from the discourses and practices of domination that suppressed and oppressed the very great majority of human beings in their world? The binarism of slave and free was then no concept good to think with[6]: the material conditions that enabled the enjoyment of Roman liberty by a select group of men in the late Republic were supported inter alia by the slaughter over ten years of perhaps a million Gauls and the enslavement of perhaps a million more, totaling perhaps one-fifth of the population of northern Europe at the time. Such was the foundation of Roman republican liberty and the achievement of republican virtue.

In what follows, I concentrate on a number of issues that might be embraced under two rubrics. The first, naturally enough, is liberty: how did the Romans define it; through what theoretical resources was it articulated and defended; and in what form were Roman understandings of liberty inherited and manipulated in the eleventh and twelfth centuries? My comments here will be brief: the historical issues are simple enough; hence, consideration of them may provide scope for the voicing of methodological considerations involved in the field more generally.

The second rubric covers a more involved, more complex problem, namely, how to assess the stakes in politics and republican political theory when someone commits the ontological mistake of attributing singularity and personhood to a collective, namely, the *populus*, the citizen body. To anticipate conclusions reached below, I shall argue that this move in argument was instrumental in enabling the redescription of the person of the emperor *as* the state, with all the consequences of that move for the history of domination. It likewise compromised and constrained the capacity of Republican thinkers to imagine, and certainly to solve, the problem of majoritarianism, as also to provide normative descriptions of the sources of law and the legitimacy of magistrates.[7]

These issues of the liberty of the individual and the personhood of the state became under the imperial republic inextricably intertwined, because the attribution of sovereignty to the person of the emperor required, in the language of the day, the assignment to him of *maiestas*; and that act placed inevitable and enormous pressure on preexisting patterns of social differentiation and the languages of status and freedom that had developed to describe, explain and justify them.

Interlude: The Rediscovery of Republican Rome

Allow me to open by naming four texts essential to modern understandings of the Roman Republic, which became available to theorists in, and historians of, the republican tradition in most cases well after its major tenets and languages had solidified.

The most important and hence named outside chronological order is Cicero's *De re publica*, which was discovered in December 1819 and received its *editio princeps* in 1822.[8] It would be difficult to overemphasize the importance of this fact, that the only work of normative political theory written in Rome under the Republic was simply unavailable to the Republican tradition until, on any modern account, the tradition itself had lapsed into senescent irrelevance.[9] This is not to say that Cicero's text had *no* influence in the interim: Cicero's account of Carneades' visit to Rome clearly fascinated both Lactantius and Augustine, who therefore preserve fragments of *De re publica* book 3. Similarly, Cicero's insistence that a *populus* was not any group of individuals, gathered together for any reason, but one united by common interest and shared commitment to a particular normative order, was taken up by both Ulpian and Augustine, and so reached high and late medieval intellectual culture by two routes. A number of Italian glossators of the eleventh and twelfth centuries, as well as an anonymous twelfth-century glossary of legal concepts preserved at Turin, echo Cicero's formulation by defining a *populus* as a *collectio multorum ad iure vivendum; quae nisi iure vivat, non est populus*, "a gathering of many in order to live according to law, which, if it does not live according to law, is not a *populus*."[10] This definition, in varying formulations, may likewise be found in the so-called Berlin commentary on Martianus Cappella and in Thierry de Chartres' commentary on Cicero's *De inventione*, both products of the later eleventh century and the early twelfth, the former Italian, the latter French.[11] Those allusions aside, deep engagement with Cicero's *De re publica* was naturally impossible.

Second, the so-called *lex de imperio Vespasiani*, better named a *lex de potestatibus Vespasiani* (it not being a law granting *imperium*), was, according to the anonymous chronicler of Cola di Rienzo, brought to light by Cola in 1347 and explicated by him in John Lateran precisely so as to legitimate arguments locating sovereignty in the people and, more particularly, the Senate, which it then vested in contingently authorized magistrates. Arguments about the nature, scope and ontology of popular sovereignty in the Republican tradition were transformed by Cola's discovery. (The understanding among Roman historians of magistracy *under the Republic* was transformed again starting in the third decade of the twentieth century as fragments of the *lex de provinciis praetoriis* were gradually discovered and even more gradually correctly interpreted.)

Third is the *lex agraria*, whose major fragments were delivered by the dukes of Urbino to Pietro Bembo, the historian of Venice and champion of Tuscan as a vernacular dialect, c. 1511 and which received its first full publication by Francesco Orsini in Antonio Augustín's collection, *De legibus et senatus consultis*, published in Rome in 1583. The *lex agraria* is a phenomenally difficult text, but it made one thing emphatically clear, which was that Roman agrarian laws were in no way whatsoever assaults on private property rights. They were fundamentally give-aways of public property into private hands. What is more, their major immediate effect on politics would have been to enfranchise the poor: to put the matter simply, at Rome the votes of landless citizens were concentrated so as to contribute to a narrow range of votes in the Roman equivalent of the American electoral college. A sufficiently large give-away of public land would have required the redistribution of the poor within the constituent units of the voting assembly and hence granted their individual votes vastly greater influence in elections and legislation.[12] Fear of that outcome motivated horrific distortion in public debate and, on several occasions, state-sanctioned murder of office holders advocating such distributions. Attempts to construe the history of republican opposition to agrarian laws as grounded in some republican idealization of private property rights became, after 1583 if not 1511, untenable as a matter of history and immoral at the level of politics.[13]

Finally, the full text of Gaius's *Institutes*, in something at least relatively close to its second-century C.E. form, was discovered in a palimpsest at Verona in 1816, three years before Angelo Mai discovered the *De re publica* in similar condition. It would, again, be difficult to overestimate the difference this discovery made to modern understandings of Roman law of the classical period. To give but one example—one to which I shall return—without Gaius it would not necessarily have been clear to readers of Justinian *Inst.* 1.2.3–4 that the phrase "edicts of magistrates" does *not* refer to any power wielded by Roman magistrates to make law. Rather stunningly, as I hope to show, a small number of twelfth- and thirteenth-century commentators on Justinian's *Institutes* drew the correct conclusion from this passage (even if, as seems likely, they did so for the wrong reasons, but that we cannot on current evidence know).[14]

Regarding this survey I make two observations. First, a full history of the Republican tradition must take into account the scholarship that unearthed, edited and interpreted these documents. As the names of Cola and Bembo make clear, this scholarship was not produced and read only in some ivory tower or Académie of antiquarians: it was, rather, produced and exploited in politics and public debate by the major figures of the day.

The second observation I would draw from this survey is one I have made before but on which I can now elaborate. The sources available to the early expositors of the Republican tradition were overwhelmingly products of Rome in the time of monarchy. Philip Pettit quotes with approval Montesquieu's characterization of England as "a nation where the republic hides under the form of monarchy" and adapts it, mutatis mutandis, to describe the political character of English republicanism.[15] But Rome of the Principate was a nation where monarchy hid under the form of a republic, and that was a far more terrifying and problematic condition. Its devastating effects on elite psychology and culture form the dominant theme of Tacitus's life work, indeed, of much of the cultural production of the early empire. Accommodation to that fact accounts for very nearly all the rest. It is time the neo-Romans came to grips with that fact.

Roman Liberty

Where liberty is concerned, I have argued in Chapter 4 that liberty at Rome—and likewise in Greece—was woefully undertheorized: its understandings remained nearly forever derivative from, indeed, one might say they were parasitic upon, the binarism of slave and free. It must furthermore be stressed that this polarity was *not* intellectually productive: in a slave-owning society of sometimes astonishing brutality, the wish that one were free rather than slave does not amount to a political-theoretical claim of great sophistication.

It is true, of course, that Cicero in *De re publica* connects *libertas* with participation in communal deliberation and power, with voting for magistrates and laws, and it may well be that since 1822, but not before, Cicero's arguments on that topic have contributed to civic republican conceptions of citizenship.[16] It is rather less clear what Cicero can have meant by this in respect to citizens at large: this is so on one level because citizens at Rome were not entitled to speak in legislative assemblies—their role in communal deliberation was restricted to that of auditor.[17] (Whether mere listening is legitimately described as "participating in common deliberation" is a question I set aside.) Nor is it clear what connection Cicero drew between this form of freedom and citizenship on another, more important level because not all citizens possessed even such freedom to participate as this.

That is so because citizenship was not in the Roman republic always conceived as a reward for service or token of membership or as a bundle of privileges and duties, public and private: it was also an instrument of domination. This can be shown from narratives of Roman conquest. In the wars of the late fourth century B.C.E., for example, and so in the period covered by Livy's first decade, the Romans often granted citizenship to defeated enemies at the moment of their surrender: but not citizenship as they themselves exercised it, namely, "with a share in communal deliberation and power." On the contrary, they granted citizenship without the right to vote.[18] That such grants were punitive is made abundantly clear by Livy's narrative of the aftermath of wars with the Hernici in 306 B.C.E.:

> Cornelius was left behind in Samnium. Marcius returned to the city in triumph over the Hernici and an equestrian statue in the forum was decreed, which was placed before the temple of Castor. To three polities of the Hernici—the Aletrinati, Verulani and Ferentinati [who had sided with Rome in the war]—because they preferred this to Roman citizenship, it was permitted that their laws should be returned to them and rights of intermarriage granted, which for a time they alone of

> the Hernici possessed. To the Anagnini, who had borne arms against Rome, was given citizenship without the vote: their rights of assembly and intermarriage were taken away and their magistrates forbidden any responsibility other than sacred ones.[19]

Shortly after this incident, Livy reports, the Romans demanded satisfaction from another rebellious ally, the Aequi:

> The Aequi responded that the demand was patently an attempt to force them under threat of war to suffer themselves to become Roman: the Hernici had shown how greatly this was to be desired, when, granted the choice, they had preferred their own laws to Roman citizenship. To those to whom the opportunity of choosing what they wanted was not granted, citizenship would of necessity be *pro poena*, as a punishment. (Livy 9.45.6–8)

This practice of distributing citizenship without the right to vote reveals the Romans' capacity to disarticulate the public or communal privileges and obligations of citizenship from each other, as well as from one or more of its purely private rights, for example, of intermarriage or contract. Far, however, from conceiving of all citizens as free from domination or as possessing scope for the exercise of citizenly virtue, the Romans were clearly capable of conceiving citizenship as a means to embrace conquered populations within structures of domination, and hence of citizenship as entailing obligations—above all, taxation and military service—without any correlative privileges whatsoever.[20]

This much is also visible in the legal tradition in the ancient world, and it remains apparent in late medieval Italian texts. So, for example, in his treatment of the law of persons in book 1 of the *Institutes*, Gaius makes clear that the varied forms of membership in the Roman community had been devised, at one or another moment in history, as the means to incorporate individuals or populations of defective status: of populations, this might be because they had had to be conquered; of individuals or freed slaves, because they had been convicted of crimes.[21] In Giovanni da Viterbo's *Liber de regimine civitatum*, written perhaps between 1250 and 1260, "citizenship" receives a definition that provides grist to the neo-Romans' mill but should likewise urge caution to the same: "Citizenship is said to be the *libertas* of the citizens or the immunity of inhabitants . . . For the word 'civitas' is a syncopation . . . hence, 'ci' and 'vi' and 'tas': 'ci' from 'citra,' 'vi' for 'vim,' 'tas' that is, 'habitas.' Hence, 'civitas' is to say 'a dwelling beyond violence.'"[22] Giovanni defends this understanding by citing four texts from Justinian's *Digest*: two concern the construal of one's home as one's most safe refuge. But the other two, quoted first and at some considerable length, concern the need to protect the weak against the predations of the strong. These passages are interesting in part because the domination against which they inveigh consists solely in forms of *iniuria*, criminal injury, and not the mere possibility of constraint, but also because both spring from texts by lawyers of the second and early third centuries C.E., specifically, Gaius and Ulpian, instructing provincial governors in their duties in ruling over formerly conquered populations. Later in the same work, in a chapter entitled "On the sort of *rector* to be selected for a *civitas* and to be elected into power," Giovanni again turns to a work of Ulpian on the duties of provincial governors: in other words, the framework Giovanni adumbrates for the selection of magistrates over a citizen population is elaborated on the basis of a Roman framework for selecting governors over the conquered and producing order among the dominated.[23]

It is of course true that already in the ancient world, the spread of Roman citizenship was rehearsed as an emancipatory narrative, and it bears observation that most authors in that tradition originated in the provinces. We are their heirs. I have myself written at length on the historical problems, that Rome remains unique among empires in having granted citizenship to nearly all its subjects, and that we are in consequence challenged to devise analytic categories to describe what sort of state it became. The citizenship so granted was republican in form, as was the state in which it was held; but the grant was made by an emperor; and no one, then or now, was under any illusions as to the reality of his domination, the freedom and citizenship of his subjects notwithstanding. The concept of freedom as non-domination seems to me wholly inapplicable to this state of affairs.

That said, the resources available in the Roman law tradition in support of neo-Roman doctrines of liberty are far fewer even than this. In a reading of the *Digest*—or, more accurately, in a reading avowedly of a single chapter of the *Digest*, 1.5 "*De statu hominis*"—so misleading as to appear tendentious, Quentin Skinner has argued that the Romans so defined freedom as to urge that "everyone in a civil association is either bond or free." In consequence, according to Skinner, the Romans believed that "a *civis* or free subject must be someone who is not under the dominion of anyone else, but is *sui iuris*, capable of acting in their own right. It likewise follows that what it means for someone to lack the status of a free subject must be for that person not to be *sui iuris* but instead to be *sub potestate*, under the power or subject to the will of someone else."[24] Skinner cites in support of this argument two sentences of the *Digest* and an excerpt of a third, the last of which offers as an example of "being in the power of others," the slave.[25] As the very next chapters of the *Digest* make clear, however, not all citizens were *sui iuris*, nor were all those who were *sui iuris* not subject to the will of someone else. So, for example, (free) citizens *of any age* whose father was alive remained "in his power" and formally did not possess legal personality; and likewise, free citizen women who were *sui iuris* nevertheless necessarily remained under the guardianship of some male, who supervised and had to approve their legal and financial acts. In practice, of course, social custom as well as legal doctrine and procedure accorded some flexibility to adult children in power, as also to women; and likewise there were mechanisms by which fathers could emancipate children and women could win freedom from guardianship. But the *default*, as well as the *norm*, was that all such citizens, who must have constituted an enormous majority of all citizens living at any given time, were "subject to the will of someone else."

The point is of sufficient importance to deserve restatement. In form, the *Digest* is a congeries of quotations, organized under rubrics. Its contents must not be quoted without proper regard for both the context from which the Justinianic editors excerpted any given passage and the structure of the corpus itself. Neglecting to do so, Skinner assimilates freedom to citizenship, citizenship to legal personality, and legal personality to non-domination. Every single one of these moves is wholly and easily falsifiable: whole classes of free persons within the empire lacked citizenship; a huge number, perhaps a majority, of citizens lacked legal personality; citizen women who were *sui iuris* were *de iure* dominated. The distinction between a Roman republican law of persons and a modern liberal one might be captured thus: in a liberal democracy, the norm is to regard all individuals as possessing legal personality, as atomized rights-bearers, and it is the denial of this status to (classes of) individuals that demands jural articulation. Under Roman law, the norm was to deny legal personality to as many citizens as possible, by subordinating them to the single personality of their oldest male agnate. In the Roman case, it was the awarding of legal personality to those with living fathers, or the freeing of women from domination, that was exceptional and which required specific legal action to be accomplished. It would be a generous but incomplete explanation of the neo-Romans' errors to say that they read the Roman sources through the lens of liberalism.[26]

In short, the binarism of slave and free is simply utterly and completely useless as a guide to the realities of domination in the Roman world of the Republic or empire, or in the Roman legal tradition.

In closing this section, I note that there survives from Rome a single definition of *libertas* by a lawyer—at least, that I know of—that by Florentinus in the late second century C.E.: *Libertas est naturalis facultas eius quod cuique facere libet, nisi si quid vi aut iure prohibetur*, "*Libertas* is the natural faculty of doing what one wants, unless it is prohibited by force or by law."[27] To the extent that this accords with any modern definition, it would, I suppose, be with negative liberty—what Pettit calls liberty as non-interference. A problem confronting civic republicans is that Florentinus goes on in the very next sentence to clarify what he means by "natural" when he speaks of a "natural faculty": "Slavery," he writes, "is an institution of the *ius gentium*, whereby someone is against nature made subject to the ownership of another." The problem is thus that, bracketing any association of liberty with citizenship or citizenly virtue, mere freedom as non-slavery was never made systematically available to all persons in any society known from the ancient world. Neither in a Ciceronian republic nor in an Aristotelian *polis* could mere freedom as a *telos* of the human condition ever be realized.

What's more, Florentinus was not alone in so describing freedom of some kind as the natural condition of human beings. But those Romans who asserted this also insisted that all known societies were slave owning, and so far as we know, in respect to those societies with whom the Greeks and Romans had contact, they were correct. More importantly, we know of *no* Greek or Roman who *ever* advocated abolition on the basis of this recognition of freedom as natural.[28] Not one. From civic republicans above all, this history demands some response. The Ciceronian republics and Aristotelian *poleis* of antiquity may well have been so organized, and their workings theorized, such that some few people got to maximize their virtue and liberty and so achieved some telos of the human condition, even as those very same intellectuals recognized that freedom of some other kind was the natural condition of all human beings. But the civic virtue of the few had, on this understanding, of necessity to be purchased through the domination of the many. Are we so sure that a tradition with roots such as these can offer resources to avoid even merely economic domination of subalterns today, of those free among us who merely listen?

Popular Sovereignty, from Azo to Rome

Allow me to pursue this trail, that of neglect or misreading of the legal tradition, into my second field of inquiry, sovereignty. Perhaps the signal hero in Quentin Skinner's history of "the rediscovery of republican values" is Portius Azo, who taught civil law at Bologna between c. 1190 and 1220.[29] Skinner emphasizes two related contentions advanced by Azo: first, that although the highest *iurisdictio* rests with the *princeps*—the first citizen, as he was denominated in the Roman monarchy in its pseudo-Republican phase—any magistrate in a city retains the power to make law; and second, that even as a citizen body transfers into an emperor its entire authority and power by means of a *lex regia*, it retains that same power—especially that of making law—for itself and in itself as a corporate whole.[30]

Neither of these claims, in either their substance or their language, is straightforward. To contextualize them properly one must attend to at least two features of their production: the form of the argument produced by Azo in defense of his contention, and the source and contextually specific meanings of the languages he deploys.

To begin, it is important to keep in mind that Azo, like virtually all Roman lawyers from the age of Augustus until the early modern period, wrote commentaries (rather than, say, monographs; and many of those "commentaries" consisted of lecture notes transcribed as Azo read a corpus of laws consecutively before students). Following established form, Azo opens his comment on any given law or extract or term by providing a terse statement of some conventional view, followed at times by an explanation how it was derived, and, rarely but significantly, by some dissent or departure of his own, itself likewise defended, often in the briefest possible terms.

So, for example, in respect to the ability retained by the populace to make law, Azo opens his gloss on the phrase *Soli imperatori &c*, "To the emperor alone and so forth," as follows: "Therefore the Roman populace does not have the power to establish law which it once had, but by the *lex regia* the populace transferred into him (namely, the emperor) all the power that it used to have. . . . Therefore it seems that today it has no power." He continues, in the sentence quoted by Skinner, "Say, rather, that it has not transferred except in that it retains it for itself."[31]

In a complex institutionalized discipline like the civil law, in Azo's day some twelve hundred years old, there were well-established rules, based on complex conventions regarding analogy, precedence and interpretation, that governed the manufacture, articulation and likewise the assessment of argument. Hence, where the power of magistrates to make law is concerned, Azo's interpretation remained a minority view in his time for two reasons: not only did no evidence from Roman legal texts available in the twelfth century justify his reading, no extant construal, however wild, of such evidence did so, either. What is more, as I have emphasized, the discovery of Gaius's *Institutes* in its near-classical form has only clarified the situation in respect to the republican tradition of the Roman Republic, in which, as now seems absolutely clear, no such magisterial power existed. The distinction between *lex*, statute, as command of the populace and mere magisterial action even in the exercise of *iurisdictio* remained there fundamental.[32]

The only possible exception to this consensus known to me is the terse assertion of a contemporary glossator to the effect that "the edicts of magistrates obtain no small share in this authority."[33] The glossator in fact quotes *Inst.* 1.2.7, substituting "magistrates" for the Justinianic "praetors." But the historical claim there advanced bears little relevance to Azo's argument for at least two reasons: first, Roman magistrates had *de facto* ceased to produce *ius honorarium* in the early second century of this era, and the magistrates in question had been those of the metropole. That said, legal theory and practice at Rome did in fact take up the question of the residual law-making capacities of municipalities in respect to the metropole, and to that topic I shall return.

Azo's arguments regarding popular sovereignty are both more involved and more important. Following tradition, Azo revisited the problem of legislative power when commenting on the chapter in Justinian's *Codex* treating *Longa Consuetudo*, "Age-old Custom," which in the Roman tradition obtained the force of law.[34] In this case, Azo observes that "according to ancient law, the populace had the power both to make law and to abrogate it through desuetude; today, all that power and all that legal authority has been transferred to the emperor." As Skinner records, Azo here intervenes with the claim, once again, that "this power was not so transferred except in that the populace retained it for itself." Azo defends this remarkable assertion by reference to two bodies of law: derogation from a contract *per pactum*, by mutual agreement, and renunciation of *praescriptio fori*, the right of certain individuals to have cases removed from secular courts to ecclesiastical ones.[35]

Alas, these are within the standards of legal scholarship of Azo's day wholly illegitimate arguments. Quite apart from issues of facticity—did Azo have any evidence that the monarch consented that sovereignty should abide also in the populace?—derogation *per pactum* was part of the civil, which is to say, private law of contract of the classical period, and *praescriptio fori* a doctrine of procedure in the civil law of the post-classical period. Neither doctrine formed a part of what Roman and medieval lawyers denoted *ius publicum*, public law, the law of magistracies and public powers; nor did either civil-law doctrine, classical or Christian, have in jurisprudence even analogical force in arguments over public law. The silence in which Azo's contentions in this field were buried in the subsequent tradition—until, that is, the work of Jean Bodin—may well be attributed to a quiet judgment on the form taken by his defense of them. Indeed, we may go further: Azo's recourse to doctrines outside public law—outside, that is to say, that which we might name republican constitutional law—itself amounts to significant testimony that he found no resources within the republican tradition, such as it was, to defend his views.[36]

Sustained inquiry into Azo's deployment of the concept of *universitas* reveals similar, perhaps even more fascinating surprises in respect to his scholarship. In considering his arguments on this topic, it is crucial to recall that corporations were entities at *private* law. "*Universitas*" was *not* a term of art in the republican thought of the Roman Republic, in respect to sovereignty, majoritarianism or magisterial power, or anything else, for that matter. What is more, on extant evidence, its usage in any form of political or legal discourse commenced only in the mid-second century C.E., some two hundred years after the Roman Republic fell and republican discourse, such as it was, had been co-opted in ideological support of monarchical domination *within* the Roman citizen body, in addition to aiding imperial domination over those without.[37] That said, the contrast drawn by Azo between individual and collective legal power featured in Roman thought at a variety of levels, in a number of articulations, and their history and their relationship to the tradition that Azo attempted to rewrite deserves attention.

To begin, the language and arguments deployed by Azo in distinguishing between individual and collective find their earliest antecedents not in legal texts but, ironically, in the rhetorical tradition whose late medieval expositors Skinner has done so much to recuperate for the history of political thought. Their first witnesses are digressions in works by Cicero and Varro, each writing between 55 and 45 B.C.E., on the relationship between individual usage, correct usage, and popular usage in respect to language. The text of Azo cited by Skinner in part reads in full as follows:

> *Dic ergo quod hic non excluditur populus, sed singuli de populo, & est simile in illo exemplo, Solus Scipio civitatem vel universitatem Romanam liberavit. Non enim excluditur hic populus, quia falsum esset: sed singuli de populo: quia plus fecit ipse quam aliquis aliorum. ideo singuli excluduntur, non universitas sive populus.*
>
> Say therefore that the populace is not excluded from this power, but individuals from among the populace are; and it is likewise in this example, Scipio by himself saved the city or the Roman people as a corporate body. For the populace is not excluded from this power, because that would be false: but individuals from among the populace; because he did more than one among others. Therefore individuals are excluded, not the corporate body as a whole or the populace.[38]

The relevant passage by Cicero occurs early in his dialogue *On the Laws*, which was drafted in the late 50s B.C.E., at a moment when Cicero (speaking in his own voice, as a character in the dialogue) distinguishes between some transcendent law that is right reason existing in nature and the statutes contingently enacted by human societies for themselves:

> *ea est enim naturae vis, ea mens ratioque prudentis, ea iuris atque iniuriae regula. Sed quoniam in populari ratione omnis nostra versatur oratio, populariter interdum loqui necesse erit, et appellare eam legem quae scripta sancit quod vult aut iubendo <aut vetando>, ut vulgus appellat.*
>
> Law is the power of nature; it is the mind and reason of the prudent man; it distinguishes justice and injustice. But since all our speech is based on popular usage, we must sometimes speak in popular terms and name that law which prescribes what it wants in writing by ordering or forbidding, as the *vulgus* names it.[39]

Cicero here draws a crude distinction between some recondite, true meaning of "law" and its popular usage, which he deems catachrestic; he predicates the distinction in usage on one between referents. Where notions of individual and collective are concerned, it is noteworthy that although Cicero's topic is legal-philosophical, his usage is largely non-constitutional and indeed largely non-political. What he seeks within this framework to determine is the responsibility of the individual in respect to the two systems of valuation, the one metaphysically superior, the other socially correct and, it would seem, pragmatically essential.

The terms deployed by Varro in his books *On the Latin Language* are far more precise and, ironically, far more legalitarian. Indeed, it is not hard to imagine that he so deploys the language of popular constitutionalism in gentle imitation of Cicero, a correspondent and friend; each seems to have admired the other's work a very great deal. In the passage in question, Varro takes up the relationship between theoretically correct and regular usage:

> (9.5) *Alia enim populi universi, alia singulorum; et de ieis non eadem oratoris et poetae, quod eorum non idem ius. Itaque populus universus debet in omnibus verbis uti analogia et, si perperam est consuetus, corrigere se ipsum, cum orator non debeat in omnibus uti, quod sine offensione non potest facere, cum poeta transilire lineas impune possit.*

> (9.5) For some [words and forms] are the usage of a people as a whole, others belong to individuals; and of these, the words of the orator and the poet are not the same, because their *ius*, their legal standing, is not the same. Therefore the people as a whole ought in all words to use regularity [*analogia*] and, if it has the wrong practice, it ought to correct itself; whereas the orator ought not to use regularity in all words, because he cannot do so without giving offense; on the other hand, the poet can with impunity leap over all the bounds.

> (9.6) *Populus enim in sua potestate, singuli in illius: itaque ut suam quisque consuetudinem, si mala est, corrigere debet, sic populus suam. Ego populi consuetudinis non sum ut dominus, at ille meae est. Ut rationi optemperare debet gubernator, gubernatori unus quisque in navi, sic populus rationi, nos singuli populo.*

> (9.6) For the people has power over itself, but individuals are in its power; therefore as each one ought to correct his own usage if it is bad, so should the people correct its usage. I am not the master—so to speak—of the people's usage, but it is of mine. As a helmsman ought to obey reason, and each one in the ship ought to obey the helmsman, so the people ought to obey reason, and we individuals ought to obey the people.[40]

The problem discussed by Varro is at some level directly analogous to that raised by Cicero: in language, Varro asserts, one might distinguish between proper usage, popular usage and individual usage, as in law Cicero had distinguished between the law of nature, statute, and individual conduct. Like Cicero, Varro asserts that in most cases, in consequence of individual legal standing, individual conduct must conform to the rule established by a political collective for itself. In this context, to speak of "the people as a whole" reflects mere constitutional realities, as well as the language of contemporary popular constitutionalism, in that Republican Latin authors always spoke of autonomous and democratically organized political communities—not least their own—in their exercise of legislative capacity using singular collectives. So, for example, in one of the earliest extant Roman laws for which we have indisputable access to its original wording (rather than, for example, paraphrase or quotation in modernized language), namely, the agrarian law of 111 B.C.E., the text of the statute refers to its own passage as follows: "The [magistrate] who will have been created or empowered by this law is to act within 250 days of those on which the *populus* or *plebs* shall have commanded this statute (*quibus h(anc) [l(egem)] populus plebesve iuserit*)."[41] Likewise, magisterial action that bound the people—most particularly in respect to the signing of treaties or commencing of war—was deemed illegitimate when it was performed *iniussu populi*, without command of the populace, or, in the broader but polemical formulation of Cicero speaking in 63 B.C.E., no magistrate can have *potestas*, power, *iniussu populi aut plebis*, "without command of *populus* or *plebs*."[42]

The language of jurisprudential literature is similar in respect very narrowly to the use of the collective *populus* to denominate the source of lawmaking sovereignty within the state. In the formulation of the jurist Ateius Capito, who served as suffect consul in the reign of Augustus in 5 C.E. and whose career therefore straddled the transformation of Rome from republic to monarchy, "*Lex*, law *qua* statute, is a general command of the *populus* or *plebs*, when a magistrate puts a question to it."[43] Capito's formulation was taken up with slight alteration by Gaius in his *Institutes* and again by Tribonian in Justinian's, and in that form is quoted by nearly every jurist in the Italian tradition of the late medieval period: "*Lex* is what the populace commands and establishes"; "*Lex* is what the *populus Romanus* has decided, when a senatorial magistrate has put a question to it."[44] Capito's and Tribonian's formulations likewise reflect the reality to which I alluded earlier, namely, that the populace did not deliberate but only voted—indeed, it could only meet—when a magistrate summoned it to assembly.[45] As we shall see, the linguistic and constitutional forms of the Roman Republic enabled the articulation, though they did not supply a precedent, for the related claims always associated with such definitions of law in the later republican tradition, namely, that monarchs constitute a preeminent source of law but are not themselves bound by it.

Returning to Varro, his usage further conforms to Republican practice in another regard, which is that he employs *universus* as an adjective: it is in his text singular because it modifies the collective singular "populace." Where *universus* is used as a substantive to designate "all people," meaning in particular "all members of the polity," it appears in Republican literature (and into the empire) in the plural, above all in the phrase *consensus universorum*: "by consent of all."[46] The plural is ideologically important: however fictitious the unanimity of the citizen body expressed by the phrase, the plural avows that all have individually assented. The concept finds memorable expression in Cicero's foundational, contractarian definition of *populus*, to which I alluded earlier: "A *populus* is not any assemblage of human beings, herded together for any reason whatsoever, but the assemblage of a multitude united by consensual commitment to a particular normative order and common interest."[47] Cicero himself further endorsed the importance of both universal consensus and individual commitment in the remarkable simile with which book 2 of *De re publica* now closes:

> In playing the lyre or the flute, and of course in choral singing, a degree of harmony (*concentus . . . quidam*) must be maintained among the different sounds, and if it is altered or discordant a trained ear cannot endure it; and this harmony, through the regulation of very different voices (*ex dissimillimarum vocum moderatione*), is made pleasant and concordant. So too the state, through the reasoned balance of the

> highest and the lowest and the intervening orders, is harmonious in the concord of very different people (*sic ex summis et infimis et mediis interiectis ordinibus, ut sonis, moderata ratione civitas consensu dissimillimorum concinit*). What musicians call harmony with regard to song is concord in the state, the tightest and best bond of safety in every republic; and that concord can never exist without justice.[48]

The problem of concord was of course one that preoccupied Cicero, and not only him; alas, nowhere in his extant works does he outline in substantive terms a mechanism by which consensus among most dissimilar individuals—the superlative is important—was to be achieved, even as the very great differences internal to the populace were respected and, indeed, protected. Cicero thus gestures toward two very great problems of politics and political theory nearly entirely neglected in scholarship on the Roman Republic, namely, its awareness of, and safeguards against, majoritarianism, and the precise nature and scope of the affective, cultural and existential commitments normatively entailed by communal membership.

Varro's language, too, gestures at this issue, and in its very fluency suggests that the language was neither novel nor restricted. But Varro's closing metaphor points in a different direction than does Cicero's: for in its complex assimilation of reason to helmsman in respect to people, but people to helmsman in respect to individual, Varro actualizes the potential latent in singular collectives such as *populus* for political language to grant agency, both political and cognitive, to collectives, and in so doing to demand of them homogeneity rather than concord. It is to the consequences of that cluster of problems under the Roman republican monarchy that I now turn.

Monarch as Magistrate and Monarch as State in Imperial Rome

The establishment of monarchy at Rome under Julius Caesar and his grandnephew Octavian, whom Caesar adopted in his will and who, after many shifts of public persona, took the name Augustus on motion of the Senate, is of course one of the most intensively studied events in all of ancient history.[49] In what follows I focus not on the events by which that transformation was effected, but rather on some of the most important ways in which the republican tradition of the empire and beyond was itself shaped by the peculiar cast of the Augustan principate. Above all, it is crucial to remember that

Augustus came to power at least in part by exploiting the forms of Republican constitutional law and persisted in power by similar means. This is one of the grand motifs of his autobiography—encapsulated in the claim that he had accepted "no magistracy established *contra morem maiorum*, against the custom of our ancestors"[50]—and the outlines by which he achieved this are given with superb precision by Cassius Dio (see especially Dio 53.17–18).[51] But we have near-contemporary evidence, too, in the form of notices on public calendars around Italy, and this evidence largely confirms these retrospective if interested depictions. Hence, Augustus could (correctly) describe the triumvirate as the result of the *populus* having "created" him as *triumvir rei publicae constituendae* (one of the board of three for organizing the state), an action we know from Appian to have occurred *stricto sensu* not by election as such, but through plebiscite, proposed by the tribune Publius Titius; and it is from the contemporaneous *Fasti Colotiani* that we know the *lex Titia* to have been carried on 27 November 43 B.C.E., and that the powers were to expire in five years, on 31 December 38.[52]

So well-crafted was this process between Augustus and his enablers in state and Senate that, in the famous phrase of Tacitus, despite the concentration in Augustus's hands of all the separate powers of Senate, magistrates, and laws, *eadem magistratuum vocabula*, "the titles of magistracies remained the same."[53] The gap thereby created between language and the realities it was called upon to describe forms a dominant theme of Tacitus's *Annals*. Another was the status dissonance and kindred disruptions to preexisting forms of social differentiation caused by the coming to be of monarchic power, not least one that could not in contemporary language be named. Over time, of course, political theory and jural-political practice caught up with events; and the reliance of Augustus on Roman republican constitutionalism delivered into the hands of lawyers in the high empire the principal means by which they sought at once to legitimate and constrain domestic imperial rule. Not least in consequence of their reliance on just these sources of the imperial period, in respect to theme, language, and argument the jurists and rhetoricians of northern Italy between the eleventh and thirteenth centuries delivered to later European history a proto-Republicanism at once obsessed with, and inextricably supportive of, monarchic power.

Consider the *lex regia*, described by Ulpian as the measure by which the *populus* delivered to and into the *princeps* all its rulership and power.[54] If indeed all the powers and prerogatives of the imperial office were delivered to the emperor in Ulpian's day through a single enactment—and there is some reason to believe that this was true—this may well have been an innovation of the third decade of the third century C.E. Certainly as late as the reign of Otho, a full century after the establishment of monarchy, emperors were still elected into an agglomeration of separate offices through separate votes of the assembly, on separate days, no less.[55] The claim by Augustus of adherence to Republican constitutional tradition was thus true in the limited but important sense that each single office and power that he held often enough had *some* precedent; but no one before had held so many such offices at the same time, nor had anyone else exploited to nearly the same extent the possibility—long available in Roman law—for the powers of a magistracy to be granted by legislative act separate from election into it. What is more, as the *lex* on the powers of Vespasian makes clear, it had long been deemed necessary to vote to successive emperors an increasing number of extra-magisterial privileges: the power to strike treaties, convene the Senate, and so forth, including, controversially, being unfettered by select statutes and plebiscites. (The evolution of a specific exemption into the blanket claim that emperors were *legibus solutus* is obviously part of the history I seek to tell, but need not be rehearsed here.) In other words, the People and Senate of Rome chose to grant by statute powers that emperors could well have arrogated, and in that perspective the *lex regia*, as it became known, should be understood as giving consolidated articulation to a long process of negotiation, in which emperors agreed to accept rather than claim powers and so conceded that the source of those powers lay in sovereign bodies other than themselves. To understand precisely what baggage this long history freighted upon the republican tradition, it is necessary to look briefly both backward and forward, to pre-monarchic theories of magistracy and sovereignty, to their transformation under the early Roman monarchs, and to their reception in the Italian communes.

In the last two centuries of the Roman Republic, the only period for which we have robust evidence speaking to these issues, theories of magistracy were remarkably underdeveloped.[56] Higher magistrates were distinguished by their possession of *imperium* and *iurisdictio*, the former being the power to command—and also to punish—Roman citizens, the latter evolving into the power to give an authoritative description of a private legal dispute and either themselves issue judgment in the matter or assign a lay judge to hear evidence relevant to the case as the magistrate had defined it.[57] Among writers of the early empire, it is true, the *imperium* of magistrates, their power of command, was understood to be analogous to, and perhaps to derive in some loose historical way from, the power that the Roman kings had once exercised, but it was throughout the Roman Republic also emphatically and rigorously distinguished from royal power in a variety of ways.[58] First, their power was constrained in three significant respects, operating both *de iure* and *de facto*: all regular higher magistracies at Rome were collegiate, and the veto of one consul, say, was understood to block action by the other; the term of office for virtually all magistracies was strictly limited to one year; and citizens retained a right of appeal, called *provocatio*, such that no citizen could be put to death *iniussu populi*, without the command of the populace.

The second constraint upon magisterial power that distinguished it utterly from royal authority as the Romans understood it is both more abstract but also more significant: what the populace vested in magistrates was not sovereignty—it was not even in some narrow sense *omne suum imperium et potestatem* or all its *ius*, to cite the formulations of Ulpian and Justinian, respectively, regarding the *lex regia*. Rather, it was in respect to some offices mere *imperium*, and in respect to others specific powers, *potestates*; and the conferral of these by one assembly was disarticulated procedurally from the conferral of the religious authority that formally enabled the taking up of any power of command.[59] Hence, the law passed by the curiate assembly after a magistrate was elected by the centuriate assembly was, strictly speaking, a *lex de imperio*; under the Republic, the term *lex regia* referred to one of a number of mostly private-law statutes still operative that were thought to date back to the time when Rome was ruled by kings. As a formal matter then, higher magistrates could not make law or bind the populace through treaty, any more than they could execute citizens. The importance of this point emerges in legal instruments: even as statutes took the form of decisions or commands of the people, *interrogante magistratu*, so in Roman treaties the agent that binds itself is the *populus*. The contrast emerges with particular clarity in treaties struck with kings: democratic peoples subscribe as collectives, while kingly power is personalized to such a degree that it is sometimes never stated whom any given king is king of.[60] The concept of sovereignty at work here would seem to be unitary, with all the implications that would have for high-imperial, legalitarian attempts to describe the power of the sovereign as that of the people, transferred to and into him by legislative act.

The Republican republican distinction between magisterial *imperium* and popular and later monarchic sovereignty is to a point captured by Cicero in a brief statement in his work *De officiis*, "On duties," in which he distinguishes the duties of magistrates, private citizens, and resident aliens:

> *Ac ne illud quidem alienum est, de magistratuum, de privatorum, de civium, de peregrinorum officiis dicere. Est igitur proprium munus magistratus intellegere se gerere personam civitatis debereque eius dignitatem et decus sustinere, servare leges, iura discribere, ea fidei suae commissa meminisse.*
>
> It would not go beyond my brief to say something also of the duties of magistrates, private individuals, citizens, and foreigners. It is the particular function of a magistrate to realize that he assumes the *persona*, the role or mask of the *civitas*, and ought to sustain its standing and seemliness, to preserve the laws, to administer justice, and to be mindful of the things that have been entrusted to his good faith. (Cicero, *Off.* 1.125; translation E. M. Atkins, with very minor modifications)

This passage was oft quoted by late medieval Italian scholars, but it was not then well understood, and their confusion has been since compounded. Their difficulty lay very precisely in the term *persona*, "theatrical mask" and, by metonymy, "role," which as a metaphor served Cicero well precisely because it respected the ontological and legal distinction he drew between magistrate and *populus*. The derivation of modern "personhood" and "personality" from the Latin *persona* has had the common effect of inducing confusion between the semantic fields of the modern terms and their etymological ancestors. In fact, the ancient and modern terms animate quite distinct conceptual structures.

All this changed late in the reign of Augustus and in that of his adopted son, Tiberius, in respect to the office Augustus occupied but had tried so hard not to name. The development was fitful and non-linear but may nonetheless be simply described. In short, the emperor was credited with *maiestas*, the word whence derives modern "majesty" but which properly means "greaterness"; it is, I believe, the only abstract noun in Latin derived from a comparative adjective. By credited I intend the following: individuals seeking in varying degrees to curry favor with the emperor or simply to eliminate enemies, accused others of disrespect toward the imperial house under charges of *maiestas*, and to the extent that emperors allowed trials to proceed, and individuals were in fact convicted, the varying orders of the governing class collaborated in bringing about an astonishing revolution in political thought.[61] In what this revolution consisted, and the nature of its effects, may be laid out as follows.

Under the Republic, *maiestas*, "greaterness," was a quality attributed by documents in political and legal discourse uniquely to the Roman people, and exclusively invoked in foreign affairs.[62] Its origins are obscure, but its importance is not: other political communities, whether free, allied or subject, were expected to respect the greaterness of the Roman people. If they did not do so, Roman magistrates were regularly commanded by the populace to see to it that in the future they did. *Maiestas* could only be held by one party to any bilateral relationship, and so the concept operated within some Roman ideology of imperialism to justify further and further expansion abroad.[63]

Furthermore, under the Republic, despite the status of the term *populus* as a singular collective, conceptions of the populace never so achieved what *we* might call personality as to enable first the location of *maiestas* in a metaphorical person and thence its transfer in and into a real one. What is more, although a slight to a Roman magistrate abroad *might* be construed as a slight to the greaterness of the Roman people, magistrates were not always so understood: hence the importance of philological precision in interpreting Cicero's *persona*. Paradoxically, in the domestic sphere the only persons known to have been charged with *maiestas*—as the crime was by shorthand known—were in fact magistrates when the actions that spurred the indictment were committed. That said, our knowledge of the statutes themselves and of the trials to which they gave rise rests almost entirely upon later reports and tendentious claims by participants to the actions. It is therefore entirely unclear whether the Republican statutes on *maiestas*—the first of which is, frankly, remarkably late, dating from c. 100 B.C.E.—offered a general description of what *maiestas* was or how it might be slighted, or instead criminalized quite specific actions; it is likewise unclear whether the authors envisaged anyone other than a magistrate being subject to the law.[64] That said, the indictment of magistrates on charges of *maiestas* surely confirms that magistrates were not understood to embody the sovereignty of the people under the Republic.

Importantly in the present context, another reason for our ignorance regarding the laws on *maiestas* of the Roman Republic is the complete lack of interest in them on the part of jurists under the monarchy. The historical perspective of the chapter devoted to *maiestas* in Justinian's *Digest* thus commences with the statute on *maiestas* passed on the motion of Julius Caesar during his dictatorship, at a moment when confusion over the location, as it were, of the people's greaterness was already in evidence. On another plane, it was likewise in respect to charges of *maiestas* that the emperor Augustus first began (quite illegally, as it happens) to hold trials *in camera*.[65] We witness an attempt to grapple at once with the distinctions important to Republican law and simultaneously with their upending under republican empire in an anonymous historical lexicon produced at Bologna or Turin in the early thirteenth century but now housed in the Vatican: "The crime of *maiestas*," it avers, "is said to be of two kinds, *contra rempublicam et contra imperium*."[66] In Republican law, this would of course be nonsense, as *maiestas* was not *de iure* housed in magistrates; but it is easy to see, in light of the pressures monarchy put on republican constitutionalism, how such confusion became nearly unavoidable.

Allowing disrespect to Augustus and later to Tiberius to be understood as a slight against the *maiestas* of the Roman people forms part of a conceptual and social revolution that received only gradual articulation in contemporary political theoretical discourse, which culminated, as I have argued, in Ulpian's *lex regia*. But that revolution had several attendant components and consequences that deserve scrutiny here. I focus on three.

First, the attribution of *maiestas* to the person of the ruler should be understood as consequent upon the attribution of personality and singularity to political collectives, and part of a longer history by which such attributions expanded in their range of application. Not for nothing do all the varied legal doctrines by which corporate decisions are described in Roman legal texts as emanating from a homogenous and singular agent—its *universitas*, its whole—spring from sources of imperial date. Far from being some neutral aspect of a Roman law of corporations, they give expression to a pernicious and rampant majoritarianism that was merely latent in the republicanism of the Roman Republic but which seeped into full articulation in civil law only after it had been fully naturalized in public law. Even so, it was still necessary in the early third century C.E. to explain that decisions made by the majority could be ascribed to all and affected all, and jurists of consequence continued to use the plural *universos* rather than the singular collective to explain this.[67] The *universitas* that Skinner sees recuperated from Roman civil law for use in debates over popular sovereignty in twelfth- and thirteenth-century Italy thus finds its origin in constitutionalist moves designed first to legitimate monarchic domination and mobilized thereafter in effect to erase minority views.

Second, we may assess the degree to which the attribution of *maiestas* to the emperor really did express the subsumption of the people's sovereignty into his person, as well as the degree to which, Augustus's protestations aside, the principate in fact amounted to more than an agglomeration of Republican offices, in the disappearance under the Principate of *provocatio*, the citizen's right of appeal. While intelligible as no more than a reflection of the realities of politics and power, the inappellate nature of both convictions *before* the emperor as well as convictions for slights to his person can also be understood in constitutional terms as reflecting the emperor's status *as* the people: to admit appeals beyond the emperor to the people would have amounted to a denial of the essential identity between his person and the people's *ius* and *potestas* that the concept of *maiestas* neatly if obliquely expressed.

Third, the attribution of *maiestas* to the *princeps* had direct consequences for Roman discourse on liberty, in ways that should alarm neo-Roman republicans. As I have said, under the Republic *maiestas* was a concept in Roman foreign relations. Locating it in an individual, even a magistrate, brought into play in a domestic context among citizens the rigorous logic of domination that Rome had long exercised as a collective over foreign peoples. Henceforth, the capstone of Roman social relations was necessarily and always governed by an absolute insistence on the greaterness of one party—one individual—in respect to all others. Leonardo Bruni's *History of the Florentine People*, whose first book was completed in 1416, bears witness to an incisive but imperfect understanding of this moment when Bruni observes of the establishment of monarchy: "From that time forth, emperors began to be chosen, and the word *imperator*, which before had meant arms and forts, was brought, as it were, within the city walls as though to signal continuous civil war. The word still referred to a legitimate function, but in reality it signified lordship and domination. Surrounded by armed troops, the citizens were cowed into subservience."[68] The problem being, of course, that Bruni himself lamented the domination of Etruria by Rome, but neither he nor his forbears in Florence or Bologna possessed significant intellectual resources outside the classical tradition for giving articulation to doctrines of popular or local sovereignty; and in taking up the Roman tradition, they reinscribed in the Florentine one armature by which to legitimate monarchic and other forms of domestic domination.

Returning to the transition to monarchy at Rome, and to the investiture of the monarch with *maiestas*, the effect of those moves was to lay bare discrepancies in power that Republican republican forms of social differentiation and ideologies of citizenly equality had worked to mask. It was, I argue, the naked and ruthless playing out of the logic of greaterness that caused Roman authors of the imperial period to thematize in political theoretical discourse freedom from domination, which only then became for them an existential problem, over against freedom from contingent acts of interference, which had been the main concern of Republican republican reflections on freedom and which remained in Roman legal philosophy the only freedom that mattered. In other words, it was the insistent domination by the emperor of the highest levels of the Roman aristocracy that made slavery intelligible as the other to their own freedom in some metaphorical mapping of the elite condition.

As a corollary to my third point, allow me to observe that on my understanding, the history of *maiestas* represents the working out in a Roman context of the insistence in the later republican tradition upon placing in both analytic and ontological correlation the freedom of individual and polity.[69] As John Pocock has repeatedly insisted, though not to this end, the Roman case itself suggests the fallacy of this logic, and likewise its dangers: for at the very roots of the Republican tradition, a free Republic that had purchased its freedom at the expense of others was ultimately forced by its own success to internalize and to domesticate the very structures of domination by which it had imagined its freedom to be preserved.[70]

Sovereignty and Autonomy in the Italian Communes

The problem of popular sovereignty and its transfer into a monarch returns us to the questions raised in the reading of Azo, namely, what power the populace retains to make law in the aftermath of such a transfer. It might be useful to commence by adumbrating a Roman Republican conception of communal sovereignty, by way of clarifying what connections and concepts the civil-law tradition was capable of supporting, as well as those it implicitly resisted granting articulation. With regard to the concerns of the later republican tradition, what most needs emphasis is the complete disarticulation in Roman thought in respect to international law of sovereignty cum freedom of action in foreign affairs, on the one hand, and autonomy, meaning above all the right to conduct civil and criminal trials of local relevance using laws authorized by local authorities, on the other. As I have argued in Chapter 4, the former was denominated *eleutheria* in Greek and *libertas* in Latin; the latter *autonomia* in Greek, and in Latin by the periphrasis *suis legibus utere*, the use of one's own laws. That is to say, what we might term external and internal sovereignty were so divorced in both the Greek and Roman international law traditions that far from being a single or unitary concept, the two forms of communal self-determination had to be expressed by two different (and etymologically unrelated) terms.[71]

Again, as is explained in Chapter 1, the Romans conceived "civil law" as the body of law a community of citizens authorized for use over itself. What is more, as a matter of domestic politics, the Romans occasionally claimed that only Roman citizens should or could have access to Roman legal forms. In consequence, conquered communities were so far from being systematically forced to use Roman law and legal forms that they were at various times and to different degrees forbidden to use them. For their part, allied communities and communities of Latin and other statuses—which is to say, communities embraced by the Roman state without having been conquered by it—were allowed to subscribe on their own initiative to select Roman statutes and occasionally required to subscribe to others. In Cicero's account, the distinction between those to which allies might and those to which allies must subscribe was drawn when the Romans felt "their state, their empire, their wars, their victory, or their health" to be at issue.[72]

Cicero drew this distinction in discussing allied, which is to say, free cities with populations legally alien in respect to Rome. By the high empire, Cicero's language and the framework to which he alluded had largely lost direct relevance, but they were nonetheless utilized in nostalgic reflections on the distinction between *coloniae* and *municipia*, colonies and municipalities. In Roman public law, a colony was merely a constituent of the Roman state. Though notionally composed of Roman citizens, colonies were not self-governing, were not entitled to elect higher magistrates, and did not make law for themselves. Municipalities, by contrast, were self-governing communities of Roman citizens. Bracketing serious conflict with Roman *ius civile*, which over centuries was increasingly understood to penetrate public-law structures of communal self-governance in order to direct the legal affairs of imperial citizens, their residents made law for themselves. When created *de novo*, municipalities were entitled to retain preexisting structures of magistracy; and early in the Roman Republic these had even retained the use of local vernaculars.

In the mid-second century C.E., at a time when the historical and juridical force of such public-law distinctions from the age of expansion had largely been forgotten, the contrast between colonies and municipalities was discussed in a speech of the emperor Hadrian, in response to a petition from an autonomous municipality that sought to surrender its autonomy in return for the more prestigious (it was felt) status of Roman colony. A passage from Hadrian's speech was later quoted and glossed by the antiquarian and miscellaneist Aulus Gellius. For both Hadrian and Gellius, the heart of the matter was that municipalities were bound by no statute of the Roman people except those which the citizens of the municipality had voted to render binding upon themselves, while colonies received their laws from the metropole.

> (8) *sed coloniarum alia necessitudo est; non enim veniunt extrinsecus in civitatem nec suis radicibus nituntur, sed ex civitate quasi propagatae sunt et iura institutaque omnia populi Romani, non sui arbitrii, habent.*
>
> But the bond of colonies is different; for they do not enter into the citizen body from outside nor are they nourished by their own roots, but they are propagated as it were from the citizen body itself and have all the laws and institutions of the Roman people, not of their own choosing.
>
> (9) *quae tamen condicio, cum sit magis obnoxia et minus libera, potior tamen et praestabilior existimatur propter amplitudinem maiestatemque populi Romani, cuius istae coloniae quasi effigies parvae simulacraque esse quaedam videntur, et simul quia obscura oblitterataque sunt municipiorum iura, quibus uti iam per ignotiam non queunt.*
>
> This status, however, although more burdensome and less free, is nevertheless considered preferable and more worthy, on account of the magnificence and greaterness of the Roman people, of whom these colonies seem to be small images, as it were, and sort-of likenesses and at the same time, because the laws of *municipia* are obscure and forgotten, through ignorance they are not able to use them. (Gellius 16.13.6–9; trans. J. C. Rolfe, adapted)

The antiquarian pedantry of Hadrian notwithstanding, it is clear that he—like Gellius—subscribes to a normative expectation to the effect that communities of citizens would exercise some limited form of juridical autonomy, while communities of subject aliens would use their own laws; as a related matter, it is also clear that their understanding represents the legacy of the empire in its Republican phase, which understood itself to dominate communities that were not free but were nevertheless *antiquo sensu* autonomous. In no case whatsoever was this local capacity to make law permitted to trump metropolitan interest, which it lay for the metropole to determine.

To these considerations regarding practice we should add others, of theory. In classical Roman legal philosophy no necessary distinction, whether moral or metaphysical, was drawn regarding the status or substantive content of the varied bodies of law known at the time. This is not to say that the Romans did not forbid certain practices among those they conquered—genital mutilation and human sacrifice are the most often noticed in ancient sources—but in general the Romans held strictly to the rule, consequent upon Cicero's definition of a *populus*, that all communities of citizens should, for various reasons, make law for themselves. The major transformation worked upon this framework in the Christian empire, and visible of course in the Justinianic codification of the sixth century C.E., was the introduction of a metaphysical and ontological schema according to which imperial law, which is to say the law made by emperors, was elevated above human law by virtue of its authorization by God. This amounted, naturally, to a revolution in legal philosophy, the delicacy and precision of its articulation in classicizing language notwithstanding.[73]

All these ingredients are visible in the legal and rhetorical literatures of the twelfth- and early thirteenth-century Italian communes, but the overwhelming tendency is far more subtle than the raw assertion of residual popular sovereignty made by Azo. Alas, on my reading, those literatures offer to neo-Roman republicans far less fuel than on Skinner's, not least by virtue of their being far more Roman than he seems to understand—if by that term we intend that they drew on such Roman sources as they had (those being overwhelmingly imperial, indeed, Justinianic in date), and interpreted them in light of hermeneutic strategies of widespread contemporaneous validity.

An exemplary participant in the rhetorical tradition is Boncompagno da Signa, who was born at Signa around 1170, studied in Florence, and taught at Bologna and Venice among other places before dying c. 1240 in Florence. His *Rhetorica Novissima* opens with a book *de origine iuris*, "On the origin of law." The singular notwithstanding, Boncompagno identifies fourteen separate such origins: the first in heaven, the second in paradise, the third with Adam, "who discovered natural law," and so forth. Two of the remaining "origins" merit reflection:

> The tenth was in the time of Justinian, a most Christian *princeps*, who was the very origin of law, for just as God divided the elements from primordial matter and brought them forth into the light, so Justinian clarified the confused origins and raw material of the laws, for the illumination of students and the glory of canon and civil law.

> The thirteenth [origin] was in municipal laws, which today Italy in particular imitates, because of its extensive liberty. But these municipal laws and plebiscites are as impermanent as lunar shadows, since, after the fashion of the moon, they wax and wane according to the judgment of their makers.[74]

Following Roman theory as he understood it, Boncompagno does not deny to local communities the capacity to make law. Rather, following civil-law doctrine as pronounced in the Justinianic codification, he assigns discrepant ontological and normative statuses to bodies of law, privileging the civil law as an imperial pronouncement—and by implication other imperial pronouncements—over against the evanescent law that localities might make for themselves.

That such is his outlook is further clarified by the arguments *pro et contra* Boncompagno outlines in the chapter he devotes to the exercise of arguing for and against varied topics: there, the argument *pro* rests first upon the value of law to both monarchy and social order, whence "whosoever speaks against the law sins under a charge of *lese maiestatis*," even as, secondarily, the monarch himself is deemed fit to pronounce law precisely because he is not bound by it. In other words, social order writ large is tied to the maintenance of a particular political order, and both are given juridical articulation by a monarch whose authority transcends them both. The argument *contra* returns to the terms deployed by Boncompagno in book one of the *Rhetorica*: the civil law governs only a hundredth part of the earth; being compromisable, it waxes and wanes proportionately with legislative action by "rustics"; and its authority and esteem are undermined by *plebiscita popularia*: "for not without shame is it compelled to be silent when a plebiscite or statute speaks." The civil law is thus to be praised insofar as it produces and supports a monarch, whose authority in turn buttresses that of the law; it is to be condemned exactly insofar as it is undermined by popular law making.[75] These arguments are, as I have said, part of a set of rhetorical exercises and have no direct basis in some political or legislative reality; nonetheless, the system of valuation to which they give articulation harmonizes with Boncompagno's more explicit statements of legal philosophy, as well as with broader currents in contemporaneous jurisprudence.

Writing a *summa* of Justinian's Code perhaps half a decade earlier, the Bolognese jurist Rogerius had opened his comments on the forms of legislation and sources of law (in respect to *Cod. Iust.* 1.7) by posing and answering the question: "Why treat concerning statutes before constitutions and edicts, when constitutions and edicts are *digniora*, more noble, insofar as they proceed from the *vox* of the *princeps*?"

> *Solutio: ideo primum posuit de legibus quam constitutionibus, quia primum conditae fuerunt leges a populo quam ab imperatore, cum dictum sit quod populus transtulit ei et in eum potestatem omnem: sic ergo inspexit ad originem potius quam ad dignitatem.*
>
> Answer: He treats concerning statutes before constitutions for this reason, because statutes were established first by the people before they were established by the emperor, when it is said that the people transferred to him and into him all *potestas*: thus he looks to origin [that is, priority in time] rather than to grade of dignity.[76]

A similar concern with the metaphysical status of varied kinds of law is visible in the anonymous thirteenth-century lexicon now housed at the Vatican that I have already quoted. The author of that text, like Boncompagno and Rogerius, correlates this hierarchy of laws with a hierarchy of sources of law: *ius gentium*, meaning the varied doctrines of positive law shared among the peoples of the world, "is a creation of human labor through the operation of natural reason, and so is termed *ius non simpliciter*, because it is a product of both industry and labor." *Naturale ius*, in contrast, by virtue of its ultimate derivation *ab ipsa divina dispositione*, is *ius simplex*.[77]

Conclusions of Diverse Kinds

Neither Boncompagno nor Rogerius denied to localities that were constituents of empire the power to make local law. Far from it. Nor did they feel any compulsion to do so, for the architecture of Roman public law that they had received and which they espoused readily granted such. It had done this in the Republican empire, and continued throughout its varied lives to do so because nothing within its conceptual foundations required the coupling of this concession regarding legislative authority with any other, regarding either magisterial power or the nature or location of sovereignty within the state.

That said, theirs was obviously not a purely Republican republican outlook.

That was so in part because they acknowledged the transcendent moral authority of one body of law over against that of all other states, and it was so because they, like virtually all their peers, understood that authority to descend from the divine.

To state the matter thus is to invite the question whether the jurists and rhetoricians of the Italian communes were not anti-republican, or at least non-republican, in so subscribing to monarchy. Setting aside the issue how democratic a normative republicanism can or should be,[78] I have argued only that monarchy at Rome possessed an essentially republican form. This was true of its authorizing acts—in the constitution of the monarch's power through the agglomeration of traditional Republican offices, and in the awarding to him of those offices, as well as further, extra-magisterial powers, through comitial actions. It was also true of the forms of domination that monarchy institutionalized and embedded in Roman life: by virtue of acts describable in Republican language without violence to its foundational metaphors or meanings, imperial forms of domination once exercised by the free Republic over other peoples were, under the monarchy, quite literally domesticated, and exercised henceforth by Romans over themselves.

I have likewise urged, however, that one should not overstate this moment in Roman life as amounting to a corruption of republican ideals in respect to either the liberty of individuals or the scope available for the exercise of citizenly virtue. On the contrary, the political role of the very great majority of such citizens as possessed Ciceronian virtue consisted almost exclusively in listening to their betters. They had also to die for them, of course, and win for them the glory and wealth that would sustain their dominance. For that bulk of the population that was excluded from the exercise of virtue, indeed, that was deemed to have no share of virtue whatsoever—all women, as well as children of both sexes—the Roman and later civil law of persons demanded their continual subjection to the will of others. To all those, and likewise to all male citizens with living fathers, the law denied legal personality.

I do not wish to imply that the normative projects of the modern republican movement are necessarily and hopelessly implicated in traditions of imperial and gendered domination. That said, it merits observation in this context that the invocation of tradition was itself a commonplace of Roman Republican politics. Hence, when advocating the creation of an extraordinary, even revolutionary *imperium* for Gnaeus Pompey, Cicero faced opponents who urged that it was wholly out of keeping with the practice of their ancestors. Nothing is so in keeping with the example and institutions of our ancestors, he responded, as constant innovation.[79] Cicero carried the day, and the groundwork was laid for monarchy. What is more, that monarchy, which is to say, the Roman Republic in its monarchic phase, is very largely the only Roman Republic the Italian communes knew.

Quentin Skinner has defended the recourse to historical argument by modern republicans in the following terms:

> Before embarking on this task, one obvious query about this way of proceeding needs first to be answered. It might well be asked why I propose to examine the historical record at this juncture instead of attempting directly to develop a more inclusive philosophical analysis of negative liberty. My answer is not that I suppose such purely conceptual exercises to be out of the question. On the contrary, they have I think been among the most probing and original contributions to the contemporary debate. It is rather that, in consequence of certain widespread assumptions about the best method of studying social and political concepts, it is apt to seem much less convincing to suggest that a concept *might* be coherently used in an unfamiliar way than to show that it *has in fact* been put to unfamiliar but coherent uses.[80]

It remains to be seen whether the concepts of liberty and citizenship *as they were in fact* put to use in the ancient and medieval Roman tradition can serve without compromise the modern one. I have my doubts. For the ancient and medieval tradition was not intended to serve, nor did it in fact serve, any emancipatory purpose. The political ideology of the Roman Republic, as also of its empire, including their theoretical and jural apparatuses, worked rather in support of domination by a rarified elite over varied foreign and domestic subalterns. Its successful propagation outside the governing class and among later academic lawyers reflects above all the success achieved by the elites whom those ideologies supported, in inducing the disenfranchised and the dominated into playing the game by their rules: by accepting as honorable derivative and deracinated constituents of elite subjectivity—so-called citizenship and so-called virtue—those who were excluded from power and agency by the working out of republican ideals ultimately collaborated with the powerful in burnishing a political theoretical apparatus that worked to their disadvantage, while hiding its systemic and structural flaws from scrutiny. No more.

Appendix

Work-arounds in Roman Law: The Fiction and Its Kin

1. Gaius *Inst.* 1.1
(the opening lines are missing in ms and are quoted from *Dig.* 1.1.9)

Omnes populi qui legibus et moribus reguntur partim suo proprio, partim communi omnium hominum iure utuntur: nam quod quisque populus ipse sibi ius constituit, id ipsius proprium est vocaturque ius civile, quasi ius proprium civitatis; quod vero naturalis ratio inter omnes homines constituit, id apud omnes populos peraeque custoditur vocaturque ius gentium, quasi quo iure omnes gentes utuntur. populus itaque Romanus partim suo proprio, partim communi omnium hominum iure utitur.

All peoples who are governed by statutes and customs observe partly their own peculiar law and partly the common law of all human beings. The law that a people establishes for itself is peculiar to it, and is called ius civile, being, as it were, the special law of that civitas, that community of citizens, while the law that natural reason establishes among all human beings is followed by all peoples alike, and is called ius gentium, being, as it were, the law observed by all peoples. Thus the Roman people observes partly its own peculiar law and partly the common law of humankind.

2. Cicero *De re publica* 1.39

populus autem non omnis hominum coetus quoquo modo congregatus, sed coetus multitudinis iuris consensu et utilitatis communione sociatus.

> A people is not any coming-together of human beings, herded together for any reason whatsoever, but a coming-together of many, united by consensual commitment to a particular normative order and common utility.

See also *De re publica* 1.41 and 6.17 Powell:

> *Nihil est enim illi principi deo, qui omnem mundum regit, quod quidem in terris fiat, acceptius, quam concilia coetusque hominum* ***iure sociati****, quae civitates appellantur.*
>
> For nothing which happens on earth is more pleasing to that chief god who rules the world than the councils and comings-together of humans united by law which are called citizen bodies.

For a significant later formulation, widely deployed between the twelfth and fourteenth centuries, see De verbis quibusdam legalibus ex cod. ms. Taurinensi D. V. 19, §39, ed. F. Patteta in Gaudentius 1892, p. 131 (see also Glossae ineditae e cod. Institutionum Sessoriano 110 ad *Inst.* 1.2.1; Glossae ined. e cod. Inst. vaticano 8782 ad *Inst.* 1.2.1):

> A *populus* is a *collectio multorum ad iure vivendum; quae nisi iure vivat, non est populus*, "a gathering of many in order to live according to law, which, if it does not live according to law, is not a *populus*."

3. Cicero *Verr.* 2.2.32

> *Siculi hoc iure sunt ut, quod civis cum cive agat, domi certet suis legibus, quod Siculus cum Siculo non eiusdem civitatis, ut de eo praetor iudices ex P. Rupili decreto, quod is de decem legatorum sententia statuit, quam illi legem Rupiliam vocant, sortiatur. Quod privatus a populo petit aut populus a privato, senatus ex aliqua civitate qui iudicet datur, cum alternae civitates reiectae sunt; quod civis Romanus a Siculo petit, Siculus iudex, quod Siculus a civi Romano, civis Romanus datur; ceterarum rerum selecti iudices ex conventu civium Romanorum proponi solent. Inter aratores et decumanos lege frumentaria, quam Hieronicam appellant, iudicia fiunt.*

The Sicilians are subjects of law as follows: actions of a citizen with a fellow citizen are tried at home, according to their own laws. To adjudicate actions of a Sicilian with a Sicilian not of the same citizen body, the praetor [that is, the Roman governor] should appoint a judge by lot, in accordance with the decree of Publius Rupilius, which he fixed on the recommendation of the [commission of] ten legates [sent to advise him at the formal organization of the province], which decree the Sicilians call the Rupilian Law. To adjudicate suits brought by an individual against a community, or by a community against an individual, the senate of another *civitas* should be assigned, granting the possibility that a *civitas* might be rejected by each side. When a Roman citizen sues a Sicilian, a Sicilian is assigned to adjudicate; when a Sicilian sues a Roman citizen, a Roman citizen is assigned. In all other matters judges are accustomed to be selected from among the Roman citizens resident in the assize district. Between farmers and collectors of the grain tithe, judgments are rendered according to the grain law which they call the Hieronican.

4. Work-arounds in Roman Legislation, 1: The Contrafactual Imperative

4A. Cicero *Contra Rullum* 2.29

Quid postea, si ea lata non erit? Attendite ingenium. "Tvm ei xviri," inquit, "eodem ivre ***sint*** *qvo qvi optima lege." Si hoc fieri potest ut in hac civitate quae longe iure libertatis ceteris civitatibus antecellit quisquam nullis comitiis imperium aut potestatem adsequi possit, quid attinet tertio capite legem curiatam ferre iubere, cum quarto permittas* ***ut sine lege curiata idem iuris habeant quod haberent, si optima lege a populo essent creati****?*

What then, if the *lex* is not passed? Note his ingenuity! "Then let the decemvirs be of the same legal standing as those created according to strict procedure." If this is indeed possible, that in this polity, which excels all other polities by far in the rights of liberty, someone should be able to obtain command over citizens or administrative authority without the authorization of any electoral body, what is the point of ordering the passage of a curiate law in the third chapter, when in the fourth you permit that these officials should have the same legal status without a curiate law as they would have had if they had been created by the people according to strict procedure?

Cf. *Lex Flavia municipalis* clause 24 (another instance in which rules of appointment to magistracy are manipulated through fiction):

Rubrica. De praefecto imperatoris Caesaris Domitiani Augusti.

Si eius municipi decuriones conscriptiue municipesue imperatori Caesari Domitiano Augusto, patri patriae, duumviratum communi nomine municipum eius municipi detulerint, imperatorque Caesar Domitianus Augustus, pater patriae, eum duumviratum receperit et loco suo praefectum quem esse iusserit, is praefectus ***eo iure esto, quo esset, si*** *eum IIvirum ex hac lege solum creari oportuisset isque ex hac lege solus duumvir iure dicundo creatus esset.*

If the decuriones or conscripti or municipes of that municipium, in the common name of the municipes of that municipium, confer the duumvirate on the Emperor Caesar Domitian Augustus, father of his country, and the Emperor Caesar Domitian Augustus, father of his country, accepts that duumvirate and orders anyone to be praefectus in his place, that praefectus is to have the same rights as he would have if it had been appropriate for him to be appointed sole duumvir under this statute and he had been appointed under this statute sole duumvir for the administration of justice.

4B. Livy 22.10.2–6

Qui faciet, quando uolet quaque lege uolet facito; quo modo faxit probe factum esto. Si id moritur quod fieri oportebit, profanum esto, neque scelus esto. Si quis rumpet occidetue insciens, ne fraus esto. Si quis clepsit, ne populo scelus esto neue cui cleptum erit. Si atro die faxit insciens, probe factum esto. Si nocte siue luce, si seruus siue liber faxit, probe factum esto. Si antidea senatus populusque iusserit fieri ac faxitur, eo populus solutus liber esto.

Let him who performs the sacrifice do so whenever he wants, by whatever rite; however he shall do it, let it be considered to have been done properly. If something intended for sacrifice should die, let it be held profane and let it be understood that no crime has taken place. If someone should unknowingly hurt or kill it, let it not be a crime. If someone should steal it, let no blame attach to the people, nor to that person by whom it was stolen. If the sacrificer should sacrifice on an inappropriate day, let the sacrifice be considered to have been done properly. If the sacrifice is performed before the day on which the Senate and people order it to be done, let the people be held to be free and released from obligation.

5. Work-arounds in Roman Legislation, 2: Fiction

5A. (?) *Lex Hortensia* (287 B.C.E.)

Gaius *Inst.* 1.3: *sed postea lex Hortensia lata est, qua cautum est, ut plebiscita universum populum tenerent. itaque eo modo legibus exaequata sunt.*

But afterwards the *lex Hortensia* was passed, by which it was provided that plebiscites should bind the entire citizen body. Therefore, by that means plebiscites were assimilated to statutes.

5B. Aulus Gellius 5.19.9, on the form of adoption known as *adrogatio*; the language was putatively formulated in the early first century B.C.E.:

Eius rogationis verba haec sunt: "Velitis iubeatis uti L. Valerius L. Titio ***tam*** *iure legeque filius siet,* ***quam si*** *ex eo patre matreque familias eius natus esset, utique ei vitae necisque in eum potestas siet, uti patri endo filio est. Haec ita uti dixi, ita vos, Quirites, rogo."*

These are the words of the motion: "Do you wish and command that Lucius Valerius should be son to Lucius Titius by law and statute, **just as if** he had been born from that father and the mother of his family, and that the power of life and death over him should be his, as to a father over a son. These things that I have thus spoken, I put to you, Quirites."

5C. *Lex agraria* (*RS* 2) ll. 29–31

Whatever according to this statute as it is written down above, in the lands which [are in the land of Italy and which were the public property of the Roman people in the consulship of P. Mucius and L. Calpurnius [112 B.C.E.], it shall have been lawful for any Latin and foreigner (*Latino peregrinoque*) to do, whatever of those things] anyone shall not have done which it shall have been appropriate [for him] to do [according to this statute,] or whatever [loss] anyone of them [shall have suffered] which is provided for according to this statute, [the magistrate] or pro-magistrate before whom anyone shall have gone for a pre-trial concerning that matter, whatever suit there shall be according to this statute, the magistrate is [to grant] trial and [appoint] a judge [or *recuperatores* according to this statute to the person in question and against the person in question, just as] it were appropriate to grant trial and appoint a judge or *recuperatores* according to this statute [to the person in question] and against the person in question if anyone [were demanding] trial concerning that matter [who was a Roman citizen or who was suing from a Roman citizen . . .] . . . *item iudicium iudi[cem recuperatoresve ex hac lege ei et in eum dato* ***ita utei*** *ei] et in eum iudicium iudicem recuperatoresve ex hac lege dare oporteret,* ***sei*** *quis de ea re iudiciu[m postularet, quei | [ceivis Romanus esset quive a ceive Romano peteret].*

5D. *Lex Latina Tabulae Bantinae* (*RS* 7) ll. 12–13

eique omnium rerum ***siremps*** *lexs esto* ***quasei*** *is haace lege pequniam, quae supra scripta est, exigeret.*

and let the statute apply to that magistrate in every respect **exactly as if** he were exacting money in accordance with this statute, as is written above.

5E. Tabula Contrebiensis ll. 6–8

eidem quei supra scriptei sunt iudices sunto. sei Sosinestana ceivitas esset, tum qua Sallviensis | novissume publice depala[r]unt, qua de re agitur, sei [i]ntra eos palos Sallviensis rivom per agrum | publicum Sosinestanorum iure suo facere liceret.

Let the same persons who are written above be judges. Suppose there in fact to be a Sosinestan *civitas*: then, in the place where the

Salluienses recently and officially put in stakes, which matter is the subject of this action, if it would be permissible for the Salluienses within their rights to lead a canal within those stakes through the public land of the Sosinestani.

5F. *Lex de Gallia Cisalpina* (*RS* 28) chap. 22, ll. 40–43

siremps *lex res ius caussaque omnibus omnium rerum esto*, the law, the issue, the right of action, and the suit shall be same for all persons in every respect, ***atque utei*** *esset esseve oporteret*, as they would apply, or as it would be appropriate for them to apply . . . ***sei*** *is . . . de ieis rebus Romae apud praetorem eumve quei de ieis rebus Romae iure deicundo praeesset in iure confessus esset* . . . if that person . . . had confessed concerning these matters before the praetor at Rome or before the person who in Rome had jurisdiction over these matters.

5G. *Lex de Gallia Cisalpina* (*RS* 28) chap. 22, ll. 45–50

The praetor or the person who in Rome has jurisdiction over these matters is to render judgment and decree against him and his heir concerning all these matters thus and shall order them to be arrested and their property to be seized or proscribed and sold, ***ac sei*** *is heresve eius de ea re in iure apud eum praetorem eumve quei Romae iure deicundo praesset* . . . **just as if** he or his heir had confessed concerning this matter in a proceeding before the praetor or whoever at Rome has jurisdiction, or had not responded at all concerning this matter, or had not defended himself as would have been appropriate.

5H. *Lex de imperio Vespasiani* (*RS* 39) ll. 7–9

utique cum ex voluntate auctoritateve iussu mandatuve eius praesenteve eo senatus habebitur, omnium rerum ius ***perinde*** *habeatur servetur,* ***ac si*** *e lege senatus edictus esset habereturque;*

and that when the Senate shall be convened according to his wish or authority, by his order or mandate or in his presence, the law in all matters should be maintained and observed, **as if** the Senate had been summoned and was being convened according to statute;

5I. *Lex de imperio Vespasiani* (*RS* 39) ll. 29–32

utique quae ante hanc legem rogatam acta gesta decreta imperata ab imperatore Caesare Vespasiano Augusto iussu mandatuve eius a quoque sunt, ea ***perinde*** *iusta rataque sint,* ***ac si*** *populi plebisve iussu acta essent.*

and that whatever before the proposal of this statute has been undertaken, carried out, decreed, or ordered by the emperor Caesar Vespasian Augustus or by anyone according to his order or mandate, they be lawful and binding, **just as if** they had been undertaken according to the order of the people or plebs.

Cf. *Cod. Iust.* 8.47.2.2, a rescript of Diocletian from 286 C.E.:

Adrogatio etenim ex indulgentia principali facta ***proinde*** *valet apud praetorem vel praesidem intimata* ***ac si*** *per populum iure antiquo facta esset.*

The adrogation performed by imperial permission before the praetor or provincial governor has **exactly** the same force **as if** it had been performed by ancient law through the people.

6. Work-arounds in Roman Legislation, 3: Substitution

6A. Livy 8.23.10–12 (describing events in 327 B.C.E.):

iam Publilius inter Palaepolim Neapolimque loco opportune capto diremerat hostibus societatem auxilii mutui qua, ut quisque locus premeretur, inter se usi fuerant. itaque cum et comitiorum dies instaret et Publilium imminentem hostium muris auocari ab spe capiendae in dies urbis haud e re publica esset, actum cum tribunis est ad populum ferrent ut, cum Q. Publilius Philo consulatu abisset, ***pro consule rem gereret*** *quoad debellatum cum Graecis esset.*

Meanwhile, Publilius, having opportunely captured a position between Palaeopolis and Naples, was disrupting the arrangement for the exchange of aid between those enemies, which they had been accustomed to enjoy between each other, each place being now under threat. Therefore, as the day for elections was drawing near and it was scarcely in the public interest that Publilius be called away from the imminent hope of capturing the city, threatening as he was the enemies' walls, it was enacted through the tribunes, who brought a motion before the people, that when Quintus Publilius Philo should depart the consulate, he should conduct matters **as if** he were consul until the war with the Greeks should be successfully ended.

Cf. *Fasti triumphales capitolini* (*Inscr. Ital.* XIII.1:70–71) 326 B.C.E. = a.u.c. 428: Q. Publilius Q. f. Q. n. Philo II ann. CDXXVII *primus pro co(n) s(ule) de Samnitibus, Palaeopolitaneis k. Mai.*

Cf. Livy 38.42.8–10 (187 B.C.E.):

In Liguribus magni belli et gliscentis in dies magis fama erat. Itaque consulibus nouis, quo die de prouinciis et de re publica retulerunt, senatus utrisque Ligures prouinciam decreuit. Huic senatus consulto Lepidus consul intercedebat, indignum esse praedicans consules ambos in ualles Ligurum includi, M. Fuluium et Cn. Manlium biennium iam, alterum in Europa, alterum in Asia, uelut pro Philippo atque Antiocho substitutos regnare. Si exercitus in his terris esse placeat, consules iis potius quam priuatos praeesse oportere.

A rumor was growing stronger day by day that a great war [was] brewing ever stronger among the Ligurians. Therefore, on the day when the new consuls consulted the Senate concerning their bailiwicks and the condition of the state, the Senate decreed for both the Ligurians as their province. The consul Lepidus sought to veto this decree of the Senate: it was improper, he said, that both consuls should be shut up in the valleys of Liguria, while Marcus Fulvius and Gnaeus Manlius ruled for two years now, the one in Europe, the other in Asia, **as if** they were substitutes for Philip and Antiochus. If it were decided that armies should be in those lands, it was appropriate that consuls should command them, rather than private citizens.

6B. *Lex agraria* (*RS* 2) l. 31

quibus colonieis seive moinicipieis, seive quae ***pro*** *moinicipieis colon[ieisve* to whichever colonies or *municipia*, or any equivalents of *municipia* or colonies there may be

Cf. Livy 32.2.6:

Et Narniensium legatis querentibus ad numerum sibi colonos non esse et immixtos quosdam non sui generis pro colonis se gerere, earum rerum causa tresviros creare L. Cornelius consul iussus.

Ambassadors from the colony of Narnia complained that the colonists were not at the number assigned to them and that some persons not of their kind had become commingled with them and were conducting themselves as colonists [or, "as if they were colonists"]. The consul Lucius Cornelius was ordered to create a board of three to see to this matter.

6C. *Lex agraria* (*RS* 2) l. 66 (and elsewhere)

quoi colono eive, quei in colonei numero scriptus est

to each colonist or to each person who was enrolled among the number of colonists

6D. Cicero *Off.* 3.47, on the *Lex Licinia Mucia* of 95 B.C.E.

Male etiam qui peregrinos urbibus uti prohibent eosque exterminant, ut Pennus apud patres nostros, Papius nuper. ***Nam esse pro cive qui civis non sit rectum est non licere****, quam legem tulerunt sapientissimi consules Crassus et Scaevola; usu vero urbis prohibere peregrinos sane inhumanum est.*

They also act badly who prevent foreigners from enjoying their city and banish them, as Pennus did in our fathers' time and Papius recently. It is right not to allow one who is not a citizen to act as a citizen: those wisest of consuls Crassus and Scaevola carried that law. However, to prevent foreigners from enjoying the city is surely subhuman.

Cf. Cicero *Pro Archia* 11:

Sed—quoniam census non ius civitatis confirmat ac tantum modo indicat eum qui sit census [ita] se iam tum gessisse pro cive—eis temporibus quibus tu criminaris ne ipsius quidem iudicio in civium Romanorum iure esse versatum, et testamentum saepe fecit nostris legibus, et adiit hereditates civium Romanorum, et in beneficiis ad aerarium delatus est a L. Lucullo pro consule.

But—since the census does not confirm the right of citizenship but only indicates that he who was counted did at that time conduct himself as a citizen—allow me to point out that, at the time when you charge that not even in his own judgment did Archias carry himself in the framework of a citizen, he often made a will according to our laws; he entered upon inheritances left him by Roman citizens; and he was commended to the archives of the state by Lucius Lucullus in the latter's proconsular command.

7. The Fiction of Citizenship: Gaius *Inst.* 4.37

Item ciuitas Romana peregrino fingitur, si eo nomine agat aut cum eo agatur, quo nomine nostris legibus actio constituta est, si modo iustum sit eam actionem etiam ad peregrinum extendi, ueluti si furti agat peregrinus aut cum eo agatur. <nam si cum peregrino agatur> formula ita concipitur: iudex esto. SI PARET <LUCIUS TITIO A DIONE HERMAEI FILIO OPEUE CONSILIO DIONIS HERMAEI FILII FURTUM FACTUM ESSE PATERAE AUREAE, QUAM OB REM EUM, SI CIUIS ROMANUS ESSET, PRO FURE DAMNUM DECIDERE OPORTERET, et reliqua. item, si peregrinus furti agat, ciuitas ei Romana fingitur. similiter si ex lege Aquilia peregrinus damni iniuriae agat aut cum eo agatur, ficta ciuitate Romana iudicium datur.

Again, if an alien sues or is sued on a cause for which an action has been established by Roman statutes, there is a fiction that he is a Roman citizen, provided that it is equitable that the action should be extended to an alien, for example, if an alien sues or is sued by an *actio furti*. Thus, if he is being sued by that action, the *formula* is framed as follows: "Be X *iudex*. If it appears that a golden cup has been stolen from Lucius Titius by Dio the son of Hermaeus or by his aid and counsel, on which account, if he were a Roman citizen, he would be bound to compound for the wrong as a thief," etc. Likewise, if an alien is plaintiff in the *actio furti*, Roman citizenship is fictitiously attributed to him. Similarly an action with the fiction of Roman citizenship is granted if a plaintiff sues or is sued for wrongful damage under the *L. Aquila*.

8. Gaius *Inst.* 3.25–26

Sed hae iuris iniquitates edicto praetoris emendatae sunt. Nam eos omnes, qui legitimo iure deficiuntur, uocat ad hereditatem, ***proinde ac si*** *in potestate parentis mortis tempore fuissent, siue soli sint, siue etiam sui heredes, id est qui in potestate patris fuerunt, concurrant.*

But these injustices in the civil law were corrected by the praetor's edict. For he summons to inheritance all children deficient in statutory title **exactly as if** they had been in their father's power at the time of his death, whether they stand alone or whether *sui heredes*, that is, persons who were actually in his power, come in with them.

9. *Lex Flavia municipalis* chap. 91

R(ubrica). Quo iure in tertium denuntietur, dies diffindatur diffi<s>susue sit, res iudicetur, lis iudici{i} damni sit, res in iudicio esse desinat.

et si intra it tempus, quod legis Iuliae, quae de iudici<i>s privatis proxime lata est, kapite XII senatusue consultis ad it kaput legis pertinentibus conpr<e>hensum est, iudicatum non sit, uti res in iudicio non sit, ***siremps*** *lex {r} i(us) [c](causa)que* ***esto*** *adque{m}* ***uti esset si*** *eam rem in urbe Roma praetor p(opuli) R(omani) inter cives Romanos iudicari iussisset*

Rubric. According to what law notice for the third day may be served, the day may be postponed or have been postponed, a matter may be judged, a case may be at the peril of the iudex, a matter may cease to be under trial.

if judgment has not taken place within the time laid down in Chapter XII of the *Lex Iulia* that was recently passed concerning *iudicia privata* and in the decrees of the Senate that relate to that chapter of the statute, so that the matter be no longer under trial; the statute and law and pleading is to be as it would be if a praetor of the Roman people had ordered the matter to be judged in the city of Rome between Roman citizens.

10. Gaius *Inst.* 3.55–56

Sequitur, ut de bonis Latinorum libertinorum dispiciamus. Quae pars iuris ut manifestior fiat, admonendi sumus, id quod alio loco diximus, eos qui nunc Latini Iuniani dicuntur olim ex iure Quiritium servos fuisse, sed auxilio praetoris in libertatis forma servari solitos; unde etiam res eorum peculii iure ad patronos pertinere solita est; postea vero per legem Iuniam eos omnes quos praetor in libertate tuebatur liberos esse coepisse et appellatos esse Latinos Iunianos: Latinos ideo, quia lex eos liberos ***perinde*** *esse voluit* ***atque si*** *essent cives Romani ingenui qui, ex urbe Roma in Latinas colonias deducti, Latini coloniarii esse coeperunt; Iunianos ideo, quia per legem Iuniam liberi facti sunt, etiamsi non essent cives Romani.*

We proceed to consider the estates of [Junian] Latin freedmen. In order to make this branch of law clearer, we must call to mind that, as we have said elsewhere, those who are now termed Junian Latins were in earlier times slaves by Quiritary law (that is, civil law in the strict sense), but that they were maintained in a framework of freedom by the aid of the praetor; and therefore their property used to go to their patrons by title of *peculium*; later, owing to the *lex Iunia*, all who used to be protected in a state of freedom by the praetor came to be free and to be styled Junian Latins: Latins because the law made them free **exactly as if** they were free-born Roman citizens who, by migrating from the city of Rome to Latin colonies, had become colonial Latins, Junian because it was by the *lex Iunia* that they were made free, although they were not Roman citizens.

Further fictions relevant to personal status in the *Lex Flavia municipalis*, clauses 22 and 23:

> *Rubrica. Ut, qui civitatem Romanam consequentur, maneant in eorumdem manu mancupio potestate.*
>
> *Qui quaeue ex hac lege exue edicto imperatoris Caesaris Vespasiani Augusti imperatorisve Titi Caesaris Vespasiani Augusti aut imperatoris Caesaris Domitiani Augusti, patris patriae, civitatem Romanam consecutus consecuta erit, is ea in eius, qui civis Romanis hac lege factus erit, potestate manu mancupio, cuius esse deberet,* ***si civitate mutatus mutata non esset, esto*** *itaque ius tutoris optandi* ***habeto,*** *quod haberet* ***si a cive Romano ortus orta neque civitate mutatus mutata esset.***
>
> (Chapter 22) Rubric. That those who acquire Roman citizenship should remain in the same *manus* and *mancipium* and power of the same persons (as before).
>
> Whoever, male or female, acquires Roman citizenship under this statute or according to an edict of the Emperor Caesar Vespasian Augustus or the Emperor Titus Caesar Vespasian Augustus or the Emperor Caesar Domitian Augustus, father of his country, he or she is said to be [as before] in the power and *manus* and *mancipium* of the same person who has become a Roman citizen under this statute, in whose power and *manus* and *mancipium* he or she would have been if he or she had undergone no change of citizenship. And he or she is to have that right of *tutoris optio* which he or she would have if he or she were born from a Roman citizen and had undergone no change of citizenship.
>
> *Rubrica. Ut, qui civitatem Romanam consequerentur, iura libertorum retineant.*
>
> *Qui quaeve ex hac lege exue edicto imperatoris Caesaris Vespasiani Augusti imperatorisve Titi Caesaris Vespasiani Augusti aut imperatoris Caesaris Domitiani Augusti civitatem Romanam consecutus consecuta erit, eis in libertos libertas suos suas paternos paternas{q}ue, qui quaeue*

in civitatem Romanam non venerint, deque bonis eorum earum et is, quae libertatis causa imposita sunt, idem ius eademque condicio ***esto****, quae esset,* ***si civitate mutati mutatae non essent****.*

(Chapter 23) Rubric. That those who acquire Roman citizenship should retain rights over freedmen.

Whoever male or female acquires Roman citizenship under this statute or according to an edict of the Emperor Caesar Vespasian Augustus or the Emperor Titus Caesar Vespasian Augustus or the Emperor Caesar Domitian Augustus, is to have the same rights as they would have had if they had undergone no change of citizenship, over their own and their parents' freedmen and freedwomen, who have not acquired Roman citizenship, also over their goods and the obligations imposed in return for freedom.

11. Gaius *Inst.* 3.56

legis itaque Iuniae lator, cum intellegeret futurum ut ea fictione res Latinorum defunctorum ad patronos pertinere desinerent, quia scilicet neque ut servi decederent, ut possent iure peculii res ad patronos pertinere, neque <ut> liberti, [Latini hominis] <ut> bona possent manumissionis iure ad patronos pertinere, necessarium existimavit, ne beneficium istis datum in iniuriam patronorum converteretur, cavere [voluit], ut bona eorum ***proinde*** *ad manumissores pertinerent* ***ac si*** *lex lata non esset. itaque iure* ***quodammodo*** *peculii bona Latinorum ad manumissores ea lege pertinent.*

Realizing that as a result of this fiction the estates of deceased Latins would no longer go to their patrons, because of course they would die neither as slaves, whose property would go to their patrons *iure peculii*, nor as freedmen, whose estates would go to their patrons *manumissionis iure*, the author of the *lex Iunia* therefore deemed it necessary, in order to prevent the benefit given to them from being turned to the injury of their patrons, to provide that their estates should go to their manumitters **exactly as if** the *lex* had not been passed. Hence under the *lex* the estates of Latins go to their manumitters **in some fashion** by the law of *peculium*.

12. Paul *Quaestiones* bk. 11 fr. 1373 Lenel = *Dig.* 35.2.18.*pr.*

Filius familias qui militaverat decedens patris sui fidei commisit codicillis, ut peculium suum castrense Titio post mortem restitueret: quaerebatur, an ut heres quartam deducere possit. dixi legem Falcidiam inductam esse a divo Pio etiam in intestatorum successionibus propter fideicommissa: sed in proposito nec hereditatem esse, quamvis placeret mihi extraneo herede instituto fieri hereditatem aditione eius: nam cum apud patrem remanet, ius pristinum durat et peculium est. nec huic contrarium est, quod in testamento eius qui apud hostes decessit exercetur Falcidia: nam fictio legis Corneliae et hereditatem et heredem facit. sed me non dubitare, quin debeat id quoque indulgeri legis beneficium, ***siquidem quasi*** *patris familiae bona restituere cogitur et heres scriptus omissa ex testamento aditione exemplo edicti legatorum nomine convenietur.*

A son in power who died while serving in the military charged his father by means of a codicil with a trust, to deliver to Titius his *peculium castrense* after death. It was asked whether the heir (namely, the father) could deduct a quarter. I said that the *lex Falcidia* had been extended by the Divine Pius in respect to trusts even to cases of intestate succession. That said, in the case before us, there was no inheritance, although I would have agreed that, had someone outside the family been named heir, his acceptance would have created an inheritance. As the son in our case remained in the power of his father, the erstwhile legal framework obtained and the property was *peculium*. Nor is this contrary to the fact that the *lex Falcidia* governs the wills of those who die as prisoners of war, for the fiction of the *lex Cornelia* creates both an inheritance and an heir. But I also said that I did not doubt but that the charity of the law should also be satisfied, **if** the father were required to transfer the assets **as if** those of a *paterfamilias* and, being instituted as heir but declining acceptance under the will, he were then sued in respect of legacies on the pattern of the edict.

Compare Paul *Ad legem Falcidiam* fr. 921 Lenel = *Dig.* 35.2.1.1–2:

Lex Falcidia etiam ad eos, qui apud hostes moriuntur, propter legem Corneliam pertinere videtur, quod ea lex perinde eorum testamenta confirmat, ***atque si*** *in civitate decessissent:* ***propter quam fictionem*** *lex Falcidia et omnes testamentariae pertinent, quae tamen possint locum habere. (2) Ad eos, qui omissa causa testamenti possident hereditatem, non pertinet lex Falcidia: sed per edictum praetoris inducitur* ***potestas legis****.*

The lex Falcidia is held applicable also to those who die in enemy hands by reason of the lex Cornelia; for this latter enactment confirms their testamentary dispositions **just as if** they had died citizens. **By virtue of this fiction** the lex Falcidia and all other testamentary enactments which may be relevant are applicable. (2) The lex Falcidia has no application to those who possess an inheritance in the absence of a will; but the import of the statute is introduced through the praetor's edict.

13. Gaius *Inst.* 3.194

Propter hoc tamen, quod lex ex ea causa manifestum furtum esse iubet, sunt, qui scribunt furtum manifestum aut lege intellegi aut natura: lege id ipsum, de quo loquimur, natura illud, de quo superius exposuimus. sed uerius est natura tantum manifestum furtum intellegi; neque enim lex facere potest, ut qui manifestus fur non sit, manifestus sit, non magis quam qui omnino fur non sit, fur sit, et qui adulter aut homicida non sit, adulter uel homicida sit; at illud sane lex facere potest, ut ***proinde*** *aliquis poena teneatur,* ***atque si*** *furtum uel adulterium uel homicidium admisisset, quamuis nihil eorum admiserit.*

Nevertheless, because of this, namely, that the statute orders that in such cases the theft be manifest, there are those who will say that theft may be understood to be manifest on the basis of statute or in reality: by statute in the situation we are now discussing, and in reality in the circumstance we described above. The truer answer is that manifest theft is understood as such in reality. For statute can no more bring it about that a non-manifest thief is manifest, than it can make someone who is altogether not a thief into a thief, or someone who is not an adulterer or a homicide into an adulterer or a homicide. Rather, what law can do is simply this, it can make someone liable to punishment **exactly as if** he had committed theft or adultery or homicide, even if he had committed none of those things.

Notes

CHAPTER I

1. On the *lex Iulia iudicaria*, see Gaius *Inst.* 4.103–5. A significant exception to this overall trend was the opening of the court governing charges of extortion against magistrates to foreign plaintiffs. On this, see Chapter 3 n. 13 and especially Ando, "Three revolutions in government," forthcoming.

2. Further actions and formulations that act upon or give expression to this supposition include grants of autonomy in the constitution of a province or restitution of systems of law in the aftermath of surrender (on which processes see Ando, "Rites of others," forthcoming), as well as the opposition between grants of Roman citizenship and the right "to use one's own laws" operational in Roman narratives of the settlement of Italy (on which see, e.g., Chapter 5, pp. 87–88, 107).

3. See Appendix passage 2. Further texts in the reception history of Cicero's definition are cited in Chapter 5 nn. 10–11.

4. For a preliminary exploration of metonymy in Latin and what it can reveal narrowly of Roman political thought, as well as Roman cognition more generally, see Ando 2011, "Law and the landscape of empire." On racialism in Athenian law and ideologies of citizenship, see Lape 2010.

5. Sherwin-White 1973, 397–468.

6. Nicolet 1982 = idem 1991; Ando 2000; and Ando 2010, "Imperial identities."

7. For a reading of the jurisdictional rules in the *lex de Gallia Cisalpina* and the *lex Flavia municipalis*, see Rodger 1996.

8. Reasonably detailed evidence for the process called by Romans "reduction into the form of a province" exists under the Republic for Sicily, Achaea, and Asia. It can be supplemented by accounts of the settlement of territories not formally annexed, such as Macedon after the second Macedonian war. On geographic aspects of Roman governance, see Nicolet 1982 = idem 1991; Ando 2006; and idem, *The Ambitions of Government*, forthcoming. Recognition of another legal system could also occur outside this framework, motivated by whatever contingency, such as is attested in the Tabula Contrebiensis.

9. On this topic see Ando 2010, "Imperial identities," and idem, *The Ambitions of Government*, forthcoming, as well as Chapter 5, pp. 107–9.

10. See, e.g., *Lex de Gallia Cisalpina* (RS 28), chapter 20, ll. 7–19 at 15–16: *tum*

mag(istratus) prove mag(istratu) IIvir IIIIvir praefec(tus)ve, quoquomque d(e) e(a) r(e) in ius aditum erit.

11. The likelihood is naturally that these were members of whatever population group had previously inhabited the site where the colony was founded and who were in some fashion integrated into the life of the settlement. One record that explicitly describes such a situation in strikingly similar language is Livy 32.2.6, which is quoted at Appendix passage 6B.

12. The so-called *lex de imperio Vespasiani* is perhaps the most intensively studied of all Latin epigraphic texts. Among a vast literature, see Mantovani 2005 and the now classic survey of Brunt 1977.

13. On legal fictions at Rome the bibliography is more or less limited to two superb essays published in the same year, Thomas 1995 and Richardson 1995.

14. On conflict of law theory, see Tetley 1999 and Briggs 2008, 1–52. There has been no systematic effort to study ancient private law in light of modern conflicts of law or international private-law theory. Perhaps the most suggestive of available studies are Johnston 1987 and Rodger 1991.

15. Julian *Digest* bk. 90 fr. 842 Lenel = *Dig.* 1.3.11.

16. Julian *Digest* bk. 15 fr. 259 Lenel = *Dig.* 1.3.12. See also Ulpian *Ad edictum aedilium curulium* bk. 1 fr. 1757 = *Dig.* 1.3.13: *Nam, ut ait Pedius, quotiens lege aliquid unum vel alterum introductum est, bona occasio est cetera, quae tendunt ad eandem utilitatem, vel interpretatione vel certe iurisdictione suppleri.* "For, as Pedius says, whenever something or another has been brought within the scope of the law, this is a good opportunity for other things, which further the same interest, to be folded in either by interpretation or *a fortiori* by judicial decision."

17. Ulpian *Ad edictum* bk. 15 fr. 518 = *Dig.* 5.3.20.6d: *aptanda igitur nobis singulis verbis senatus consulti congruens interpretatio.*

18. Cf. Gaius *Inst.* 1.128, on the *fictio legis Corneliae*; and Gaius *Inst.* 2.197 on the *senatusconsultum Neronianum.*

19. Gaius *Inst.* 2.133. Compare Gaius *Inst.* 2.263: there the supplement to the civil law arises from a *senatusconsultum*. Prior to the emperor Augustus, *fideicommissa*, trusts, had moral force only, and commonly took the form of requests to heirs. Augustus made them enforceable by a new procedure (in fact, a *cognitio extra ordinem*). But because trusts had no requisite form—and indeed could be imposed on an heir even in intestacy—while the constraints on legacies were numerous, more and more people had recourse to trusts alone. To bring the devolution of property back under the normative moral and economic control of the state, some correction was necessary. Thus it was provided by *senatusconsultum* in the age of Nero, according to Gaius, that "the actions which would lie at civil law in favor of and against the heir should also be granted in favor of and against him to whom an inheritance is made over under a trust. In consequence of this *senatusconsultum*, the stipulations (in civil law) mentioned above have fallen out of use, and the praetor now gives *actiones utiles*, in favor of and against the recipient of an inheritance *as though* in favor of and against an heir, and these actions are published in the edict" (*actiones, quae iure ciuili heredi et in heredem conpeterent, ei et in eum darentur, cui ex fideicommisso*

restituta esset hereditas; per quod senatus consultum desierunt illae cautiones in usu haberi. praetor enim utiles actiones ei et in eum, qui recepit hereditatem, ***quasi*** *heredi et in heredem dare coepit, eaeque in edicto proponuntur*).

20. Julian *Digest* bk. 84 fr. 819 Lenel = *Dig.* 1.3.32.pr.: *De quibus causis scriptis legibus non utimur, id custodiri oportet, quod moribus et consuetudine inductum est: et si qua in re hoc deficeret, tunc quod proximum et consequens ei est: si nec id quidem appareat, tunc ius, quo urbs Roma utitur, servari oportet.*

21. The understanding of metaphor and modeling here deployed is owed largely to Black 1962.

22. Gaius *Inst.* 3.56, 3.58. For a thorough treatment of Roman law on slavery, see Buckland 1908.

23. Papinian *Definitiones* bk. 2 fr. 46 Lenel = *Dig.* 1.1.7.1.

24. Gaius *Inst.* 3.56: *Quae pars iuris ut manifestior fiat, admonendi sumus, id quod alio loco diximus, eos qui nunc Latini Iuniani dicuntur olim ex iure Quiritium servos fuisse, sed auxilio praetoris in libertatis forma servari solitos.*

25. For extra-legal evidence for Augustus's worries regarding the purity of the citizen body, see Dio 56.33.1–3.

26. On Latin as a legal status, see Oakley 1998, 538–42 and 567–68, and Kremer 2006.

27. One might compare the arguments elaborated by jurists about invalid or impossible conditions in wills and testaments: these must be regarded as never having been written—*pro non scripto*—for the will to possess validity (see, *exempli gratia*, *Dig.* 28.7.20 or 29.7.2.1). The language of scholarship consolidates elsewhere around fiction: for a codicil to function as a testament, for example, its contents must be regarded *perinde ac si*, exactly as if they had been written in a will (again, *exempli gratia*, see *Dig.* 29.7.2.2 or 29.7.14).

28. Further problems arose when a Junian Latin received Roman citizenship, which he might do by one of several procedures. On this contingency see Gaius *Inst.* 3.72–73.

29. Paul *Ad legem Falcidiam* fr. 921 Lenel = *Dig.* 35.2.1.1. Compare Julian *Digest* bk. 62 fr. 759 Lenel = *Dig.* 28.6.28: *Lex Cornelia, quae testamenta eorum qui in hostium potestate decesserunt confirmat, non solum ad hereditatem ipsorum qui testamenta fecerunt pertinet, sed ad omnes hereditates, quae ad quemque ex eorum testamento pertinere* ***potuissent, si*** *in hostium potestatem non pervenissent. quapropter cum pater in hostium potestate decessit filio impubere relicto in civitate et is intra tempus pubertatis decesserit, hereditas ad substitutum pertinet,* ***perinde ac si*** *pater in hostium potestatem non pervenisset.*

30. Garnsey 1970; MacMullen 1990, 204–17; Millar 2004, 120–50.

31. This is a special theme of Thomas 1995.

32. Gaius *Ad edictum provinciale* 7 fr. 168 Lenel = Dig. 7.5.2.1: *Quo senatus consulto non id effectum est, ut pecuniae usus fructus* ***proprie*** *esset (nec enim naturalis ratio auctoritate senatus commutari potuit), sed remedio introducto coepit* ***quasi*** *usus fructus haberi.*

33. Ulpian *Lex Iulia et Papia* bk. 1 fr. 1978 Lenel = *Dig.* 1.5.25. In Lenel's reconstruction, the passage continues with consideration of two further, similar cases, themselves excerpted at *Dig.* 40.16.4 and *Dig.* 40.10.6: *Si libertinus per collusionem fuerit pronuntiatus*

ingenuus, collusione detecta in quibus causis ***quasi libertinus*** *incipit esse. medio tamen tempore, antequam collusio detegatur et post sententiam de ingenuitate latam, utique* ***quasi ingenuus*** *accipitur. Libertinus si ius anulorum impetraverit, quamvis iura ingenuitatis salvo iure patroni nactus sit, tamen ingenuus intellegitur: et hoc divus Hadrianus rescripsit.* "If a freedman has through collusion been pronounced of free birth and the collusion is discovered, from that time he is treated *as if* a freedman in all respects. Nonetheless, in the intervening time after the judgment for free birth and before discovery of the collusion, he is certainly taken to be *as if* free born. If a freedman has sought and obtained the right to rings, although he has acquired the rights of free birth—his patron's rights being protected—nonetheless he is understood as a freeborn person: so the divine Hadrian ruled by rescript." In such cases of suit for free birth, jurists (and judges) had to guard against deceit, of which perhaps the easiest form was to bring suit without the awareness of interested parties or potential witnesses. In the case of a fraudulent suit, the annulment of a verdict granting rights of free birth took the form of a fiction that the earlier judgment had not occurred, an act similar to the erasure of clauses from wills by treating them "as if they had not been written." See Callistratus *De cognitionibus* bk. 4 fr. 27 Lenel = *Dig.* 40.16.3: *Cum non iusto contradictore quis ingenuus pronuntiatus est, perinde inefficax est decretum, atque si nulla iudicata res intervenisset, idque principalibus constitutionibus cavetur.* "When someone has been pronounced of free birth in the absence of a person with the right to contest the suit, the decision is *just* as ineffective *as if* there had been no judgment in the case at all, and this is provided in imperial constitutions." Finally, to the simple formulation by Ulpian with which I opened, compare in another domain Servius *Ad Aen.* 2.116, discussing human sacrifice: *VIRGINE CAESA. non vere, sed ut videbatur. et sciendum in sacris simulata pro veris accipi: unde cum de animalibus quae difficile inveniuntur est sacrificandum, de pane vel cera fiunt et pro veris accipiuntur.* " 'The maiden killed': not truly, but in seeming. Indeed, one should know that in rites the pretend is taken for the true: whence, when it is necessary to sacrifice an animal but they are hard to find, the sacrifice is made from bread or wax and these are accepted in the place of the true things."

34. Celsus *Dig.* bk. 26 fr. 219 Lenel = *Dig.* 1.3.17: *Scire leges non hoc est verba earum tenere, sed vim ac potestatem.*

35. See Paul *Ad legem Falcidiam* fr. 921 Lenel = *Dig.* 35.2.1.2 = Appendix passage 12.

CHAPTER 2

1. For accounts of these terms, with intelligent assessments as to their utility, see Schulz 1946, 262–66, 278–99; Jolowicz and Nicholas 1972, 469–77.

2. See, e.g., *Labeo Ad edictum praetoris peregrini* fr. 4 Lenel = Dig. 4.3.9.4a or Gaius *Ad edictum provinciale* bks. 6–32 frr. 53–388 Lenel. Such distinctions as are drawn between Roman and provincial practice in the fragments preserved by the Justinianic compilers not surprisingly never rest upon no longer operative distinctions in the juridical

status of persons or communities. See, e.g., fr. 87 Lenel = *Dig.* 3.4.1: *item collegia Romae certa sunt . . . qui et in provinciis sunt.*

3. Modern literature on legal pluralism has played almost no role in scholarship on the Roman Empire, to considerable loss.

4. In addition to Chapter 1 of this work, I have reflected on the social-theoretical implications of Roman reflections on *ius civile* in Ando 2008, *The Matter of the Gods*, 59–92, and Ando 2010, "The ontology of religious institutions."

5. Julian *Digest* bk. 59 fr. 740 Lenel = *Dig.* 1.3.10: *Neque leges neque senatus consulta ita scribi possunt, ut omnes casus qui quandoque inciderint comprehendantur, sed sufficit ea quae plerumque accidunt contineri.* Ulpian *Ad Sabinum* bk. 30 fr. 2747 Lenel = *Dig.* 19.5.4: *Natura enim rerum conditum est, ut plura sint negotia quam vocabula.* Celsus *Digest* bk. 8 fr. 72 Lenel = *Dig.* 19.5.2: *Nam cum deficiant vulgaria atque usitata actionum nomina, praescriptis verbis agendum est.* To this last compare Julian *Digest* bk. 14 fr. 238 Lenel = *Dig.* 19.5.3: [*in factum civilis actio,*] *in quam necesse est confugere, quotiens contractus existunt, quorum appellationes nullae iure civili proditae sunt.*

6. See Ando, "The rites of others," forthcoming, and Ando 2010, "The ontology of religious institutions."

7. On the rights of victors, see especially Servius *Ad Aen.* 1.6. On the importance of local legal orders see Chapter 1, pp. 2–6.

8. On this episode, see Chapter 1 p. 4 and Chapter 5 pp. 87–88.

9. *Collatio* 6.4.6: *sed posthac religionem sanctitatemque in conubiis copulandis volumus ab unoquoque servari, ut se ad disciplinam legesque Romanas meminerint pertinere et eas tantum sciant nuptias licitas, quae sunt Romano iure permissae.* "That said, we desire that henceforth in contracting marriages religious and moral scruple should be observed by all, to the end that they should be mindful of the need to conform themselves to the laws and lifestyle of Rome and should know that only those marriages are licit that are permitted by Roman law."

10. The remarks here are indebted to an extended study of the late Republican and Julio-Claudian laws on jurisdiction, likewise aimed at recovering from them Roman thought in respect to territoriality. See Ando 2011, "Law and the landscape of empire." On conceptions of the empire as they can be recovered from legal instruments and diplomatic practice, see Ando 2008, "Aliens."

11. Pliny *Ep.* 10.49–50, on which see Ando 2009.

12. Ulpian *De officio proconsulis* fr. 2197 Lenel; *Collatio* 1.11.2; *Dig.* 48.8.4.1.

13. *Cod. Iust.* 4.55.5 (Honoré Palingenesia 709/8/90): *Qui exportandus a domino de civitate sua venit, nec in urbe Roma morari debet: qui autem de provincia certa, nec in Italia. si itaque contra legem constitutam factum probare potes, utere iure, quod propterea tibi competit.*

14. In addition to the text cited in n. 13, see, e.g., Ulpian *Ad edictum* bk. 60 fr. 1393 Lenel = *Dig.* 5.1.19.4: *Illud sciendum est eum, qui ita fuit obligatus ut in Italia solveret, si in provincia habuit domicilium, utrubique posse conveniri et hic et ibi: et ita et Iuliano et multis aliis videtur.*

15. Salvian *De gubernatione Dei* 4.54, 5.47; Eugippius *Vita sancti Severini* 31.6. On these passages, see Ando 2009, 109–11.

16. On *subtilitas,* see the brilliant suggestion of Schulz 1946, 292 n. 7, urging that *suptilitate iuris* in Ulpian *Ad Sabinum* bk. 48 fr. 2951 Lenel = *Dig.* 45.1.36 is an interpolation for *ipso (civili) iure.*

17. Millar 1999 = idem 2004, 435–64.

18. See, e.g., *Cod. Theod.* 16.5.7: *Si quis Manicheus Manichaeave ex die latae dudum legis ac primitus a nostris parentibus in quamlibet personam condito testamento vel cuiuslibet titulo liberalitatis atque specie donationis transmisit proprias facultates . . . quoniam isdem sub perpetua inustae infamiae nota* ***testandi ac vivendi iure Romano omnem*** *protinus eripimus* ***facultatem*** *neque eos aut relinquendae aut capiendae alicuius hereditatis habere sinimus potestatem.*

19. See, e.g., Ulpian *Inst.* bk. 1 fr. 1915 Lenel = *Dig.* 1.1.6, where the category of "unwritten law" is not only flagged as Greek but written in Greek.

20. One possible instance of the use of such language is Cicero *pro Cluentio* 166: *alterum veneficii crimen Oppianico huic adulescenti, cum eius in nuptiis more Larinatium multitudo hominum pranderet, venenum Habiti consilio paratum* ("The second charge of poisoning is that Habitus instigated an attempt to poison young Oppianicus here, at a dinner which Oppianicus, after the custom of Larinum, gave to a large number of people on his marriage").

21. Paul *Quaestiones* bk. 1 fr. 1269 Lenel = *Dig.* 1.3.37: *Si de interpretatione legis quaeratur, in primis inspiciendum est, quo iure civitas retro in eiusmodi casibus usa fuisset: optima enim est legum interpres consuetudo.*

22. Invocations of local custom prior to the Antonine Constitution focus on issues of discretion in Roman courts, namely, on the discretion afforded judges in whether they might take account of local norms. See, e.g., Callistratus *De cognitionibus* bk. 4 fr. 28.6 Lenel = *Dig.* 22.5.3.6: *Testes non temere evocandi sunt per longum iter et multo minus milites avocandi sunt a signis vel muneribus perhibendi testimonii causa, idque divus Hadrianus rescripsit. sed et divi fratres rescripserunt: quod ad testes evocandos pertinet,* ***diligentiae iudicantis est explorare, quae consuetudo in ea provincia, in quam iudicat, fuerit****. nam si probabitur saepe in aliam civitatem testimonii gratia plerosque evocatos, non esse dubitandum, quin evocandi sint, quos necessarios in ipsa cognitione deprehenderit qui iudicat.* "Witnesses should not lightly be summoned from long distances, still less soldiers called away from their military duties, as the deified Hadrian said in a rescript. The deified brothers also wrote, 'So far as summoning witnesses is concerned, the careful judge should find out what the practice is in the province in which he is judge.' If it is found that several witnesses are often summoned to another *civitas* to give evidence, the witnesses whom the judge thinks necessary for the *cognitio* should undoubtedly be summoned."

23. *Cod. Iust.* 6.24.7 (Honoré Palingenesia 1457/17/17) 3 December 285: *Nec* ***apud peregrinos*** *fratrem sibi quisquam per adoptionem facere poterat. cum igitur, quod patrem tuum voluisse facere dicis, irritum sit, portionem hereditatis, quam is adversus quam supplicas velut adoptatus frater heres institutus tenet, restitui tibi curae habebit praeses provinciae.* "Not even among foreigners can one make another brother to himself through adoption.

Since therefore you say that your father willed this, his act is void and the governor of the province shall take care that the portion of the estate held by the person who was instituted heir under the title, as it were, of adoptive brother, against whom you have filed suit, shall be restored to you."

24. *Inst.* 2.6.12, referring to the law studied here, *Cod. Iust.* 7.31.1.

25. For an exploration of the history of ancient government in these terms, see Ando, "Three revolutions in government," forthcoming; see also idem 2010, "Imperial identities," 40–45.

CHAPTER 3

1. Contrast the argument of the second speaker, whose argument rests on the weighing of reputation (*De armis*, bk. 2 chap. 1): "For when marshaled against the authority of the most famous men, the weightiest judgments, and the force of undefeated arguments, what service might the most obscure testimonies, the shoddiest pieces of hostile evidence, or utterly worthless carpings perform for those opposed by a unanimous judgment? Paulus Diaconus, Zonaras, Orosius, Cedrenus, and others whose names the prosecutor wouldn't have the audacity to mention—these are his witnesses who are to be opposed to Dionysius, Polybius, Plutarch, Livy, whom he regards as suspect historians and lying encomiasts of the Romans."

2. Although I number among those who for evidentiary reasons resist the extraction from Roman sources of any code of "the laws of war," that project has obviously a very long pedigree. Perhaps the most impressive short statement of the achievements of this tradition is Lammert 1935; see also Bederman 2001. Kindred to those works and often overlapping are those investigating just-war doctrine at Rome: see especially Drexler 1959; and Riggsby 2006, 157–89, 215–16. For a more skeptical treatment, see P. A. Brunt 1990, especially 305–22. Where international law in the Roman period is concerned, and in particular doctrines of sovereignty, I have suggested elsewhere that we would do well to stand apart from the relatively meager and underconceptualized reflections contained in Roman literary texts and study instead the vastly more varied and fascinating evidence for the practice of diplomacy and content of diplomatic instruments (Ando 2008, "Aliens").

3. For an exemplary study of the development of Roman historical writing, with particular reference to the invention in the late Republic of documentary records for the remote past, see Frier 1999.

4. Richardson 2008; Woolf 1998, 48–76; Ando 2008, *The Matter of the Gods*, 120–49; see also P. A. Brunt 1990, 288–323, 433–80.

5. Scheid 2006 is a superb effort in this vein. A related body of work seeks to show the influence of concepts derived from private law upon public law and constitutional theory: an early and remarkable essay in this tradition is Moatti 2001. See also Ando 2009.

6. The most recent essay in this vein known to me is Nótári 2006, 142–49; see also idem 2008, 98–103.

7. The fetial ritual and the history of the priesthood have generated an enormous

bibliography. The two most extensive recent studies are Rüpke 1990, 97–124 and Zack 2001, 13–73. Rüpke takes the radical (but it seems to me correct) view that the fetial ritual (and of necessity fetial law) is entirely an invention of the late Republic; Zack takes Roman claims regarding the historicity of the priesthood at face value. Among a huge modern literature reconstructing the contents of so-called fetial law, see especially Samter 1909 and Catalano 1965, 3–48.

8. *ILS* 61: *Fert. Erresius, rex Aequeicolus. Is preimus ius fetiale paravit; inde p. R. discipleinam excepit.*

9. I observe that Oakley 2005, 46–47, treating just these events, accepts the historicity of not only the fetials but also just-war doctrine at Rome in the late fourth century B.C.E. For a very different assessment of the reliability of Livy's narrative in particular, see Briquel 2006.

10. On this change, and on Roman warfare in this period more generally, see Rich 1976; on its implications for the rituals of declaring war, see McDonald and Walbank 1937, 192–97, together with Walbank 1949.

11. Literary asides: see, e.g., Cicero *Verr.* 2.5.49, where *in fetialium manibus* is shorthand for "international law." For the declaration of war against Cleopatra, see Dio 50.4.4–5. On the late Republican evidence, see especially Ferrary 1995, 413–20.

12. Rüpke 1990, 103–7 offers a devastating review of the reliability of the (late) evidence for (early) practice.

13. John Richardson has pointed out to me that the *legis actio sacramento* appears to have been the action according to which trials under the early *leges de repetundis*, namely, the *lex Calpurnia* and *lex Iunia* were conducted (the evidence derives from the Gracchan *lex repetundarum* ll. 21–23 [*RS* 2]: *neiue eum* [*quei condemnatus siet, quod cum eo lege Calpu*]*rnia aut lege Iunia sacramento actum siet aut quod h(ace) l(ege) nomen* [*delatum sie*]*t*). The opening thereby offered to aliens to use the *legis actio sacramento* in Roman courts—if that is what occurred—undoubtedly exists in causal relation in one direction or another with the homologies visible between the *legis actio sacramento* and fetial ritual. Further on these laws, see Ando, "Three revolutions in government," forthcoming.

14. Varro *Ling.* 5.180; Gaius *Inst.* 4.13: the monies are designated the *summa sacramenti* or *praedes*.

15. Cicero *Caec.* 97; *Dom.* 78; *De oratore* 1.42.

16. Broughton 1987 and Ferrary 1995.

17. Pomponius *Encheiridion* liber singularis fr. 178.7 Lenel = *Dig.* 1.2.2.7.

18. My reading of these texts is indebted to Scheid 2006.

19. Nock 1939 (reprinted in Ando 2003, 84–97) regards this use of imperatives in addresses to gods as a distinctive and important feature of Roman religion and gives the phenomenon classic treatment.

20. On the oaths of foreign parties, see, briefly, Ando, "The rites of others," forthcoming.

21. In issuing this indictment, it is important to remember that Roman politicians could and did denounce their peers, or particular actions, for not having satisfied even these minimal standards: see, e.g., Cicero *Pis.* 85; Livy 38.45.3–7. Indeed, it may well be

that the preeminent use of the so-called laws of war—or laws on magisterial misconduct, for that matter—lay with Romans attacking other Romans. To the extent that empirical inquiry can settle the matter, one should begin with careful consideration of P. A. Brunt 1990, 53–95, 487–506.

22. I have recently made two attempts to analyze when, why, and to what effect Romans came to describe the rules of cult and regulations of religion as bodies of law: see Ando 2008, *The Matter of the Gods*, 59–92 and idem 2009; each cites relevant bibliography.

23. Livy 9.11: on the content of this passage and its place within Roman thought on law in international relations, see Ando 2008, "Aliens," 493.

CHAPTER 4

1. Swain 1940; Momigliano 1982, reprinted in idem 1986, 31–57; cf. Fuchs 1938, 62–73. The theme also has an important reception outside the Graeco-Roman world: on this, see Metzler 1989, citing earlier bibliography.

2. Dionysius of Halicarnassus *Ant. Rom.* 1.2; see also Appian *Praef.* 29–44.

3. Polybius 1.3.3–5, on which see Ando 1999, especially 24.

4. *Rhet. ad Herennium* 4.34.

5. Plutarch *Mor.* 207d. On the figure of Alexander in Roman politics of the Principate see Kühnen 2008.

6. Namely, the fragment attributed to the *Chronicle* of Aemilius Sura in the text of Velleius Paterculus 1.6.6, deleted as an interpolation by Delbenius in the Aldine edition of 1571. It was accepted as genuine by Swain 1940 and Alonso-Núñez 1989; Peter 1906, 2: ccx, 161. See also n. 10 below on Appian *Lib.* 628–30.

7. On this use of the term see, e.g., Barfield 2001.

8. Woolf 1998, 48–76; Ando 2000; Ando 2008, *The Matter of the Gods*, 138–39.

9. Pocock 2003.

10. Homer *Il.* 6.448–49 (trans. after R. Lattimore). It is ascribed to Scipio at Appian *Lib.* 628–30 but merely quoted, apparently from Polybius but without the ascription to Scipio, at Diodorus 32.24. On the reconstruction of the text of Polybius at this point, see Walbank 1957–79, 3:722–25.

11. Isidore *Etym.* 2.21.4. For treatments, see Wirszubski 1950, 31–44; Richardson 1991, 4; and Pocock 2003, 276–78.

12. On the stress placed upon the boundary between individual and collective in the collapse of Republican government at Rome, both in political language as well as constitutional realities, see Millar 1988 = idem 2002, 183–99.

13. The obiter dictum of Cato cited from Malcovati, *ORF3* p. 218 n. 249 by Wirszubski 1950, 38 (*Iure, lege libertate, re publica communiter uti oportet; gloria atque honore, quomodo sibi quisque struxit*) makes explicit the tension between public and private (or communal and individual) that I take to be implicit in Scipio's utterance, but Cato does so in a way that denies that the tensions exist in the way that I suggest: his lists in effect assert the communal and individual to be articulable as non-overlapping domains.

14. For an analysis of the period, including extensive citation of secondary literature, see Ando 2010, "From Republic to Empire."

15. Ando 2010, "From Republic to Empire," addresses the question of what relationship modern social historians should see between constitutional language and constitutional change at Rome and broader currents in the history of political culture and political subjectivity in the Roman empire between the second century B.C.E. and the early second century C.E.

16. On this question regarding Athens see Raaflaub 1998; regarding Rome, see Millar 2002, 109–61.

17. Cf. Davies 1994.

18. Ando 2008, "Aliens."

19. Hansen 1995.

20. Jones 1960, 51–65; Robert 1973; Oliver 1979; Millar 1993 = idem 2006, 106–35; Ager 1996.

21. Welles 1965, not cited by Davies 1994, 61, who laments the absence of significant studies.

22. See, e.g., *ILS* 8779, a decree of Pergamum for Publius Servilius Isauricus: ἀποδεδωκότα τῇ πόλει τοὺς πατρίους νόμους καὶ τὴν δημοκρατίαν ἀδούλωτον, "he restored to the city its ancestral laws and its democracy unenslaved."

23. Herodotus 6.42 (Ἀρταφρένης . . . μεταπεμψάμενος ἀγγέλους ἐκ τῶν πολίων συνθήκας σφίσι αὐτοῖσι τοὺς Ἴωνας ἠνάγκασε ποιέεσθαι, ἵνα δωσίδικοι εἶεν καὶ μὴ ἀλλήλους φέροιέν τε καὶ ἄγοιεν) and 43 (τοὺς γὰρ τυράννους τῶν Ἰώνον καταπαύσας πάντας ὁ Μαρδόνιος δημοκρατίας κατίστα ἐς τὰς πόλιας).

24. On the history of this period see especially Badian 1995.

25. For an attempt to understand the history of the Greek city in Asia and the East in this framework, see Ando 2010, "Imperial identities."

26. See especially Davies 1995; cf. Beck 1997. For a much more positive view of the institutional and political robustness of the Greek leagues see Funke 2007, "Polisürbergreifender Machtbildung," and idem 2007, "Staatliche Neuformierung." Hans Beck and Peter Funke are currently leading an international effort to update J. A. O. Larsen's historical study of the Greek federal states, which should establish this debate on a much sounder empirical foundation.

27. On the relationship between geographic dispersal and Hellenicity, see Hall 2002; and cf. Ferrary 2001, "Géographie de l'hellénisme," and Ando 2010, "Imperial identities." Two fine studies of the evolving ideologies of citizenship at Athens in the third and second centuries B.C.E. are Osborne 1976 and Lape 2004.

28. The uncitizen of the Hellenistic period has received little attention. At some level, the phenomenon has roots in the hostility to the insularity of *polis*-culture voiced already in the first Sophistic (see, e.g., Xenophon *Memorabilia* 2.1.13: Aristippus does not confine himself within a citizen-community, but is everywhere a foreigner [οὐδ' εἰς πολιτείαν ἐμαυτὸν κατακλείω, ἀλλὰ ξένος πανταχοῦ εἰμι]). For a related problem, imperial valorizations of exile, see Whitmarsh 2001, 133–80, together with Ando 2004, 95–96.

29. For cosmopolitanism in the Hellenistic and Roman periods, see Badian 1958 and Ando 1999, 24. On cosmopolitanism's afterlife see Pagden 2000.

30. On the legal framework see Bernhardt 1971. For a wider ranging perspective see Momigliano 1951.

31. On the success of Greek translations of Roman concepts, see Ando 1999, 7–8, 14–16; for bibliography on language difference in relations between Greeks and Romans, see Ando 2010, "Imperial identities," 25–31.

32. Richardson 1991.

33. For now, see Ando 2008, *The Matter of the Gods*, 95–148; idem 2010, "The ontology of religious institutions"; and idem, "The rites of others," forthcoming.

34. Exceptions include its predication of the reputation (the *nomen*) of Alexander the Great by Livy (9.18.6) and of oxen by Varro (*De re rustica* 2.5.4).

35. Thomas 1991 presents an idiosyncratic but frequently brilliant investigation of *maiestas*. I stress the distinction between theory and practice in Roman doctrines of sovereignty because the ritual forms of Roman diplomacy seem to me to have evolved so as to recognize other states as homologous in structure and status to Rome itself (Ando 2008, "Aliens").

36. Rhodes and Lewis 1997, 18: "The Athenians were slow to develop standard formulae for use in their public documents. They never reached a stage where all decrees of a certain period could be relied on to contain exactly the same elements, arranged in the same order and expressed in the same way." Rhodes 2008 surveys the epigraphic evidence for just this issue, namely, the transformation of alliance into empire, in light of contemporary standards for dating the relevant texts: where relevant, I cite both his dates and those of *IG* i^3.

37. In the regulations establishing the obligations of Erythrai to the Panathenaia: *IG* i^3.14 (*IG* i^3 date c. 453/2; Rhodes fixes an early date of the late 450s) = Tod 29 = *GHI* 40.

38. *IG* i^3.19 (*IG* i^3 date c. 450/49; Rhodes fixes a late date of the late 420s), the proxenos decree for Akheloion: note the reference to πόλες ὁπόσον Ἀτεναίοι κρατοῦσι. See also *IG* i^3.27 (*IG* i^3 date c. 450/49; Rhodes fixes a late date of the late 420s) and 156. Athenian magistrates: *IG* i^3.1453 & 1454 ter (Rhodes offers a late date c. 425) = Tod 67 = *GHI* 45, the coinage decree. The contribution of member cities to the fund for common defense is likewise soon identified as being paid to Athens (*IG* i^3.68 = *GHI* 68, ll. 5–6; almost certainly datable to 426). On the change in terminology see Meiggs 1972, 171–72 and 425–27; for the dating of these decrees see Mattingly 1996, 5–52, 87–106 and 147–79 and Rhodes 2008.

39. For a survey of practice, see Henry 1977, 1–18, and Rhodes and Lewis 1997, 11–29.

40. First in *GHI* 14, late sixth century B.C.E. On the universality of this language see Rhodes and Lewis 1997, 4.

41. *IG* ii^2.18: Ἔδοξεν τῆι βουλῆι· Κινησίας εἶπε· περὶ ὧν Ἀνδροσθένης λέγει, ἐπαινέσαι Διονύσιον τὸν Σικελίας ἄρχοντα καὶ Λεπτίνην τὸν ἀδελφόν τὸν Διονυσίου. *IG* ii^2.31 ll. 5–9: ἐπαινέσαι μὲν Ἑβρύζελμιν τὸν βασιλέα τὸν Ὀδρυσων, ὅτι ἐστὶν ἀνὴρ ἀγαθὸς περὶ τὸν δῆμον τὴν Ἀθηναίων, καὶ εἶναι αὐτῶι ἅπερ τοῖς προγόνοις ἅπαντα.

42. Note the heading to Tod 157 = *IG* ii^2.127: Συμμαχία Ἀθηναίων πρὸς Κετρίποριν τὸν Θρᾶικα καὶ τοὺς ἀδελφοὺς καὶ πρὸς Λύπειον τὸν Παίονα καὶ πρὸς Γράβον τὸν Ἰλλυριόν. See also ll. 37ff.: Ὀμνύω Δία καὶ Γῆν . . . φίλος ἔσομαι Κετριπόρι καὶ τοῖς ἀδελφοῖς τοῖς Κετριπόριος καὶ σύμμαχος, καὶ πολεμήσω μετὰ Κετριπόριος τὸν πόλεμον τὸν πρὸς Φίλιππον ἀδόλως παντὶ σθένει κατὰ τὸ δυνατόν.

43. *GHI* 70 = *SEG* 39.9 from 424/23 B.C.E.; Tod 118 = *IG* ii^2.34, 35, from 384 B.C.E.

44. On the dating of texts, see Mattingly 1996, 103–6; for the evidence of Athenian practice in dating (but treated with excessive credulity, it seems to me), see Cadoux 1948 and Henry 1979.

45. Loraux 1986; see also eadem 1984, on autochthony and gender; and eadem 2000, 47–64 and 125–34. Davies 1995.

46. Meier 1990, 186–221; Gernet 1981, 216–39; Csapo and Miller 1998.

47. On Athenian perceptions of Cleisthenic reforms see Anderson 2003. On historiography in the fifth century see Fowler 1996. On the contribution of historical knowledge to local political cultures in late classical and Hellenistic Greece see Chaniotis 1988 and Gehrke 2003.

48. On the treaties see Walbank 1957–79, 1:337–55.

49. The data for a proper history of early Roman date-keeping are probably lacking, but see Livy 2.8 with Ogilvie 1965, 253–54; and Feeney 2007, 140–42, on the dedication of the temple of Jupiter Capitolinus and the problematic information of early lists of magistrates; Livy 7.3, with Oakley 1998, 73–82 and Feeney 2007, 76, on the supposedly archaic practice of putting a nail in the threshold of that temple each year on the ides of September, with Livy's revealing uncertainty about the titulature of the magistrates responsible; and Pliny *Nat.* 33.19 with Feeney 2007, 89 and 140–41 on Gnaeus Flavius's use of the dedication date of the temple to date his own acts. Regarding the evolution of *fasti* as a form of historiography at Rome, see Rüpke 1995 and idem 1997, and cf. Feeney 2007, 167–77.

50. An important exception might be literary records of surrenders, which regularly led to the restoration of autonomy and property to the former population—a gift of "freedom," "so long as the Roman people and Senate shall wish." A limited body of documentary evidence from the second century B.C.E. suggests that in this case, later literary accounts preserve much of the form and spirit of the legal instruments themselves. The evidentiary problems of these texts being substantial, I have subjected them to scrutiny elsewhere: see Ando, "The rites of others," forthcoming.

51. On the aftermath of the Social War and its implications for first-century B.C.E. histories and ethnographies of Italy, see Ando 2002.

52. Polybius 18.35, where the phrase πρότερον ἢ τοῖς διαποντίοις . . . πολέμοις undoubtedly translates the Latin term *bella transmarina*.

53. Cicero 2 Verr. 2.2: *primum quod omnium nationum exterarum princeps Sicilia se ad amicitiam fidemque populi Romani applicavit. Prima omnium, id quod ornamentum imperii est, provincia est appellata. Prima docuit maiores nostros quam praeclarum esset exteris gentibus imperare.* To this passage compare Polybius 18.35.1–2.

54. See especially Festus s.v. Vellona p. 30L; Servius *ad Aen.* 9.52. On these texts, see Ando 2008, *The Matter of the Gods*, 115–16 and 127–28, and idem 2008, "Aliens."

55. On diplomacy in the late Republic and early empire, see Shaw 1986; Millar 1988 = idem 2004, 196–228; and Ando 2008, "Aliens."

CHAPTER 5

1. For an overview of contemporary republicanism, with many salient historiographic excursus, see Laborde and Maynor 2008. I have been encouraged in this project by a number of readings critical of historical aspects of neo-Roman scholarship that for reasons of relevance are not cited below: among these I single out Worden 1994 and 2009, Geuna 2006, and McCormick 2010. For a quite different (and very useful) critique of the unitary "Roman tradition," see Straumann 2009. On Pettit's invocations of and allusion to Roman material, see Markell 2008, 24–27. The effort here undertaken has significant affinities with Janet Coleman's exemplary essay, "El concepto de república" (2005), and I thank Professor Coleman for bringing it to my attention.

2. See, e.g., Skinner 2002, *Visions of Politics*, 190–91 (quoted below at n. 80) and especially 196: "The missing line of argument I should like to reinstate is the one embedded in the classical and especially the Roman republican theory of citizenship. Before becoming engulfed by more individualistic styles of political reasoning, the Roman vision of freedom and civic equality enjoyed a brief but brilliant revival within the republican regimes of early modern Europe." See also Pettit 1997, 5, 7, and 10; and likewise, describing both his own and Skinner's practice, Pettit 2002, 339–40.

3. On the Republican law of persons, see Ando, "Three revolutions in government," forthcoming. It is high time we had a proper modern history of belonging in the Roman world.

4. Pocock 2003, 276–79, treating Carlo Sigonio's reading of Appian, is an important exception to this generalization.

5. In this respect, the reading of the medieval legal tradition by Ullman 1975, 83–116 is a model of judgment.

6. Pettit 1997, 22, 31–35; Skinner 2002, *Visions of Politics*, 287–90, 312–17, and elsewhere.

7. For the claim (not in my view substantiated) that Republicanism provides safeguards against majoritarianism, see Pettit 1997, 31.

8. As is well known, Cicero originally drafted *De re publica* together with the books of *De legibus*, almost undoubtedly as a single work, but eventually separated the two. Because it aims at something like an immanent critique, *De legibus* has found fewer readers as the structures of Roman law—particularly Roman public law—have lost relevance to contemporary political theory and constitutional debate. For the same reasons, however, it was widely read in the late Middle Ages. On that history, see Lebrecht Schmidt 1974, especially 199–408. Lebrecht Schmidt is concerned above all with the establishment of the text, but naturally much is revealed about the reading public and their intellectual formation by careful examination of the use, copying, transmission, and so forth of the text itself.

9. For one vision of this moment in the late eighteenth and early nineteenth centuries, see Rahe 1994.

10. De verbis quibusdam legalibus ex cod. ms. Taurinensi D. V. 19, §39, ed. F. Patteta in Gaudentius 1892, 131; Glossae ineditae e cod. Institutionum Sessoriano 110 ad *Inst.* 1.2.1; Glossae ined. e cod. Inst. vaticano 8782 ad *Inst.* 1.2.1.

11. *The Berlin Commentary on Martianus Capella's* De nuptiis Philologiae et Mercurii, book II (ed. Westra and Kupke 1998), 72.7 (51.3): *Maia, id ist hominum pluralitas, genuit eloquenciam, et ideo vult ut tantum impendant sapientes studiis ut congregent homines ad iure vivendum, quantum impenderunt eloquencie.* Thierry of Chartres (ed. Fredborg 1988), *ad* Cicero *Inv.* 1.1: *SAPIENTIA SINE ELOQUENTIA PARUM PRODESSE CIVITATIBUS PROSIT CIVITATIBUS, id est ad congregandum homines ut iure vivant, quod maxime per eloquentiam administrantur.* See also *ad.* 1.2 (*NAM FUIT QUODDAM TEMPUS, etc. . . . eloquentia volens Tullius ostendere primo ruditatem hominum bestialem, quae in principio mundi fuit, breviter et commode descripsit, ut per eloquentiam iunctam sapientiae tunc primo et propter hoc inchoatam ostendat et ruditatem illam hominum fuisse depulsam et civitates constituas et multa alia commoda, quae in littera ostenduntur*), ad 1.7 (*Quidam libri habent POSITUM IN CONSULTATIONE, sed hoc posset esse etiam si unus ab alio consilium acciperet, ideo subiungitur quod reliquum est. Civilem vero dixit, quoniam omnis deliberatio aut de publicis est aut de privatis, ex quibus civitas constat*), and *ad* 2.168 (*UT IN RE PUBLICA, etc. Ponit exempla eius utilitatis quae est in corpore, velut in corpore civitatis sunt haec utilia: AGRI, PORTUS et cetera, quibus incolumis civitas servatur, ne periculum incurrat, aut libertas retinetur, ne dominio subiaceat*). Thierry is clearly an important transitional moment between a classical, Republican contractarianism and a Hobbesian one.

12. The relationship between land ownership, census classification, and voting in the late Republic has received very little attention in recent decades, despite the remarkable attention devoted in that period to late Republican politics. For a very suggestive essay on these themes, see Rees 2009.

13. Immoral, that is, because based on a lie. To rehearse such an interested and falsifiable representation while neither exposing it nor discussing its more likely antidemocratic motivations is the most base form of scholarship.

14. See Abbreviatio Institutionum ex cod. ms. Taurinensi D. V. 19, ed. F. Patteta in Gaudentius 1892, 121: *Principum placita sunt quod imperatores constituunt, eaque legis habent vigorem. Populus enim in eos omne suum imperium et potestatem concessit. . . . Magistratuum quoque edicta non modicam iuris obtinent auctoritatem.*

15. Pettit 1997, 20.

16. Cicero *Rep.* 1.43 and especially 1.47.

17. For two very distinctive approaches to the nature of public debate in the Roman Republic, see Morstein-Marx 2004, with the qualifications to his approach suggested by Tan 2008, as well as Connolly 2007 and cf. Coleman 2005, 29–30. On the importance of this point for histories of Roman freedom, see Wirszubski 1950, 34–35.

18. That the Romans distributed citizenship without the right to vote is acknowledged by Pettit 1997, 27–28, but he connects the existence and distribution of *civitas sine suffragio* to the foundation of colonies too far from Rome for the vote to be exercised.

Nothing of the sort is true. On the history of *civitas sine suffragio*, see Humbert 1978, 151–220; and Oakley 1998, 538–59, especially 544–54.

19. Livy 9.43.22–24 (see also Livy 9.9.6): *Cornelius in Samnio relictus: Marcius de Hernicis triumphans in urbem rediit statuaque equestris in foro decreta est, quae ante templum Castoris posita est. Hernicorum tribus populis, Aletrinati Verulano Ferentinati, quia maluerunt quam ciuitatem, suae leges redditae conubiumque inter ipsos, quod aliquamdiu soli Hernicorum habuerunt, permissum. Anagninis quique arma Romanis intulerant ciuitas sine suffragii latione data: concilia conubiaque adempta et magistratibus praeter quam sacrorum curatione interdictum.*

20. *Contra* Pettit 1997, 27–28 (discussed above, n. 18) and 36.

21. Gaius *Inst.* 1.13–14, 22.

22. Giovanni da Viterbo, *Liber de regimine civitatum*, ed. Caietano Salvemini in Gaudentius 1901, 215–80, chapter II, "De interpretatione civitatis" (p. 218), citing Gaius *Ad edictum provinciale* bk. 4 fr. 112 Lenel = *Dig.* 4.7.3.*pr.*, and Ulpian *De officio proconsulis* bk. 1 fr. 2152 Lenel = *Dig.* 1.16.9.5.

23. Giovanni, *Liber de regimine civitatum*, Gaudentius 1901, 215–80, chapter XI, "Qualis rector querendus sit civitati et eligendus in potestatem," citing Ulpian *De officio proconsulis* bk. 1 fr. 2152 Lenel = *Dig.* 1.16.9.4.

24. Skinner 2002, "Classical liberty," 9. Skinner reads the same passages of the *Digest*, in conjunction with metaphorical uses of legal terminology among "historians and moralists," to make similar claims in respect to Roman liberty in Skinner 1998, 39–46.

25. Skinner 2002, "Classical liberty," 9 n. 3.

26. For a similar critique of neo-Roman theory in respect of ancient concepts of citizenship, see Coleman 2005, 41–42.

27. Florentinus *Inst.* bk. 9 fr. 25 Lenel = *Dig.* 1.5.4.

28. See on this problem Garnsey 1996.

29. Skinner 2002, *Visions of Politics*, 13–17.

30. My language here alludes to the ur-text on sovereign authority in the civil-law tradition, Ulpian *Inst.* bk. 1 fr. 1916 Lenel = *Dig.* 1.4.1: *Quod principi placuit, legis habet vigorem: utpote cum lege regia, quae de imperio eius lata est, populus ei et in eum omne suum imperium et potestatem conferat.*

31. Azo 1966, *Lectura super codicem*, 44. Azo here glosses *Cod. Iust.* 1.14 ("De legibus et constitutionibus princip. et edictis"), title no. 12, a law of Justinian of 529: *Soli Imperatori, &c. Ergo populus Romanus non habet potestatem legis condendae, quod olim habebat: sed lege † regia in eum transtulit populus omne ius quod habebat: ut Instit.de iur. natural.§.sed & quod. Videtur ergo quod hodie nullum ius habeat. Vel dic quod non transtulit ita quin sibi retineret.*

32. This is not to say that the edicts of magistrates did not play a decisive role in virtually all aspects of the formulary system. The issue is rather how magistrates as sources of law were understood in relation to others. On this topic see Chapter 1, p. 8 and Chapter 2, p. 21.

33. Abbreviatio Institutionum in Gaudentius 1892, 121: *Magistratuum quoque edicta non modicam iuris obtinent auctoritatem.*

34. The status of *consuetudo* in Roman law was naturally more easily stated as a principle than it was untangled in practice.

35. Azo 1966, *Lectura super codicem*, 671, commenting on *Cod. Iust.* 8.53, *QUAE SIT LONGA CONSUETUDO*, title 2, a law of Constantine from 319 C.E. (a text now numbered 8.52.2).

36. Such scholarship as exists on Azo's influence is almost entirely non-historical in orientation. Myron Piper Gilmore exemplifies practice in this field—indeed, he is rather more diligent than most—in citing from Loyseau, Bodin, and Odofredus an apocryphal story to the effect that a dispute between Azo and Lothair on sovereignty grew so heated that the emperor was summoned to resolve it (Gilmore 1941, 15–19). There is a long tradition of such stories: compare that regarding Frederick Barbarossa, who is supposed to have encountered Bulgarus and Martinus on the road and asked them whether he was *dominus mundi* (the story is summarized in Pennington 1993, 15–16; the text may be found in Walther 1976, 82 n. 41). A proper historical study would attempt to situate these anecdotes in the context of their composition and ask why and how later writers retrojected to these moments in the early twelfth century the rise of a monarchic constitutionalism.

37. Among its uses, see especially Gaius *Inst.* 2.11, Marcian *Inst.* bk. 3 fr. 71 Lenel = *Dig.* 1.8.6.1 (*Universitatis sunt non singulorum veluti quae in civitatibus sunt theatra et stadia et similia et si qua alia sunt communia civitatium. ideoque nec servus communis civitatis singulorum pro parte intellegitur, sed universitatis et ideo tam contra civem quam pro eo posse servum civitatis torqueri divi fratres rescripserunt. ideo et libertus civitatis non habet necesse veniam edicti petere, si vocet in ius aliquem ex civibus*) and Ulpian *Ad Edictum* bk. 8 fr. 303 Lenel = *Dig.* 3.4.2. Note that Marcian appeals to a more purely republican conception of the *populus* as collective possessor of goods in order to explain the legal signification of *universitas*: that which belongs to a collective belongs to it in the same way that in communities of citizens theaters and stadiums and other similar things are common to all the citizens. Marcian thus appeals to a more purely Republican discourse but does not cite the classic formulation of Cicero, *res publica res populi* (*Rep.* 1.39; see also 1.41). On Gaius and Ulpian see below at nn. 44 and 67, respectively.

38. Skinner 2002, *Visions of Politics*, 16, citing Azo 1966, *Lectura super codicem*, 44.

39. Cicero *De legibus* 1.19; translation from Zetzel 1999, with minor modifications.

40. Varro *Ling.* 9.5–6; translation from Kent 1938. Varro's language receives a stunning imitation in remarks by Augustine on the structure of the universe, where again the framework of the law provides the ground for metaphorical elaboration (Augustine, *De diversis quaestionibus* 79.1): *Omnis anima partim privati cuiusdam sui potestatem gerit, partim universitatis legibus sicut publicis coercetur et regitur. Quia ergo unaquaeque res visibilis in hoc mundo habet potestatem angelicam sibi praepositam, sicut aliquot locis divina scriptura testatur, de ea re cui praeposita est aliter quasi privato iure agit, aliter tamquam publice agere cogitur* ("Every soul wields a power that is its own, unto itself; at the same time, every soul is constrained and ruled by laws of the universe—as it were, public laws. Since, therefore, every single visible thing in this world has an angelic power placed in supervision of it, as numerous passages of divine scripture testify, regarding that thing over

which it has supervision, the angelic acts sometimes as if by private or individual right; at other times, it is compelled to act in another way, as it were, in public").

41. *Lex agraria* = Crawford 1996, no. 2, l. 78. Among later quotations of texts from the second century B.C.E. that may respect second-century diction, see Titius fr. 2 in Malcovati 1976. A number of second- and first-century B.C.E. formulations offer the Senate in partnership with populace—*iniussu populi ac senatus* or *dum poplus senatusque Romanus velet vel sim.*—and this has prompted the question whether sovereignty was understood to be lodged in both bodies, but most of those alternative formulations arise in the context of foreign religions (e.g., *ILS* 15 or *ELRH* U2, on which see Ando, "The rites of others," forthcoming). The evidence from legislation seems to me decisive: see Mommsen 1887, vol. 3, part 2, pp. 1255–56.

42. Cicero *De lege agraria* 2.27. See also Cicero *Verr.* 3.17 and *Pro Balbo* 34 (*de quo foedere populus Romanus sententiam non tulit, qui iniussu suo nullo pacto potest religione obligari*); Sallust *Cat.* 29.2–3, discussing the *senatus consultum ultimum (Itaque, quod plerumque in atroci negotio solet, senatus decrevit, darent operam consules, ne quid res publica detrimenti caperet. Ea potestas per senatum more Romano magistratui maxuma permittitur: exercitum parare, bellum gerere, coercere omnibus modis socios atque civis, domi militiaeque imperium atque iudicium summum habere; aliter sine populi iussu nullius earum rerum consuli ius est*); as well as Livy 38.45.3–7 and 9.10.9.

43. Gellius 10.20.2 = Ateius Capito fr. 22 Huschke-Seckel-Kübler: *Ateius Capito, publici privatique iuris peritissimus, quid "lex" esset, hisce verbis definivit: "Lex" inquit "est generale iussum populi aut plebis rogante magistratu."*

44. Gaius *Inst.* 1.3: *Lex est quod populus iubet atque constituit. plebiscitum est quod plebs iubet atque constituit. plebs autem a populo eo distat, quod populi appellatione universi cives significantur, connumeratis etiam patriciis; plebis autem appellatione sine patriciis ceteri cives significantur.* Justinian *Inst.* 1.2.4: *Lex est, quod populus Romanus senatore magistratu interrogante, veluti consule, constituebat. plebi scitum est, quod plebs plebeio magistratu interrogante, veluti tribuno, constituebat. plebs autem a populo eo differt, quo species a genere: nam appellatione populi universi cives significantur connumeratis etiam patriciis et senatoribus: plebis autem appellatione sine patriciis et senatoribus ceteri cives significantur.*

45. In addition to the texts cited earlier, recall the claim advanced by the consul in a public assembly in Livy's narrative of the Bacchanalian controversy in the early second century B.C.E. (39.13–15 at 15.11): "your ancestors" had not wanted any assembly to be held except under statal control—namely, when a standard was raised or at the summons of a magistrate: in sum, the consul urged, *maiores vestri* had provided, *censebant*, that "wheresoever the multitude was, there should be a *legitimus rector multitudinis*."

46. On *consensus* in Roman thought, see Instinsky 1940, as well as Ando 2000, passim.

47. Cicero *Rep.* 1.39: *populus autem non omnis hominum coetus quoquo modo congregatus, sed coetus multitudinis iuris consensu et utilitatis communione sociatus.* See also *Rep.* 1.41 and 6.17 Powell: *Nihil est enim illi principi deo, qui omnem mundum regit, quod quidem in terris fiat, acceptius, quam concilia coetusque hominum* ***iure sociati****, quae civitates*

appellantur. See further Cicero *Leg. Man.* 41, *Off.* 1.124, and *Pro Cluentio* 146. On *Rep.* 6.17 see Augustine *Civ.* 2.21 and 19.21, and cf. *Lib. arbitrio* 1.5.11, 1.6.15, and *Serm. Dolbeau* 23.7.

48. Cicero *Rep.* 2.69; translation from Zetzel 1999.

49. Edmondson 2009 provides invaluable bibliographic guidance. For an historical survey see Ando 2010, "From Republic to Empire." Syme 1939 remains an indispensable study. Augustus's extraordinary autobiography should now be read in Scheid 2007, a monument of concision and acute good sense.

50. Augustus *Res Gestae* 6.1: *nullum magistratum contra morem maiorum delatum recepi.*

51. For a detailed analysis of the public-law issues at stake in the early Principate, see Ferrary 2001, "Pouvoirs." An abridged translation by Jonathan Edmondson of this now fundamental article is available in idem 2009, 90–136.

52. Augustus *Res Gestae* 1.4; Appian *Bellum Civile.* 4.7.27; *Fasti Colotiani: Inscr. Ital.* XIII.1: 273–74; see also Livy *Periochae* 120 and Dio 46.55. The relevant texts are generously quoted at Scheid 2007, 29–30. See also Millar 2002, 243–44.

53. Tacitus *Ann.* 1.1.1, 2.1, and 3.7.

54. For the text see n. 30. For its quotation by the twelfth-century *Abbreviatio Institutionum* see n. 14; for its quotations by Azo, see Azo 1966, *Lectura super codicem*, 44, on *Cod. Iust.* 1.14.12, as well as 671 on *Cod. Iust.* 8.52.2; see also Azo 1966, *Summa super codicem*, 8–9, treating *Cod. Iust.* 1.14. Elsewhere in the glossatorial tradition, see *Ad Cod. Iust.* 1.17.1.7, Justinian to Tribonian, late December 529 (*Cum enim lege antiqua, quae regia nuncupabatur, omne ius omnisque potestas populi Romani in imperatoriam translata sunt potestatem, nos vero sanctionem omnem non dividimus in alias et alias conditorum partes, sed totam nostram esse volumus, quid possit antiquitas nostris legibus abrogare?*) and 6.23.3, a constitution of Alexander Severus from December 231 (*Ex imperfecto testamento nec imperatorem hereditatem vindicare saepe constitutum est. Licet enim lex imperii sollemnibus iuris imperatorem solverit, nihil tamen tam proprium imperii est, ut legibus vivere*).

55. See *Scriptores Historiae Augustae, Vita Severi Alexandri* 8.1 and Dio 53.17–18, especially 17.11 and 18.4, together with Ando 2000, 156 n. 115.

56. Perhaps the most interesting recent work on Roman Republican magistracy is Stewart 1998, but hers is a reconstructive history of institutions: the Republic produces no body of constitutional theory until perhaps its final decades. Hence, although Stewart provides a history of the development of principles of collegiality and of differentiation as magistracies multiplied, that history rests on the aggregation and analysis of records of elections, assignment of bailiwicks and historical action, not on readings of juridical literature.

57. See, e.g., Pomponius *Encheiridion* liber singularis fr. 178 Lenel = *Dig.* 1.2.2.16: *Exactis deinde regibus consules constituti sunt duo: penes quos summum ius uti esset, lege rogatum est: dicti sunt ab eo, quod plurimum rei publicae consulerent. qui tamen ne per omnia regiam potestatem sibi vindicarent, lege lata factum est, ut ab eis provocatio esset neve possent in caput civis Romani animadvertere iniussu populi: solum relictum est illis, ut coercere possent et in vincula publica duci iuberent.* On jurisdiction, see Varro *Ling.* 6.61: a *iudex*, a lay

judge, *ius dicat* "speaks a decision" *accepta potestate*, "having received the power to do so" (from the magistrate with *jurisdictio*).

58. For construals of consular power as royal in scope, see Livy 8.32 and Ampelius 50.2.

59. Cicero gives a polemical but not wholly distorted view of the structures of magistracy in 63 in *De lege agraria* 2.26–34, when he accuses an opponent of so breaching standard protocols in the creation of a special magistracy as to confer regal power.

60. On this point see Chapter 4, pp. 75–76.

61. For an exceedingly important attribution of *maiestas* to the imperial house in official discourse of the Tiberian age, see the decree of the Senate on Gnaeus Piso, lines 32–33: *neclecta maiestate domus Aug(ustae), neclecto etiam iure publico* (Eck, Caballos, and Fernández 1996, 40–41 and 162).

62. The only potential exception known to me is Livy 9.18.6, where Livy complains that contemporary Greeks frivolously extol the "greaterness" of Alexander's reputation.

63. On *maiestas* see Chapter 4, pp. 73–74, with the bibliography cited there. One might compare the language and legal apparatus developed at Rome for differentiating among holders of *imperium* when that power of command was specifically assigned with overlapping bailiwicks: one was simply described as "greater" than the other. What is more, as Jean-Louis Ferrary has convincingly demonstrated, there was no such thing as a blanket grant of "greater *imperium*": it was always understood that something had to be greater in relation to something else (Ferrary 2001, "Pouvoirs," 133–141 = Edmondson 2009, 113–21).

64. Ferrary 1983, 556–72; Seager 1967; and idem 2001. Beyond the statutes *de maiestate*, in a speech of 56 B.C.E. Cicero describes a law of Catulus *de vi*, on violence, as pertaining to "*imperium, maiestas*, the condition of the fatherland and the safety of all" (*Cael.* 70). It may be that this law, which criminalized specific forms of violence, embraced individuals; that said, the events surrounding its passage in 102 B.C.E. (as it seems) are known for violent attacks by magistrates on other magistrates. For a reasoned inquiry into the context of its passage, see B. Kelly 2005.

65. J. M. Kelly 1957, 24–46.

66. Excerptis Cod. Vaticani Reg. 435 in Gaudentius 1892, §127, reading in full: *Crimen maiestatis duobus modis dicitur: contra rempublicam et contra imperium. Contra imperium dicitur crimen perduellionis, quoniam hoc solo casu concedit lex humana duellum fieri. Perduellio dicta quasi duellum, quia in duas partes populus Romanus dividebatur.*

67. Ulpian *Ad Edictum* bk. 76 fr. 1673 Lenel = *Dig.* 50.17.160.1: *Refertur ad universos, quod publice fit per maiorem partem*; Marcellus *Dig.* bk. 14 fr. 169 Lenel = *Dig.* 50.16.95: *Potest "reliquorum" appellatio et universos significare.*

68. Bruni 2001, bk. 1 chap. 70.

69. See, e.g., Skinner 2002, *Visions of Politics*, 198–99, 205 on Machiavelli; and Pettit 1997, 37, on Harrington.

70. Pocock 2003, 205–14 and cf. 153–54. On the purchase of freedom through empire, see Isidore *Etym.* 2.21.4, quoting Scipio: *ex innocentia nascitur dignitas, ex dignitate honor, ex honore imperium, ex imperio libertas* ("From virtue is born esteem; from esteem,

public honor; from public honor, power of command; and from power of command, freedom"). On this dictum, see Wirszubski 1950, 31–44; Pocock 2003, 276–78; and Chapter 4, p. 67.

71. For evidence and bibliography on these issues, see Chapter 4, p. 70; see also Chapter 1, pp. 2–6, and Chapter 2, p. 23.

72. For an ancient description of this framework, see Cicero *Pro Balbo* 20–22. For reflections on the legal landscape that issued from this understanding and its importance for modern theories of empire, see Ando 2008, *The Matter of the Gods*, 59–92; idem 2010, "The ontology of religious institutions"; idem 2011, "Law and the landscape of empire."

73. This paragraph summarizes a long and complex history, on which see Ando 2008, *The Matter of the Gods*, 59–92.

74. Boncompagno da Signa, *Rhetorica Novissima*, ed. Augustus Gaudentius in Gaudentius 1892, 253: *Decima fuit tempore Iustiniani principis Christianissimi, qui fuit ipsa iuris origo; quia sicut Deus a materia primordiali elementa divisit et produxit in lucem, ita Iustinianus confusas origines et materias legum clarificavit ad illuminationem studentium et gloriam iuris canonici et civilis. . . . Tertiadecima fuit in legibus municipalibus; quas hodie Italia specialiter imitatur propter omnimodam libertatem. Sed iste leges municipales atque plebiscita sicut umbra lunatica evanescunt, quoniam ad similitudinem lune crescunt iugiter et decrescunt secundum arbitrium conditorum.*

75. Boncompagno in Gaudentius 1892, 289.

76. Rogerius, *Summa Codicis*, ed. Johannis Baptista Palmerius in Gaudentius 1888, 14.

77. Excerptis Cod. Vaticani Reg. 435 in Gaudentius 1892, §122: *Ius gentium est quia naturali ratione inductum et sic diffinitur: ius gentium est industria humana naturali ratione inducta et ideo dicitur ius non simpliciter, quia inductum est industria et natura. Naturale ius sic diffinitur: naturale ius est condicio regis creatis ab ipsa divina dispositione inposita, et ideo dicitur simplex ius, quia non ex industria hominia sed ex sola divina dispositione inductum est.*

78. On this question see McCormick 2010.

79. Cicero *De lege Manilia* 60: *At enim ne quid novi fiat contra exempla atque instituta maiorum. Non dicam hoc loco maiores nostros semper in pace consuetudini, in bello utilitati paruisse; semper ad novos casus temporum novorum consiliorum rationes adcommodasse* . . . ("I am also urged that nothing new should be done contrary to the precedents and practices of our ancestors. I will not bother to point out here that our ancestors obeyed custom in times of peace, but necessity in times of war, always developing new plans and policies to meet the new crises of the day").

80. Skinner 2002, *Visions of Politics*, 191; italics in the original.

Bibliography

Ager, S. L. 1996. *Interstate Arbitration in the Greek World, 337–90 B.C.* Berkeley: University of California Press.

Alonso-Núñez, J. M. 1989. "Aemilius Sura." *Latomus* 48:110–19.

Anderson, G. 2003. *The Athenian Experiment: Building an Imagined Political Community in Ancient Attica, 508–490 B.C.* Ann Arbor: University of Michigan Press.

Ando, C. 1999. "Was Rome a polis?" *Classical Antiquity* 18:5–34.

Ando, C. 2000. *Imperial Ideology and Provincial Loyalty in the Roman Empire.* Berkeley: University of California Press.

Ando, C. 2002. "Vergil's Italy: Ethnography and politics in first century-Rome." D. S. Levene and D. Nelis, eds. *Clio and the Poets: Augustan Poetry and the Traditions of Ancient Historiography.* Leiden: Brill. 123–42.

Ando, C., ed. 2003. *Roman Religion.* Edinburgh: Edinburgh University Press.

Ando, C. 2004. Review of T. Whitmarsh, *Greek Literature and the Roman Empire: The Politics of Imitation* (Oxford: Oxford University Press, 2001). *Classical Philology* 99:89–98.

Ando, C. 2006. "The administration of the provinces." D. S. Potter, ed. *A Companion to the Roman Empire.* Oxford: Blackwell. 177–92.

Ando, C. 2008. "Aliens, ambassadors and the integrity of the empire." *Law and History Review* 26:491–519.

Ando, C. 2008. *The Matter of the Gods.* Berkeley: University of California Press.

Ando, C. 2009. "Diana on the Aventine." H. Cancik and J. Rüpke, eds. *Die Religion des Imperium Romanum.* Tübingen: Mohr Siebeck. 99–113.

Ando, C. 2010. "From Republic to Empire." M. Peachin, ed. *The Oxford Handbook of Social Relations in the Roman World.* Oxford: Oxford University Press. 37–66.

Ando, C. 2010. "Imperial identities." T. Whitmarsh, ed. *Local Knowledge and Microidentities in the Imperial Greek World.* Cambridge: Cambridge University Press. 17–45.

Ando, C. 2010. "The ontology of religious institutions." *History of Religions* 50:54–79.

Ando, C. 2011. "Law and the landscape of empire." S. Benoist, ed. *Figures d'empire, fragments de mémoire.* Paris. 25–47.

Ando, C. Forthcoming. *The Ambitions of Government.* Berkeley: University of California Press.

Ando, C. Forthcoming. "The rites of others." J. Edmondson and A. Keith, eds. *Essays in honor of Elaine Fantham.* Toronto: University of Toronto Press.

Ando, C. Forthcoming. "Three revolutions in government." S. Procházka, L. Reinfandt and S. Tost, eds. *Official epistolography and the language(s) of power.* Vienna.

Ando, C., and J. Rüpke, eds. 2006. *Religion and Law in Classical and Christian Rome.* Stuttgart: Franz Steiner Verlag.

Azo, Portius. 1966. *Lectura super codicem = Azonis ad singulas leges XII. librorum codicis Iustinianei, commentarius et magnus apparatus nunquam antea in lucem editus.* Corpus Glossatorum Juris Civilis, vol. 3. Centro Studi di Storia del Diritto Italiana, Università de Torino; Augustae Taurinorum ex Officina Erasmiana.

Azo, Portius. 1966. *Summa super codicem.* Corpus Glossatorum Juris Civilis, vol. 2. Centro Studi di Storia del Diritto Italiana, Università de Torino; Augustae Taurinorum ex Officina Erasmiana.

Badian, E. 1958. "Alexander the Great and the unity of mankind." *Historia* 7:425–44.

Badian, E. 1995. "The ghost of empire: Reflections on Athenian foreign policy in the fourth century B.C." W. Eder, ed. *Die athenische Demokratie im 4. Jahrhundert v. Chr. Vollendung oder Verfall einer Verfassungsform? Akten eines Symposims 3.-7. August 1992, Bellagio.* Stuttgart: Franz Steiner. 79–106.

Barfield, T. J. 2001. "The shadow empires: Imperial state formation along the Chinese-nomad frontier." S. Alcock, T. N. D'Altroy, K. D. Morrison, and C. M. Sinopoli, eds. *Empires: Perspectives from Archaeology and History.* Cambridge: Cambridge University Press. 10–41.

Beck, H. 1997. *Polis und koinon: Untersuchungen zur Geschichte und Struktur der griechischen Bundesstaaten im. 4 Jahrhundert v. Chr.* Stuttgart: Franz Steiner.

Bederman, D. J. 2001. *International Law in Antiquity.* Cambridge: Cambridge University Press.

Bernhardt, R. 1971. "Imperium und Eleutheria: Die römische Politik gegenüber den freien Städten des griechischen Ostens." Dissertation. Die Universität Hamburg.

Black, M. 1962. *Models and Metaphors: Studies in Language and Philosophy.* Ithaca, N.Y.: Cornell University Press.

Boedeker, D., and K. A. Raaflaub, eds. 1998. *Democracy, Empire and the Arts in Fifth-Century Athens.* Cambridge, Mass.: Harvard University Press.

Briggs, A. 2008. *The Conflict of Laws.* Oxford: Oxford University Press.

Briquel, D. 2006. "La guerre à Rome au IVe siècle: Une histoire revue et corrigée, remarques sur le livre 9 de Tite-Live." E. Caire and S. Pittia, eds. *Guerre et diplomatie romaines IVe-IIIe siècles av. J. C. Pour un réexamen des sources.* Aix-en-Provence: Publications de l'Université de Provence. 27–40.

Broughton, T. R. S. 1987. "Mistreatment of foreign legates and the fetial priests: Three Roman cases." *Phoenix* 41:50–62.

Bruni, L. 2001. *History of the Florentine People.* J. Hankins, trans. Cambridge, Mass.: Harvard University Press.

Brunt, P. 1977. "Lex de imperio Vespasiani." *Journal of Roman Studies* 67:95–116.

Brunt, P. A. 1990. *Roman Imperial Themes.* Oxford: Clarendon Press.

Buckland, W. W. 1908. *The Roman Law of Slavery.* Cambridge: The University Press.

Cadoux, T. J. 1948. "The Athenian archons from Kreon to Hypsichides." *Journal of Hellenic Studies* 68:70–123.

Catalano, P. 1965. *Linee del sistema sovrannazionale romano*. Turin: G. Giappichelli.

Chaniotis, A. 1988. *Historie und Historiker in den griechischen Inschriften*. Stuttgart: Franz Steiner.

Coleman, J. 2005. "El concepto de república: Continuidad mítica y continuidad real." *Res Publica* 15:27–47.

Connolly, J. 2007. *The State of Speech: Rhetoric and Political Thought in Ancient Rome*. Princeton, N.J.: Princeton University Press.

Crawford, M., ed. 1996. *Roman Statutes*. 2 vols. London: Institute of Classical Studies.

Csapo, E., and M. Miller. 1998. "Democracy, empire and art: Towards a politics of time and narrative." D. Boedeker and K. A. Raaflaub, eds. *Democracy, Empire and the Arts in Fifth-Century Athens*. Cambridge, Mass.: Harvard University Press. 87–125.

Davies, J. K. 1994. "On the non-usability of the concept of 'sovereignty' in an ancient Greek context." L. A. Foresti et al., eds. *Federazioni e federalismo nell'Europa antica. Bergama, 21–25 settembre 1992*. Milan: Università Cattolica del Sacro Cuore. 51–65.

Davies, J. K. 1995. "The fourth century crisis: What crisis?" W. Eder, ed. *Die athenische Demokratie im 4. Jahrhundert v. Chr. Vollendung oder Verfall einer Verfassungsform? Akten eines Symposims 3.-7. August 1992, Bellagio*. Stuttgart: Franz Steiner. 29–36.

Drexler, H. 1959. "Iustum bellum." *Rheinisches Museum* 102:97–140.

Eck, W., A. Caballos, and F. Fernández, eds. 1996. *Das senatus consultum de Cn. Pisone patre*. Vestigia 48. Munich: C. H. Beck.

Eder, W., ed., 1995. *Die athenische Demokratie im 4. Jahrhundert v. Chr. Vollendung oder Verfall einer Verfassungsform? Akten eines Symposims 3.-7. August 1992, Bellagio*. Stuttgart: Franz Steiner.

Edmondson, J., ed. 2009. *Augustus*. Edinburgh: Edinburgh University Press.

Feeney, D. 2007. *Caesar's Calendar: Ancient Time and the Beginnings of History*. Berkeley: University of California Press.

Ferrary, J.-L. 1983. "Les origins de la loi de majesté à Rome." *Comptes rendus de l'Académie des inscriptions et belles letters* 1983:556–72.

Ferrary, J.-L. 1995. "Ius fetiale et diplomatie." E. Frézouls and A. Jacquemin, eds. *Les relations internationals: Actes du Colloque de Strasbourg 15–17 juin 1993*. Paris: De Boccard. 411–32.

Ferrary, J.-L. 2001. "À propos des pouvoirs d'Auguste." *Cahiers du Centre Gustave Glotz* 12:101–54.

Ferrary, J.-L. 2001. "Rome et la géographie de l'hellénisme: Réflexions sur 'hellènes' et 'panhellènes' dans les inscriptions d'époque romaine." O. Salomies, ed. *The Greek East in the Roman Context: Proceedings of a Colloquium Organized by the Finnish Institute at Athens May 21 and 22, 1999*. Helsinki: Finnish Institute at Athens.

Fowler, R. L. 1996. "Herodotus and his contemporaries." *Journal of Hellenic Studies* 116:62–87.

Fredborg, K. M., ed. 1988. *The Latin Rhetorical Commentaries by Thierry of Chartres*. Toronto: Pontifical Institute of Mediaeval Studies.

Frier, B. W. 1999. *Libri Annales Pontificum Maximorum: The Origins of the Annalistic Tradition*. 2nd ed. Ann Arbor: University of Michigan Press.

Fuchs, H. 1938. *Der geistige Widerstand gegen Roms*. Berlin: de Gruyter.

Funke, P. 2007. "Alte Grenzen - neue Grenzen. Formen polisübergreifender Machtbildung in klassischer und hellenistischer Zeit." R. Albertz, A. Blöbaum and P. Funke, eds. *Räume und Grenzen. Topologische Konzepte in den antiken Kulturen des östlichen Mittelmeerraumes*. Munich: Utz. 187–204.

Funke, P. 2007. "Die staatliche Neuformierung Griechenlands. Staatenbünde and Bundesstaaten." G. Weber, ed. *Kulturgeschichte des Hellenismus*. Stuttgart: Klett-Cotta. 78–98.

Garnsey, P. 1970. *Social Status and Legal Privilege in the Roman Empire*. Oxford: Clarendon Press.

Garnsey, P. 1996. *Ideas of Slavery from Aristotle to Augustine*. Cambridge: Cambridge University Press.

Gaudentius, A., ed. 1888. *Bibliotheca Iuridica Medii Aevi: Scripta Anecdota Glossatorum*, vol. 1. Bologna: In aedibus Societatis Azzoguidianae.

Gaudentius, A., ed. 1892. *Bibliotheca Iuridica Medii Aevi: Scripta Anecdota Glossatorum*, vol. 2. Bologna: In aedibus Petri Virano olim Fratrum Treves.

Gaudentius, A., ed. 1901. *Bibliotheca Iuridica Medii Aevi: Scripta Anecdota Glossatorum*, vol. 3. Bologna: In aedibus successorum Monti.

Gehrke, H. J. 2003. "Bürgerliches Selbstverständnis und Polisidentität im Hellenismus." K.-J. Hölkeskamp, J. Rüsen, E. Stein-Hölkeskamp, and H. Th. Grütter, eds. *Sinn (in) der Antike*. Mainz am Rhein: Philipp von Zabern. 225–54.

Gernet, L. 1981. *The Anthropology of Ancient Greece*. J. Hamilton and B. Nagy, trans. Baltimore: Johns Hopkins University Press.

Geuna, M. 2006. "Skinner, pre-humanist rhetorical culture and Machiavelli." A. Brett and J. Tully, eds. *Rethinking the Foundations of Modern Political Thought*. Cambridge: Cambridge University Press. 50–72.

Gilmore, M. P. 1941. *Argument from Roman Law in Political Thought 1200–1600*. Cambridge, Mass.: Harvard University Press.

González, J. 1986. "The Lex Irnitana: A new copy of the Flavian municipal law." *Journal of Roman Studies* 76:147–243.

Hall, J. 2002. *Hellenicity: Between Ethnicity and Culture*. Chicago: University of Chicago Press.

Hansen, M. H. 1995. "The 'autonomous city-state': Ancient fact or modern fiction?" M. H. Hansen and K. Raaflaub, eds. *Studies in the Ancient Greek polis*. Historia Einzelschriften 95. Stuttgart: Franz Steiner. 21–43.

Henry, A. S. 1977. *The prescripts of Athenian decrees*. Leiden: Brill.

Henry, A. S. 1979. "Archon-dating in fifth century Attic decrees: The 421 rule." *Chiron* 9:23–30.

Humbert, M. 1978. *Municipium et civitas sine suffragio: L'Organisation de la conquête jusqu'à la guerre sociale.* CÉFR 36. Rome: École Française de Rome.

Instinsky, H. U. 1940. "Consensus Universorum." *Hermes* 75:265–78.

Johnston, D. 1987. "Three thoughts on Roman private law and the lex Irnitana." *Journal of Roman Studies* 77:62–77.

Jolowicz, H. F., and B. Nicholas. 1972. *Historical Introduction to the Study of Roman Law.* 3rd ed. Cambridge: Cambridge University Press.

Jones, A. H. M. 1960. *Studies in Roman Government and Law.* Oxford: Blackwell and Mott.

Kelly, B. 2005. "The law that Catulus passed." K. Welch and T. W. Hillard, eds. *Roman Crossings: Theory and Practice in the Roman Republic.* Swansea: Classical Press of Wales. 95–118.

Kelly, J. M. 1957. *Princeps Iudex: Eine Untersuchung zur Entwicklung und zu den Grundlagen der kaiserlichen Gerichtsbarkeit.* Weimar: Böhlau.

Kent, R. G., ed. and trans. 1938. *Varro. On the Latin Language.* 2 vols. Cambridge: Harvard University Press.

Kremer, D. 2006. *Ius Latinum: Le concept de droit latin sous la République et l'Empire; Romanité et modernité du droit.* Paris: De Boccard; Rome: École française de Rome.

Kühnen, A. 2008. *Die Imitatio Alexandri in der römischen Politik (1. Jh. v. Chr.–3. Jh. n. Chr.).* Münster: Rhema.

Laborde, C., and J. Maynor, eds. 2008. *Republicanism and Political Theory.* Oxford: Blackwell.

Lammert, F. 1935. "Kriegsrecht." *Realencyclopädie der Classischen Altertumswissenschaft*, Supplementband 6:1351–62.

Lape, S. 2004. *Reproducing Athens.* Princeton, N.J.: Princeton University Press.

Lape, S. 2010. *Race and Citizen Identity in the Classical Athenian Democracy.* New York: Cambridge University Press.

Lebrecht Schmidt, P. 1974. *Die Überlieferung von Ciceros Schrift "De legibus" in Mittelalter und Renaissance.* Munich: Wilhelm Fink.

Loraux, N. 1984. *The Children of Athena: Athenian Ideas about Citizenship and the Division between the Sexes.* C. Levine, trans. Princeton, N.J.: Princeton University Press.

Loraux, N. 1986. *The Invention of Athens: The Funeral Oration in the Classical City.* A. Sheridan, trans. Cambridge, Mass.: Harvard University Press.

Loraux, N. 2000. *Born of the Earth: Myth and Politics in Athens.* S. Stewart, trans. Ithaca, N.Y.: Cornell University Press.

MacMullen, R. 1990. *Changes in the Roman Empire.* Princeton, N.J.: Princeton University Press.

Malcovati, E., ed. 1976. *Oratorum Romanorum Fragmenta liberae rei publicae.* 4th ed. Turin: In aedibus Io. Bapt. Paraviae et Sociorum.

Mantovani, D. 2005. "Les clauses 'sans précédents' de la *Lex de imperio Vespasiani*: Une interprétation juridique." *Cahiers du Centre Gustave Glotz* 16:25–43.

Markell, P. 2008. "The insufficiency of non-domination." *Political Theory* 36:9–36.

Mattingly, H. B. 1996. *The Athenian Empire Restored: Epigraphic and Historical Studies*. Ann Arbor: University of Michigan Press.

McCormick, J. 2010. *Machiavellian Democracy*. Cambridge: Cambridge University Press.

McDonald, A. H., and F. W. Walbank. 1937. "The origins of the Second Macedonian War." *Journal of Roman Studies* 27:180–207.

Meier, C. 1990. *The Greek Discovery of Politics*. Cambridge, Mass.: Harvard University Press.

Meiggs, R. 1972. *The Athenian Empire*. Oxford: Clarendon Press.

Metzler, D. 1989. "Über das Konzept der 'Vier großen Königreiche' in Manis Kephalaia (cap. 77)." *Klio* 71:446–59.

Millar, F. 1988. "Cornelius Nepos, 'Atticus,' and the Roman Revolution." *Greece and Rome* 35:40–55.

Millar, F. 1988. "Government and diplomacy in the Roman empire during the first three centuries." *International History Review* 10:345–77.

Millar, F. 1993. "The Greek city in the Roman period." M. H. Hansen, ed. *The Ancient Greek City-State*. Copenhagen: Royal Danish Academy of Sciences and Letters. 232–60.

Millar, F. 1999. "The Greek east and Roman law: The dossier of M. Cn. Licinius Rufinus." *Journal of Roman Studies* 89:90–108.

Millar, F. 2002. *Rome, the Greek World, and the East*. Vol. 1, *The Roman Republic and the Augustan Revolution*. H. M. Cotton and G. M. Rogers, eds. Chapel Hill: University of North Carolina Press.

Millar, F. 2004. *Rome, the Greek World, and the East*. Vol. 2, *Government, Society, and Culture in the Roman Empire*. H. M. Cotton and G. M. Rogers, eds. Chapel Hill: University of North Carolina Press.

Millar, F. 2006. *Rome, the Greek World, and the East*. Vol. 3, *The Greek World, the Jews, and the East*. H. M. Cotton and G. M. Rogers, eds. Chapel Hill: University of North Carolina Press.

Moatti, C. 2001. "*Respublica* et droit dans la Rome républicaine." *Mélanges de l'École française de Rome, Series Moyen âge* 113:811–37.

Momigliano, A. 1951. Review of C. Wirszubski, *Libertas as a Political Idea at Rome during the Late Republic and Early Principate* (Cambridge: Cambridge University Press, 1950). *Journal of Roman Studies* 41:146–53.

Momigliano, A. 1982. "The origins of universal history." *Annali della Scuola Normale Superiore di Pisa*, serie 3, vol. 12, fasc. 2:533–60.

Momigliano, A. 1986. *On Pagans, Jews, and Christians*. Middleton, Conn.: Wesleyan University Press.

Mommsen, T. 1887. *Römisches Staatsrecht*. 3 vols. in 5. Leipzig: S. Hirzel.

Morstein-Marx, R. 2004. *Mass Oratory and Political Power in the Late Roman Republic*. Cambridge: Cambridge University Press.

Nicolet, C. 1982. *L'inventaire du monde: Géographie et politique aux origines de l'Empire romain*. Paris: Gallimard.

Nicolet, C. 1991. *Space, Geography and Politics in the Early Roman Empire*. A translation of Nicolet 1982. Ann Arbor: University of Michigan Press.

Nock, A. D. 1939. "A feature of Roman religion." *Harvard Theological Review* 32:83–96.

Nótári, T. 2006. "Comments on the origins of the Legis Actio Sacramento in Rem." *Acta Juridica Hungarica* 47:133–55.

Nótári, T. 2008. *Law, Religion and Rhetoric in Cicero's "Pro Murena."* Passau: Schenk.

Oakley, S. P. 1998. *A Commentary on Livy Books VI–X*. Vol. 2, *Books VII and VIII*. Oxford: Clarendon Press.

Oakley, S. P. 2005. *A Commentary on Livy Books VI–X*. Vol. 3, *Book IX*. Oxford: Oxford University Press.

Ogilvie, R. M. 1965. *A Commentary on Livy Books 1–5*. Oxford: Clarendon Press.

Oliver, J. H. 1979. "Greek applications for Roman trials." *American Journal of Philology* 100:543–58.

Osborne, M. J. 1976. "Athenian grants of citizenship after 229 BC." *Ancient Society* 7:107–25.

Pagden, A. 2000. "Stoicism, cosmopolitanism, and the legacy of European imperialism." *Constellations* 7:3–22.

Panciera, S. 1994. "La lex luci Spoletina e la legislazione sui boschi sacri in età romana." *Monteluco e i monti sacri: atti dell'Incontro di studio, Spoleto, 30 settembre–2 ottobre 1993*. Spoleto: Centro italiano di studi sull'Alto Medievo.

Pennington, K. 1993. *The Prince and the Law, 1200–1600*. Berkeley: University of California Press.

Peter, H. 1906. *Historicorum Romanorum reliquiae*. 2 vols. Stuttgart: Teubner.

Pettit, P. 1997. *Republicanism: A Theory of Freedom and Government*. Oxford: Oxford University Press.

Pettit, P. 2002. "Keeping republican freedom simple: On a difference with Quentin Skinner." *Political Theory* 30:339–56.

Pocock, J. G. A. 2003. *Barbarism and Religion*. Vol. 3, *The First Decline and Fall*. Cambridge: Cambridge University Press.

Raaflaub, K. A. 1998. "The transformation of Athens in the fifth century." D. Boedeker, and K. A. Raaflaub, eds. *Democracy, Empire and the Arts in Fifth-Century Athens*. Cambridge, Mass.: Harvard University Press. 15–41.

Rahe, P. A. 1994. "Antiquity surpassed: The repudiation of classical Republicanism." D. Wootton, ed. *Republicanism, Liberty, and the Commercial Society, 1649–1776*. Stanford, Calif.: Stanford University Press. 233–69.

Rees, W. 2009. "'*Ex Italia convenerunt*' (Cic. *Dom*. 12.30): Italian participation in Roman political life (133–44 BC)." A. Keaveney and L. Earnshaw-Brown, eds. *The Italians on the Land: Changing Perspectives on Republican Italy Then and Now*. Cambridge: Cambridge Scholars Publishing. 85–106.

Rhodes, P. J. 2008. "After the three-bar *sigma* controversy: the history of Athenian imperialism reassessed." *Classical Quarterly* 58:500–506.

Rhodes, P. J., with D. M. Lewis. 1997. *The Decrees of the Greek States*. Oxford: Clarendon Press.

Rich, J. W. 1976. *Declaring War in the Roman Republic in the Period of Transmarine Expansion*. Collection Latomus 149. Brussels: Latomus.

Richardson, J. S. 1991. "Imperium Romanum: Empire and the language of power." *Journal of Roman Studies* 81:1–9.

Richardson, J. S. 1995. "The Roman mind and the power of fiction." L. Ayres, ed. *The Passionate Intellect: Essays Presented to Professor I. G. Kidd*. Rutgers University Studies in Classical Humanities 7. New Brunswick: Transaction Publishers. 117–30.

Richardson, J. S. 2008. *The Language of Empire: Rome and the Idea of Empire from the Third Century BC to the Second Century AD*. Cambridge: Cambridge University Press.

Riggsby, A. 2006. *Caesar in Gaul and Rome: War in Words*. Austin: University of Texas Press.

Robert, L. 1973. "Les juges étrangers dans la cité grecque." T. J. Panagopoulos, ed. *Xenion: Festschrift für Pan. J. Zepos*. Athens: Ch. Katsikalis. 765–82. Reprinted in L. Robert, *Choix d'écrits*, ed. D. Rousset. Paris: Les Belles Lettres, 2007.

Rodger, A. 1991. "The Lex Irnitana and procedure in civil courts." *Journal of Roman Studies* 81:74–90.

Rodger, A. 1996. "Jurisdictional limits in the Lex Irnitana and the Lex de Gallia Cisalpina." *Zeitschrift für Papyrologie und Epigraphik* 110:189–206.

Rüpke, J. 1990. *Domi militiae: Die religiöse Konstruktion des Krieges in Rom*. Stuttgart: Franz Steiner.

Rüpke, J. 1995. "*Fasti*: Quellen oder Produkte römischer Geschichtsschreibung?" *Klio* 77:184–202.

Rüpke, J. 1997. "Geschichtsschreibung in Listenform: Beamtenlisten unter römischen Kalendern." *Philologus* 141:65–85.

Samter, E. 1909. "Fetiales." *Realencyclopädie der classischen Altertumswissenschaft* 2.2: 2259–65.

Scheid, J. 2006. "Oral tradition and written tradition in the formation of sacred law in Rome." C. Ando and J. Rüpke, eds. *Religion and Law in Classical and Christian Rome*. Stuttgart: Franz Steiner Verlag. 14–33.

Scheid, J., ed. 2007. *Res Gestae Divi Augusti: Hauts faits du divine Auguste*. Paris: Belles Lettres.

Schulz, F. 1946. *History of Roman Legal Science*. Oxford: Clarendon Press.

Seager, R. 1967. "Lex Varia de maiestate." *Historia* 16:37–43.

Seager, R. 2001. "*Maiestas* in the late Republic: Some observations." J. W. Cairns and O. F. Robinson, eds. *Critical Studies in Ancient Law, Comparative Law and Legal History*. Oxford: Hart Publishing. 143–53.

Shaw, B. 1986. "Autonomy and tribute: Mountain and plain in Mauretania Tingitana." P. Baduel, ed. *Desert et montagne: Homage à Jean Dresch. Revue de l'Occident Musulman et de la Méditeranée* 41–42:66–89.

Sherwin-White, A. N. 1973. *The Roman Citizenship*. 2nd ed. Oxford: Oxford University Press.

Skinner, Q. 1998. *Liberty before Liberalism*. Cambridge: Cambridge University Press.

Skinner, Q. 2002. "Classical liberty and the coming of the English Civil War." M. van

Gelderen and Q. Skinner, eds. *Republicanism: A Shared European Heritage.* Vol. 2, *The Values of Republicanism in Early Modern Europe.* Cambridge: Cambridge University Press. 9–28.

Skinner, Q. 2002. *Visions of Politics.* Vol. 2, *Renaissance Virtues.* Cambridge: Cambridge University Press.

Stewart, R. 1998. *Public Office in Early Rome: Ritual Procedure and Political Practice.* Ann Arbor: University of Michigan Press.

Straumann, B. 2009. "Is modern liberty ancient? Roman remedies and natural rights in Hugo Grotius' early works on natural law." *Law and History Review* 27:55–85.

Swain, J. W. 1940. "The theory of the four monarchies: Opposition history under the Roman empire." *Classical Philology* 35:1–21.

Syme, R. 1939. *The Roman Revolution.* Oxford: Clarendon Press.

Tan, J. 2008. "*Contiones* in the age of Cicero." *Classical Antiquity* 27:163–201.

Tetley, W. 1999. "A Canadian looks at American conflict of law theory." *Columbia Journal of Transnational Law* 38:299–373.

Thomas, Y. 1991. "L'institution de la majesté." *Revue de synthèse,* IVe serie, nos. 3–4:331–86.

Thomas, Y. 1995. "Fictio legis: L'empire de la fiction romaine." *Droits: Revue française de théorie juridique* 21:17–63.

Ullmann, W. 1975. *Law and Politics in the Middle Ages: An Introduction to the Sources of Medieval Political Ideas.* Ithaca, N.Y.: Cornell University Press.

Walbank, F. W. 1949. "Roman declaration of war in the third and second centuries." *Classical Philology* 44:15–19.

Walbank, F. W. 1957–79. *A Historical Commentary on Polybius.* 3 vols. Oxford: Clarendon Press.

Walther, H. G. 1976. *Imperiales Königtum, Konziliarismus und Volkssouveränität.* Munich: Wilhelm Fink.

Welles, C. B. 1965. "Greek liberty." *Journal of Juristic Papyrology* 15:29–47.

Westra, H. J., and T. Kupke, eds. 1998. *The Berlin Commentary on Martianus Capella's "De nuptiis Philologiae et Mercurii," Book II.* Leiden: Brill.

Whitmarsh, T. 2001. *Greek Literature and the Roman Empire: The Politics of Imitation.* Oxford: Oxford University Press.

Wirszubski, C. 1950. *Libertas as a Political Idea at Rome during the Late Republic and Early Principate.* Cambridge: Cambridge University Press.

Woolf, G. 1998. *Becoming Roman: The Origins of Provincial Civilization in Gaul.* Cambridge: Cambridge University Press.

Wootton, D., ed. 1994. *Republicanism, Liberty, and the Commercial Society, 1649–1776.* Stanford, Calif.: Stanford University Press.

Worden, B. 1994. "Marchamont Nedham and the beginnings of English Republicanism, 1649–1656." D. Wootton, ed. *Republicanism, Liberty, and the Commercial Society, 1649–1776.* Stanford, Calif.: Stanford University Press. 45–81.

Worden, B. 2009. "Hobbes and the halo of power." *New York Review* 56:12.

Zack, A. 2001. *Studien zum "römischen Völkerrecht": Kriegserklärung, Kriegsbeschluss,*

Beeidung und Ratifikation zwischenstaatlicher Verträge, internationale Freundschaft und Feindschaft während der römischen Republik bis zum Beginn des Prinzipat. Göttingen: Duehrkohp and Radicke.

Zetzel, J. E. G. 1999. *Cicero: "On the Commonwealth" and "On the Laws."* Cambridge: Cambridge University Press.

Index

Acknowledgments

This book has had a long gestation. It took final form in response to my election to a chaire d'État at the Collège de France, which I held in March 2010. The dedication to John Scheid is an expression of thanks not simply for that opportunity but for his conduct as friend and scholar across many years.

I owe similar debts to Claudia Moatti and Yan Thomas, the former a friend, the latter an acquaintance only by correspondence before his untimely death. Their welcome into the world of French legal scholarship was an act of generosity from which I continue to benefit and for which I remain profoundly grateful.

Lectures or seminars organized around this volume's themes were delivered at the University of Southern California, the University of California at Los Angeles School of Law, Oxford University, Cambridge University, the University of Chicago, New York University School of Law, the University of Kentucky, Indiana University, the University of British Columbia, the University of Otago, and the University of Canterbury. To the audiences on those occasions I offer once again my thanks.

An earlier version of Chapter 3 appeared in Benedict Kingsbury and Benjamin Straumann, eds., *The Roman Foundations of the Law of Nations: Alberico Gentili and the Justice of Empire* (Oxford University Press, 2010), while an earlier version of Chapter 5 appeared in *History of Political Thought*, volume 31 (2010). In addition, like many in the field, I have relied heavily upon the translations in Alan Watson, ed., *The Digest of Justinian*, 4 vols. (Philadelphia: University of Pennsylvania Press, 1985). I wish here to acknowledge the debt that I owe to Professor Watson and the many scholars who contributed to that remarkable effort. I have similarly relied upon the translations of epigraphically preserved Roman statutes in Crawford 1996 and the translation of the Flavian municipal law by Michael Crawford published in González 1986. The debt remains even when, for the sake of analytic clarity or stylistic continuity, I have modified those translations or produced my own.

For comments on select chapters I am grateful to John Dillon, Peter Funke, Sabine MacCormack, Jennifer Pitts, Benjamin Straumann, and Peter White, and likewise to Ruth Abbey and Ari Bryen for readings of the whole. Kate Milco helped to reformat the manuscript in accordance with the guidelines of the Press and did so with care, accuracy, and dispatch. Finally, Kate Milco and Thomas Keith helped to correct the proofs, and the text is much cleaner thanks to their exceptional care.

John Richardson read the manuscript for the University of Pennsylvania Press. John's contributions to the study of Roman law are many, and it was a very great privilege to have the benefit of his erudition and sympathetic engagement.

Work on this volume was supported by the Mellon Foundation, the University of Chicago, and the Max Weber Kolleg of the University of Erfurt. While in Erfurt, my son Theodore and I were the beneficiaries of food, friendship, and great good cheer from Jo Weeks and Ben, Maud, and Greg Woolf. The volume received support of a different kind from Jerry Singerman, who has made every aspect of publication a pleasure.

Finally, Ruth and Theodore deserve special thanks for putting up with all my comings and goings, my love of Lenel, and all the books.

www.ingramcontent.com/pod-product-compliance
Lightning Source LLC
LaVergne TN
LVHW091517200926
848483LV00005B/438/J